Real **Encouragement for Every Homeschool Day!**

365 day Homeschool MOM with The Familyman

Todd Wilson

ISBN 978-1-937639-16-7

All inquiries should be addressed to: Familyman Ministries, 611 S. Main St., Milford, IN 46542

Printed in the United States of America

To My Sister, Wendy

who feels the pressure of homeschooling and often wonders if she's doing enough for her children. You are.

Hope this book reminds you of that 365 days of the year.
Your big brother,
Todd

Introduction

Hey Mom,

If you've homeschooled for any length of time…say 2 days or more, then you know that the pressures you face while homeschooling your children are huge. In fact, I've yet to meet a mom who doesn't feel like she's failing her children, husband, and God as she homeschools.

It saddens me, when I read their emails, talk to them at homeschool conventions, or view their posts on Facebook, and although they may smile on the outside, inside they're about to call it quits and toss in the towel.

I believe in homeschooling, and for the last bunch of years our business has been devoted to encouraging homeschool moms and dads. We travel the country speaking at homeschool conventions, support groups, and homeschool family camps. I've also written for just about every homeschool magazine published, homeschool blogs, and have spent the last 7 years writing a weekly email for The Old Schoolhouse Magazine, called The Homeschool Minute.

After all these years of writing, the articles and snippets begin to pile up, and we decided to compile them into one, big volume of daily homeschool encouragement.

This book, 365 Day Homeschool Mom, is filled with pure, undiluted homeschool encouragement from the first word to the last. There is not one iota of discouragement contained within these pages. I won't tell you how to do school, what to eat, or how many children to birth (or how to birth them). And anyone who says otherwise is fair game for my swashbuckling sword.

The book is designed to be read daily: it's a daily dose of encouragement for the homeschool mother's soul. The topics were assigned to me and sometimes they overlap. Most days, the entries will be short and other days, they'll be a little longer. There are also some helpful resources included that have been a great source of encouragement to our family over the years. I hope this will become one of the greatest resources out there for homeschool moms.

Along the way you'll meet my family (all eight children) and my beautiful wife of 25 years. You'll get little glimpses into the REAL, honest world of the Wilson home and travel with us as we zigzag across the country in our big, old RV called the Familyman Mobile (like the Bat mobile). You'll play in the snow with us and enjoy a hot day on the beach. You'll read themes and topics that repeat throughout the year, because they need to be repeated (homeschooling moms are slow learners). In short, it will be…easy, down-to-earth, and fun.

Don't sweat it if you miss a few days…or months, just jump right back in on the correct day and start again.

Be real,

Todd

A Real Worldview

Hey Mom,

Let me say right up front that I think like a man. I don't make smiley, winky, or frowny faces out of punctuations marks. I never LOL, quote poetry, or talk about the beauties of childbirth. I can't...I'm a man. But I am real and will give you a ringside seat into the real and sometimes-ugly world of our home and school.

I'm not sure I can even write a coherent sentence at the moment because I'm sitting in our RV surrounded by 8 children in a Wal-Mart parking lot just south of Springfield, MO. We live in an RV (and Wal-Mart parking lots) about 3 months per year as we travel to many state homeschool conventions around the country. Today, we head to Lansing, MI for the INCH state convention.

Actually, a Wal-Mart parking lot is the perfect setting to discuss having a biblical worldview. The truth is we tend to wrongly associate "a biblical worldview" with a glossy-covered textbook, a DVD curriculum, or a seminar where a man in a crisp, white shirt and a patriotic tie discusses current events and the Bible. More accurately, a Biblical worldview is passed on in places like Wal-Mart parking lots.

For example: this morning, I'll run into Wal-Mart and return with a cartful of stuff. Here's the worldview part. RV's park about a mile from the store and the temptation is to leave the cart for someone else to deal with. BUT everyone knows (including my children) that the carts are to be returned to the cart-corral. So after I've unloaded the cart, my children will see me push the cart the mile back to its corral, and I will have shown them a biblical worldview that Wilson's obey rules (that God has put in place) and put others' needs above our own.

That's an example of how you teach a Biblical worldview. You model biblical living to your children on a day-to-day basis. You let them see how to trust God when the car doesn't start, how to be kind when the sales clerk isn't, and how to ask forgiveness when you've just acted like a creep during school. And it starts today...on January 1st.

As the old saying goes, "More Biblical worldview is caught than taught."

That's what this man thinks.

Be real!

Make Them Get Along

Hey Mom,

How do you help siblings get along? My answer may seem a little harsh, and I certainly don't mean it to be (you know my sensitive nature and all) but… you can't. Now don't get me wrong; I'm not saying, "You can't EVER", but I am saying, "You can't ALL THE TIME."

That's just the way it is. Look at all the examples in the Bible. Those brothers and sisters were always prodding, poking, teasing, fighting, arguing, or throwing each other in a well In fact, one of the very first brothers on the whole planet KILLED his brother.

I'm guessing when people are that close…emotionally, physically, and in every other way…it causes friction. While growing up, I was a lot meaner to my brothers and sisters than I was to any of my 'school' friends. I've noticed that my children are great around other kids, cousins, and strangers, but at times, they fight like cats and dogs.

Now, don't get depressed and wonder…so what's the point? Why try?

The point is that our children need us to train them in the midst of the arguing, poking, prodding, and fighting. They need us to model and teach them about kindness, forgiveness, peacemaking, and longsuffering.

Don't allow them to AVOID conflict or each other. Don't give them separate rooms, space, friends, and activities. Force them to play together, live together, and work together. They'll still argue and bicker, but they will learn to love one another and will grow up to be best friends.

So, keep loving, working, forgiving, and encouraging your children to get along, but when they don't, don't believe for one moment that your children are the only ones that argue, poke, prod, or fight and that you're failing. You're doing just fine. Just…

Be real.

JANUARY 3

God's Unit Study

Hey Mom,

I'm in way over my head now. I'm not even going to pretend that I know how to develop a unit study. Actually, when I hear the words unit study…it makes me tired. It sounds like more work and high expectations. I imagine an already over-worked mother working way into the night on a large-scale replica of the inner nose made entirely of cereal boxes, tuna fish cans, and scotch tape.

I know my wife has tried unit studies, but they never worked out quite like the books made them sound.

Now, after reading my introduction, you might think I'm against unit studies, but 'oh contraire' (I love saying that). I'm really in favor of unit studies and have been doing one for many years.

It's called LIFE.

In fact, it's a curriculum designed by God and delivered to my doorstep…or RV step each day. Take today, for example. Today, God decided that my family needs to work on living together in an unselfish way. For the first hour of the day, we've been hollering, arguing, and being about as ugly as a homeschool family can be. This is God's unit study for my family.

All my wife and I have to do is to lead the rest of the troops in learning the lesson, which is a lot harder than building a model of the nose.

So, Mom, you might need to throw away the tuna fish cans and be on the lookout for the LIFE unit study God gives you today instead…it should be hand-delivered any minute now. Believe me; if that's all you teach your children today, you will have taught them well.

Be real.

JANUARY 4

The Homeschooler's Best Friend

Hey Mom,

This is going to be a short one. I'm parked in a McDonald's parking lot at about a 30-degree angle and my laptop is about to slide off the table. I know women authors have gobs of advice for growing and nurturing friendships…it probably has a lot to do with tea parties, scrapbooking, and "feelings."

My only thought about friends is…make your husband your best friend. Don't let any other girl friendship displace your man from being number one. It's easy to let happen, because "he" doesn't think, feel, or understand like a woman. So it's easy to give up on him and…move on.

I know my wife will sometimes say, "I'll call my sister, she'll understand."

When she does, I can't help feeling a little like second-rate goods. I know other husbands feel that way too. A friend of my wife's announced her pregnancy to my wife before she told her own husband. I know he wouldn't have screamed and sounded as excited as my wife did…but that's beside the point.

So, Mom, don't let another friendship overshadow your friendship with your husband. Here's a little way to tell if one already has: ask your husband who he thinks you'd rather talk to and be with—him or "her."

If he says "her," do whatever it takes to show him he's number one on your friendship list.

Gotta go, I'm getting parking lot sick.

Be real.

JANUARY 5

Insane and Proud of It!

Hey Mom,

The way the world looks at it…homeschooling a kindergartener is sweet, homeschooling a third grader is ideal, homeschooling a seventh grader is noble, BUT homeschooling a highschooler is INSANE!!!

After all, how are we going to prepare them for college?!! What about calculus, transcripts, college, or graduate school?!!

Yes, homeschooling is fine to a point…but doing high school at home crosses the line.

Sadly, many homeschoolers have adopted this same thinking. Moms cruise through the early grades, but somewhere around 7th grade, doubts begin to erode their game plan, and they are plagued with the idea that maybe 'the system' can do a better job for high school.

Baloney!!! (I seem to say that a lot.)

High school is the perfect time to homeschool. My friend and Harvard graduate, Greg Sabouri, of Teaching Textbooks, is convinced that homeschooling does a better job of preparing high school students for college and careers than any other type of schooling.

I agree, plus there are a dozen other reasons for homeschooling through high school that have nothing to do with academics (take a stroll down memory lane of your own high school experience).

So, if you agree that it's best to homeschool through high school, then stick to your guns, plug your ears, and dare to be INSANE!!!

Be real.

The One-Eyed Monster

Hey Mom,

TV can be bad...but I love it. I know this sounds contradictory, but I was raised on television. I was fed a steady diet of educational television, was greeted by it when I stepped off the school bus each day, spent Saturday mornings glued to it, and gathered around it with my family each night like colonial families gathered around the fire.

So when my wife and I got married, one of our first purchases was a TV. Even though we guarded our eyes and our home, TV was the one porthole of sludge into our family. Even though we didn't watch crummy programs, they were still only a channel or two away. Plus, TV was a huge time waster and when our children came along, we found they liked watching Barney (& a host of others) better than doing...anything.

That's when we decided to get rid of the thing and boy, was that ever hard...not for them, but for ME! But it was the best decision we ever made. I'm convinced every time I see the one-eyed monster that we made the right decision. The commercials, the programs, and even the news, shock me. I would never purposely expose my children to that kind of sludge, but I know a lot of families who do...not because they're bad, but because they like watching TV. It's fun and easy...but it's still bad.

But guess what? We have one now. At first it was for videos only, then we needed to upgrade so my brother-in-law could watch the super bowl at our house. Now we have Netflix streaming, and I sometimes feel like we've thrown in the towel. But here's the deal: plans change, life gets harder, and sometimes...you just need a TV.

I'm not making excuses, and you still need to guard, limit, and fight the one eyed-monster because it will consume your family. And Mom, I know your idea may be different than your husbands, but you just may have to let God work through him and allow him to think differently.

The temptation is to think he is bad, lazy, or a TV addict, but maybe that's not the case. Maybe he just feels differently than you. He may not be as "spiritual" as the people on Facebook or in Homeschool articles, but that's OK. He's your man and God wants you to love him no matter what.

At the same time, can I encourage you to talk to your husband about taking the one-month TV challenge? Unplug it for one whole month. It'll be the best thing you ever do as a family. I guarantee it.

Be real.

PS - I hope my wife doesn't read this.

Chores a Necessary Pain

Hey Mom,

The thing to remember about chores is that their purpose isn't to make our lives easier but to train our children for the future. We all know it's easier to sweep under the kitchen table ourselves than to have one of our children do it.

All I would have to do is get the broom and dustpan, sweep the floor, put the chairs back in place, and then return the broom and dustpan to the peg on the wall. But hey, I'm a parent who wants the best for my children; so instead, I make a chore chart, post the chore chart, and enforce the chore chart, teaching them what's expected along the way.

Sometimes it looks like this:

Twenty minutes after dinner, I notice that the floor is covered with food. I check the chore chart and see who the guilty party's name is next to "sweep kitchen".

"So and So," I call, "you need to sweep the kitchen."

"I am," he answers like he meant that he was going to do it AT that moment.

"How can you say I am when you're not doing it now and have not done it in the past?"

"Well, I was going to do it," he responds.

"I want you to get it done now," I insist.

"I will," he answers, like he doesn't even know what we're talking about.

"Now!" I say.

A few minutes later, the floor is swept, but the broom and dustpan are lying on the floor and the chairs are scattered about.

"So and So," I call again, "you need to put the broom and dustpan away and straighten the chairs."

"Sorry, I forgot," he or she responds.

A few minutes later, the chairs are in place and the broom is put away but the dustpan is still on the floor. That's usually when I start to rant and rave about the merits of being a team and that we must each do our job well in order for things to run smoothly. So you see…what would have taken me 5 minutes to accomplish, instead takes ME and them 45 minutes. So what should I do?

Keep training. Keep assigning chores and making the kids do them because they're part of our family, part of the Wilson team, and because I know that if I don't train them to work now, they won't do it when they grow up.

Gotta go now and check the chore chart.

Be real.

Those Pesky Relatives

Hey Mom,

Dealing with negative family members is kind of a given when you homeschool. I mean who doesn't have an "Aunt Nellie" who at Christmas gatherings asks, "So how much longer are you going to homeschool? You certainly aren't going to do it in High school…are you?"

Now you could pray that God would take Aunt Nellie 'home' before your kids get to the high school years, fake a cold and miss the next 20 Christmases, or wear dark glasses and a fake mustache and hope she doesn't recognize you, but that would be too easy.

Instead, you need to take "Aunt Nellie by the horns" and stand firm in the convictions you hold.

First of all, resist the urge to quote all the homeschooling statistics compiled by Dr. Brian Ray* and remain silent. Instead, let your children do the talking.

The truth is people see a difference between your children and other children. It's not that they obey every time or never act up…but there's just something different about them. I've had those Aunt Nellie's and they soon become spokesmen for homeschooling, just because of your children.

Secondly, tell your husband that you need him to be your knight-in-shining armor. When challenges and questions arise from family members, you need him to step up to the plate and allow you to hide behind him. Tell him that you need him to be the one delivering the answers (if possible).

For example, he might need to say, "Yes, Aunt Nellie, we are still homeschooling and we'll keep doing it until we feel like it's no longer the best option for our family."

He may even need to pull your aunt, parents, or in-laws aside and say, "When you say those things, you really discourage my wife. I know you don't mean to, but you need to stop." He won't think that sounds like a lot of fun, but let him know that you need your knight to come to your rescue.

Got it? Who knows? Maybe you'll get lucky and Aunt Nellie will die before the next family gathering. I know that's terrible, but it would be convenient.

Be real.

**National Home Education Research Institute - www.nheri.org*

JANUARY 9

Some Learn Touchily

Hey Mom,

Just pulled in the driveway late last night from a long, hot week traveling in the RV. Our house is a mess, and my computer just started making a weird noise. So what do I have to say about discovering your children's learning styles?

First, you need to take them to a learning center (found in most major cities) where they'll undergo several days of intensive studies to discover their learning style. Then, have a learning specialist come to your house and spend several weeks observing your homeschool.

Finally, after several months and a couple of thousand dollars, you will be told that your child is a 'kinesthetic' learner. Once you learn what that means and how to adjust your curriculum to meet his style, you'll be on your way to producing a well-adjusted child.

Sounds easy…NOT.

Yeah, I'm just kidding. Maybe it's the RV hangover or the time bomb buzzing sound coming from my computer that's made me a little cynical about this topic. Or, maybe it's because I see so many stressed out moms running to and from the next curriculum available wondering if it will do a better job educating their child.

The truth is…you're a homeschooling mom. You're around your children all day long. You probably already know how your child best learns…whether he learns audibly, visually, or "touchily." In other words, when you catch him learning, is he standing on his head, listening to something, feeling an object, or watching how something is done?

You don't need an expert to tell you what you can easily observe. In fact, DON'T listen to the experts; just DO what you know to be best.

I gotta stop and turn off this computer.

Be real.

JANUARY 10

If the Shoe Fits…

Hey Mom,

What is it with women and shoes? A man needs just a few pairs…black, brown and athletic. My wife, on the other hand, has more pairs of shoes than the whole men's department at the local Pilcher's Shoe Store. The weird thing about it though is that she rarely wears some of them because they don't fit that comfortably.

"Why do you keep these shoes?" I ask.

She looks at me as if I'm from another planet and answers, "Because they go with my brown, swooshy skirt."

"But I thought you said they hurt your feet."

"So."

You're probably wondering what on earth this has to do with homeschool co-ops, so here's my point. Homeschool co-ops are like women's shoes. There are all types of them to choose from, but sometimes the ones that appear the best...don't really fit you that well. Instead of offering comfort, encouragement, and support, they leave you feeling tired, worn out, or like a failure.

So here's what to look for when picking a co-op. First, pick one that is made up of members who homeschool for the same primary reason you do. Second, if the group sounds like it might require too much work from you...it will. Pass it by. Thirdly, and most importantly, pick one in which the members aren't afraid to be honest. You want and need to belong to a group that is real and will allow you to be real as well...because everyone knows that the best shoes are the ones that may look a little worn and smell a bit, but they feel so good.

Be real...and on behalf of your husband, get rid of some of those shoes,

JANUARY 11

Becoming Bella

Hey Mom,

My favorite example of encouragement is one that happened many summer Olympics ago. It was the year that the women's gymnastics team was going for the all-around gold, and it was down to them and one other team.

Everything hinged on the final vault event, and if the Americans won that, they got the gold; if not, they got the bronze. Petite American, Kerri Strug, stepped to the line and vaulted into the air, landing in a bone-jarring heap on the mat. She had twisted her ankle badly, and the U.S. had lost the gold (or so we thought).

Amazingly, fifteen minutes later, she was back at the line with her leg all wrapped up below the knee. She was going to make another attempt. While the crowd was going nuts at the idea of the little girl attempting the impossible, I was observing a great example in encouragement.

The camera panned to her coach...a thick-accented, large-mustached man whose eyes were fixed on Kerri.

"You can do it, Kerri," he hollered. "You can do it!"

He didn't tell her how to do it or how not to do it, he simply cheered, "You can do it! You can do it!!!" And she did…and the rest is history.

That's what your friends need to hear from you regarding homeschooling. They need you to cheer them on and say, "YOU CAN DO IT!!!" Sometimes they might ask for and need advice or suggestions, but most of the time, they just need someone (you) to come alongside them, believe in them, and tell them that they can do it!

Be real.

PS -By the way, we offer a great pack of funny and encouraging cards to help you encourage others in homeschooling. You can find them on our website at www.familymanweb.com in the homeschool product category.

JANUARY 12

The Joy of Blue Milk

Hey Mom,

I know you're just dying to see what the Familyman has to say about cooking. In all actuality, I'm kind of cooking-challenged. About all I can cook is PB&J and macaroni and cheese (from the box). So, although I can't cook, share helpful recipes, or tell the difference between paprika and cilantro, I do have an opinion on cooking.

It's actually very simple. Cooking should bring you joy not guilt. I'm not suggesting that everyone has to love cooking. Some people just don't find great pleasure in cooking, but I do know that cooking was never meant to be a means of heaping guilt upon the cook. But, that's what it has become in some circles.

I am continually amazed at how many articles about cooking a certain way fill Christian/homeschool magazines and Facebook. They're mostly about herbs, organic foods, baking, grinding, squishing (all natural of course), and overall, a more spiritual way to cook. Moms on Facebook post pictures of the scrumptious, homemade meals…like everyone cares about what they're having for dinner.

The more I talk to moms and observe their conversations, the more I see the huge weight of responsibility that is being dished out and served with heaping amounts of guilt. Moms are being pushed into baking their own bread (because what kind of mother would serve her family store-bought, evil bread?) A mom buys a bread maker, only to find out that good moms don't use bread makers; they knead it with their own hands. So then she sells the bread maker on EBay, and buys 50lbs of wheat flour, only to find out then that real moms don't buy their flour, they grind their own wheat. On and on it goes.

The mom tries harder, only to find out that there's still more she should do, until she throws in the towel and buys bread from a store again but forbids her children to ever mention it around certain people.

Does that sound like joy? Hardly. Now, hear me clearly. I'm not against healthy or organic eating, baking, grinding, or squishing. If you love to do it, great! Just don't make others feel like they have to do it too.

But if trying to cook that way just brings more guilt into your life or if you only do it because you think it's more spiritual, then you've believed one of the lies that homeschooling moms believe...and you need to stop it. Because... it's OK to buy bread from a store, pop a frozen pizza in the oven, or even eat cereal that turns the milk blue.

Be real.

JANUARY 13

The Heart of a Father

Hey Mom,

As I write this, we've just been blasted by the first winter storm of the season. I just spent thirty minutes side by side with my big boys digging out enough to get our second vehicle out of the driveway. The sun is shining, the air is crystal clear and the thermometer reads minus 11. The best part of the day is that we called it a snow day which means we can put off the first day of school in the New Year a day longer.

I know my wife was pleased by my firm decision NOT to do school today. She's been dreading getting back into the swing. Of course she's not alone. It doesn't matter if you live in North Dakota or Hawaii; just about every homeschooling mom faces the doldrums of winter homeschooling.

The truth is I don't even think it's so much about the weather as it is the nagging lie that asks, "What's the point?" The question reminds me of Dennis.

When I was a kid growing up in a small town in Indiana there lived a young guy named Dennis. Every small town in Indian has a Dennis. He was odd and loud. He walked around town with a short flat-top hair style and always seemed to have a rolled up sports program in his hand. No one ever really talked to him, but if he saw you at a ballgame or on the street he would almost always point and say in his loud voice, "What's the point?"

All the kids knew Dennis and to get a laugh would point to the palm of their hand and say in their best Dennis-voice, "What's the point?"

Homeschooling moms remind me of Dennis and his question. Moms come up to me and say, "So, my kids can read and know some math facts, a few important dates, and that Jonah was swallowed by a big fish NOT a whale," they say. "Day after day we face bad attitudes, unfinished lessons, disastrous messes, and the same-old-same-old. What's the point?"

I know you ask that, because sometimes my wife asks the question…not as though she expects me to answer her but more as a regretful sigh. BUT this time I will answer. I will tell you what the point is, fellow homeschoolers, because there is a point. A BIG point!!!!

The reason you get out the books most days, go through the same old lessons, and cover a few pages of semi-important information is NOT because all those subjects you are covering matters, but because those children you are covering them with matter!!

Do you realize that every day you spend with your children doing anything (including the boring homeschool stuff) provides invaluable training and learning? You're teaching them how to live and they're getting it. Of course homeschooling isn't the only way to achieve that…but it is the best way!!! That's the point. You get to be with your children and they get to be with YOU! What a great way to grow up…especially in these cold, gray days of winter.

Here's the deal, my fellow Dad, your wife will struggle with that ugly lie almost every day of her homeschooling existence. It's your job and duty to reminder her of the lie shattering truth that what she does every day with your children MATTERS, not because she's teaching them certain facts, or skills, but because she's able to be with them every day.

You keep reminding your wife that your children are going to be fine, and that they will do great in the future. Keep reminding her that your kids are going to get the subject that she thinks they never will. You keep reminding her how blessed your children are to be home with their mom every day. You keep reminding your wife how blessed you are to have such a capable wife. You've got to KEEP reminding her because she keeps forgetting.

That's the point. Don't make me use my Dennis-voice.

Be real.

JANUARY 14

What Time is It?

Hey Mom,

Now we've come to the meat of the homeschooling matter – character. That's what we all want in our children – godly character. Unfortunately, we tie ourselves up in knots trying to ensure that our kids will have plenty of godly character to get them through the adult years.

Of course we want that for our children, but in reality, it's not the sit down kind of 'character lessons' from which they'll learn. It's the very fabric of who we are that is the real influence and mold for what they'll become.

I was reminded of that myself as I went tooling up I-75 just north of Orlando last week. It was about 7 o'clock in the evening and the sun was just above the horizon when my phone rang. It was my son Ben.

"Hey Dad," he began without any other greeting, "what time is it?"

After a slight hesitation, we both blurted out, "My FAVORITE time to drive."

He knows me. He knows that's what I always say when I'm behind the wheel of our RV as the sun hangs low in the sky and the air is cooler. A thousand miles separated us, but he knew that's what I was feeling right then.

In thirty years, when he's a dad and I'm old, he'll be driving down the road as the sun sinks and think this is Dad's favorite time to drive. He'll think about me, our RVing days, and our life on the road as a family.

You know that thought may not seem like much, but it's huge. My influence on my children is huge. Your influence is huge. Don't worry so much about whether you're doing enough teaching or character training. You homeschool. You're there every day for your kids, modeling what you want them to live.

Be real.

JANUARY 15

Don't Ever Say the S Word Again!

Hey Mom,

I can't believe I even need to say anything about socialization. I mean, we all KNOW that the old, "What about lack of socialization?" question just doesn't hold water...I mean none...not even a teaspoonful of it.

You know that. I know that. We all know that...BUT when the question comes, we still find ourselves thinking, Well, maybe they've got a point... maybe they do need to be around other kids more.

Mom, stop it!!!! Don't fall for that old lie. Your kids are fine; they certainly don't need to be around kids all day long to be socialized. You know it. Don't waiver. Don't get weak in the knees. Stand firm, not only in your response to the 'questioner', but even more importantly, in your own mind and convictions.

Don't let your husband fall for the lie either. Truth is, dads fall for the lie even more than wives. Oftentimes, it's the dad who hears one of the 'questioners' and then all of a sudden becomes a 'questioner' too.

"You know maybe it would be good for "Josh" to take a couple of classes just so he can be around other kids and learn how to interact," a dad might say to his wife.

Now hear this!!! There is no uncertainty! Your kids are perfectly socialized, and they don't need other kids to be better socialized.

It's the TRUTH. Believe it, cling to it, and don't make me come over there and write another article about it!

Be real.

JANUARY 16

Sugar and Spice

Hey Mom,

I'm sure you've noticed this, but raising daughters is different than raising sons. Not that one is better than the other, but they're just so different. While sons are climbing, running, and sword fighting, most daughters are trying on clothes, sitting, and reading.

I absolutely love my boys to death, but there is something special about my two adorable daughters. They're girls after all.

And while we do train our sons and daughters to the same standards of obedience, kindness, gentleness, and self-control, there are some differences in what we train them for.

In fact, I believe that while Titus 2 may be the passage that most women hate, it's also the perfect curriculum guide for raising daughters. Mom, you are the older woman and your daughter is the younger woman.

Here's what you need to teach and encourage your daughter in:

-Loving her husband (and the men in her life until then i.e., brothers/dad/etc.)

-Loving her children (showing her how to nurture and care for small ones)

-Loving her home (and a few other things listed in Titus 2)

These things are all that really matter and will be the reason for your daughter's happiness or misery later on. The truth is your daughter will not be miserable if she fails to master algebra, but she will be miserable if she fails to learn how to love her husband and children.

And here's the crux of the matter: you don't teach these things by going through a curriculum but by loving YOUR husband, children, and home. Your girls watch you (because they're always watching) and they learn.

So, Mom make today's lesson for your daughter a lesson on loving her future husband by loving yours. Make a special dinner for your man, send him a card, or drop in and surprise him at lunchtime.

That will be a lesson your daughter will never forget…math facts should be so easy.

Be real.

JANUARY 17

Deal with Disappointment

Hey Mom,

We don't like the topic of disappointment in the homeschooling world. After all, we Christian homeschoolers don't do disappointment; we specialize in SUCCESS. We protect our children from the evil influences of the world, instill in them a Biblical worldview, and fill their little minds with the love of learning. How could there be disappointments?

Unless, of course, you mean the ones that stem from the fact that our children sometimes fight like cats and dogs, seem as spiritual as a turnip, as smart as a rock, and as loveable as a cactus. So then, maybe, we do have disappointments.

As I see it, there are four ways you can handle disappointment:

1) Hide in the closet and pray for Jesus' soon return.

2) Paint a fake smile on your face and pretend that all is well in your homeschool world.

3) Push the troops harder until either they crack or you crack.

4) Be real. Keep praying, keep trying…and adjust your measuring stick.

Trust me on this; the first three options don't work. In fact, if you play those games, you'll lose. The last option is the only one that offers hope, healing, and happiness (and they all start with H).

Sure we have disappointments…lots of them. We set our standards too high and guarantee shortcomings, but instead of tossing in the towel, let's BE REAL with each other. Let others know how things are really going. Ask them to pray for you, and then see what happens. In the Bible, James said that if we confess…and pray for one another…healing will take place.*

That, my fellow homeschooling parent is how you handle disappointment.

Be real.

**James 5:16*

JANUARY 18

Haters and Lovers

Hey Mom,

I'm not a math guy. Whenever I see a bunch of numbers all lined up, my vision clouds and my tongue swells. Now that doesn't mean I'm totally inept. I can count…pretty high and get by with your basic math skills. But don't ask me to do any algebra or anything else that involves Pythagorean's Theorem. I can't do it! And I still have flashbacks to my sophomore year in high school, looking up into the depressed face of my battle-weary algebra teacher, Mrs. Helton, as I explained why I did what I did to a certain story problem.

So here's my theory on math: people who can do math…can do math. People who can't…can't. Now don't send me mean, nasty, math-loving letters. I just don't believe that most kids will use the higher math that we assume we have to teach them (and a lot of other stuff for that matter).

Children who love math may end up doing something math-related, but those who don't…won't, and that's okay.

Now the issue comes up, what if you're a math-hater but need to teach your children math? What are you to do?

Just do the best you can (or involve your husband or a program that teaches it for you) and then don't sweat what you can't do. Teach them the basics, remember your goals, and see if any math-lovers arise in your students. Then let them go. If they've been created to do math…they will do math.

Now to all you math-lovers, you have no idea what I'm talking about. You love math, after all. But remember this, not all your children will love math. Don't try to make a math-hater into a math-lover…it won't work. You'll only frustrate yourself…and your child.

So with all that said, enjoy the gifts God has given you, accept the fact that he hasn't given you others, and love your children.

Be real.

JANUARY 19

Dousing the Guilt-Fires

Hey Mom,

I prefer to think of community involvement as community involvement of the FUTURE. The fact is we already have too much on our plate to be very involved in our community. In our family, it sometimes feels as though our own little community of Wilson's takes all our time.

Rather than fuel the guilt-fires of we should be doing more, I like to remember that we're impacting our community by pouring our lives and efforts into future citizens who will be prepared to impact their world for Christ by godly living.

If you think about it, that's community involvement. I think we have sometimes been fed a line that says, "To be truly effective, you have to be busy 'rubbing shoulders' with them (the community)."

To some extent, we all rub shoulders with our community. We go to the store, the library, and the gas station. We interact with the UPS man who comes to our house, the nurse and doctor who examine our children, and the neighbor who lives next door.

We usually have plenty of opportunities and don't need to go looking for more. We just need to make the most of the ones we have.

But with all that said, I still believe the greatest way you can impact your community is by pouring your life and beliefs into your children right now. After all, they're like arrows in the hand of a warrior penetrating the world.

Be real.

PS - I think that's what Jesus had in mind when he was talking about loving our neighbor (Luke 10:25-37). He didn't tell them to go for walks...but to love the people they came into contact with while walking.

JANUARY 20

It's Going to Be OK

Hey Mom,

Let me just state right off the bat that I'm directing this writing to the non-relaxed homeschooler, and you know who you are. You're the one who feels uptight most of the time by your school schedule, your children's lack of progress, and your own lack of discipline. You try harder but fail 'oftener'.

Deep down, you know you should take it easier, enjoy your children more, and care less about their performance, but you just can't relax!!!

You'll probably never be like 'the mom' who doesn't care what time she gets out of bed, has tea parties at 10am, and sings and smiles when her children spend the day turning the front yard into mud, and that's okay. That's the way she was designed by God, just like you were designed to be 'non-relaxed'.

With that said, you can still be a relaxed homeschooler and enjoy the benefits of being relaxed. Here's how:

1) Quit wishing God had made you more relaxed and thank Him for designing you just the way He did.

2) Acknowledge that you're not responsible to turn your children into 'what' they're going to be and then quit acting like you are.

3) Throw away all the expectations you have for your children. You do your job, and let God make your children who He designed them to be. If you don't, you'll just frustrate them and yourself.

4) Quit playing by 'their' rules, and the 'their' I'm talking about is the public school. They've proven that institutionalized school methods don't work (they're searching for something different), so don't try to replicate 'their' school in your house. It's not a good model, and you can't replicate an entire school staff by yourself anyway.

5) Make yourself do what you know is important. For example, if you feel like it's important to play a game with your child (and it is), then do it... forget math for the day and do it!!! Just do it!!!

6) Get a copy of my book Lies Homeschooling Moms Believe today and read it from cover to cover.

7) And, of course...

Be real.

JANUARY 21

You Can't So Don't Try

Hey Mom,

You cannot do it all. YOU cannot do it ALL. YOU CANNOT DO IT ALL!!!!!!

This topic of working at home (or working out of the home) and homeschooling may not apply to everyone, but the principle applies to EVERYONE. Let me state it again. YOU CANNOT DO IT ALL!

No one can. It's unrealistic and even detrimental to think and act as though you can, but sadly, that's what most homeschool moms, especially work-at-home, homeschooling moms, do.

They add a typical homeschooling routine to an already demanding schedule of working out of the home. The only problem with that is that it doesn't work. There is no way humanly possible to run a business and 'do' school like someone who doesn't run a business out of her home. So don't try.

You can't do it all.

So you need to return to the truth that homeschooling is best done as it relates to life. That doesn't mean you just do your business and ignore training your children. It means that the best way to train and educate your children is by including them in your business or work. But to do this, you may have to set aside some of the 'normal' homeschool formalities, which is okay because the beauty of homeschooling is that there is no 'normal'.

I believe that one of the real dangers of home business and home education is that you'll forget what's most important. It's easy to get so caught up in the 'business' that you neglect the relationship with your children.

But take heart, even those who don't run a business on top of homeschooling often do the very same thing.

So…we're in this thing together…struggling our way through with our eye on the goal and reminding each other, "You cannot do it all!"

Be real.

PS - My sister, who happens to be a homeschooler, has noticed a trend of working homeschooling moms who are leaving their children on their own for long periods of time and calling it homeschooling. Mom, just a note of warning: your kids need your time more than they need your money.

JANUARY 22

A Letter to the .1%

Hey Mom,

I feel ticked…angry…MAD. I'm normally a pretty even-keeled guy and reserve my rants and raves for my family, but this time 'they've' pushed too hard. I feel like Popeye when he said, "That's all I can stands, I can't stands na' more!"

Here's the deal. For the past…I don't know, while…I've been posting homeschooling cartoons on my Facebook page. I still don't get Facebook, but I thought it was a good way to encourage the majority of my friends who happened to be homeschooling moms.

Most of my homeschooling cartoons poke fun at the oddities that seem to be common to homeschoolers. I mock our fears, foibles, and quirks. Like any good cartoon, they're all a little exaggerated, and that's what makes them funny.

The cartoons get shared like hotcakes and the comments spring up like daisies. 99.9% of the comments involve lots of LOLs and nods of agreement. But the other .1% of comments makes me mad…real mad.

Just for the record, I'm not mad because I can't handle criticism. Believe me, I get plenty of criticism and even kind of like it at times, in a demented sort of way, because it means I'm engaging the reader. But this .1% is more insidious and has the power to relock the shackles my cartoons release. In fact, those negative comments kill other homeschool moms.

Here's how: I post a cartoon that pokes fun at how hard a day of homeschooling can be on moms (see example*). Almost instantly, the comments begin..."Oh, that's so me...I can relate to that one...I can't stop laughing... ROFL...ouch!!!"

I just know moms are relieved to see the comments, knowing they're normal for feeling what they feel. Then out of the blue, like a sudden cold downpour comes, "I've homeschooled for seven years, and I've never felt that way before."

KABOOM!!!

Instantly, moms are afraid to comment and begin to believe the lie that they are alone in their struggle. They feel ashamed, pushed down, and isolated, while feelings of failure and condemnation pile up around them. And what about me? What am I feeling?

Oh, I'm MAD!!!

So listen to me you...you...YOU... .1% ers, Keep your mouths shut!!! You don't fool me. You have plenty of your own struggles but are under the delusion that you have to act as though you have it all together. You may not have done what the cartoon suggested, but don't you dare say, "I've never done, or felt, that way before."

You're killing your fellow moms, alienating those who need your friendship, and are setting yourself up for a world of hurt and loneliness. In fact, you'd do yourself a favor by being a little real with some of your Facebook friends. Tell them you yelled at the kids, hate cooking organically, or yelled at your husband.

Go ahead and share your homeschooling joys, parenting successes, and pictures of your organic, made-from-scratch chicken and turnip casserole...but then the next day share your homeschooling insecurities, parenting struggles, and the photo of the sugared cereal that you served for dinner But whatever you do, don't ever, EVER say, "I've never felt that way...or acted like that!!" because it makes me MAD and it stabs at the hearts of the homeschooling moms who are just like you!

Got it? Don't make me have to write about this again!

Be real...because you ARE real.

**See cartoon on next page.*

A really dumb question

JANUARY 23

When The Pile is Low

Hey Mom,

Just to let you know, I'm running a little behind so let me cut right to the chase. Most families have financial crises at some time or another. It doesn't matter if you've got a lot or very little, those times arise when you wonder if you'll have enough. Questions plague us like: Will this be the end of life as we know it? Or, what have we gotten ourselves into?

That's okay! God is big enough to handle any financial crisis. He said He'd provide for his children and He will. The bigger problem occurs when one family member (usually the wife) blames another family member (usually the husband) for getting them into the predicament.

Harsh words are said, feelings are hurt, and walls are erected. That's bad... real bad. Financial crisis? No big deal. You'll recover if you stay on the same team. You may lose your car, your house, and your dignity, but you'll still have a husband and the love that you share, which can weather ANYTHING.

Now, on the other hand, if you turn on your husband and end up losing him, then the house, the car, and your dignity won't really matter at all. The first one is important; the others aren't. The problem is that during financial crisis we often lose our perspective and make wrong choices.

So, if you've found yourself in the middle of a financial crisis, keep praying and keep hanging onto your husband's arm. Thank him for doing the best he can, and keep talking to him. If you sense defensiveness, back off, and love your man anyway.

You may lose everything else...but you will still have what's most important and worth having.

Be real.

JANUARY 24

Making Allowance

Hey Mom,

I'm all for allowances. I think husbands should get a few bucks a week to blow on Starbucks, Coke machines, and the occasional Dunkin' Donuts. Oh, oops, my wife just said this is supposed to be about allowances for children not husbands.

In that case, you've got to be kidding!! My children already get everything FREE. I pay for their food, clothes, and the occasional bag of candy when we run to Menard's. Why would I want to give them more money just for pulling their own weight around the house?

We're a family. We work together for the good of the family, enjoying the benefits of our teamwork. I don't get extra money for taking out the trash, and they shouldn't either just for throwing their underwear in the clothes hamper instead of leaving them on the floor.

We need each other, and I make it clear at our house that everyone has a vital role to play. I want the motivation for cleaning up the schoolroom to be a willingness to serve, not a chunk of change at the end of the week.

That said, I do believe in letting our kids enjoy the fruit of their labors. From time to time, we do have extra projects (beyond normal chores) that I pay the children for doing. I want them to learn how to manage money, that hard work has rewards, and that they can enjoy the benefits of work, not only by spending but also by giving to others.

That's different than allowances...I think.

Still, I could use a couple of bucks a week.

Be real.

JANUARY 25

I'm Singing the Midwinter Blues

Hey Mom,

Sing with me...

This is the day, this is the day,

That the Lord has made, that the Lord has made.

I will rejoice, I will rejoice,

And be glad in it, and be glad in it.

This is the day...yeah; it didn't work for me either.

That doesn't mean we shouldn't start each day out with this song and truth... but sometimes, after the song is over, we still feel like singing the homeschool, midyear blues. That's normal and OK. Even schoolteachers who get paid to teach someone else's kids feel that way.

The important thing is not to act on that feeling. Don't be too quick to throw out your old curriculum in hopes that something new might work better. Don't enroll your children in 'real' school, and don't assume the fetal position in a dark corner of your closet. Instead, follow the advice of my favorite Blue fish that sang to a ready-to-give-up clown fish, "Just keep swimming."

That's the secret of beating the blues. Thank God for a great Christmas break, start school back up at your normal time, pick up those same boring books that you're sick of, prepare yourself for the usual chaos, sing 'This is the Day', and then...just keep swimming.

Before you know it, the blues will disappear and you will have made it through the day.

So, sing with me...

This is the day, this is the day,

That the Lord has made, that the Lord has made.

I will rejoice, I will rejoice...and just keep swimming!

Be real.

Slobs Unite!!

Hey Mom,

I must admit that I'm a little distracted at the moment to be discussing homeschool organization. We're waiting for a baby to arrive. The official due date was two days ago but that's come and gone. But my wife assures me that "something is starting to happen."

Apparently you ladies have some kind of dash-light that flashes when something is happening because my wife is always right. So according to my calculations…it won't be much longer.

So let me just quickly say regarding this week's topic of homeschool organization: you either ARE organized or you're NOT (it's a God thing). If you are, then you don't need me to tell you how to organize your homeschool ('cause I'm not organized). If you're NOT organized, it doesn't matter too much what anyone tells you because it probably won't work anyway. The truth is: you try, fail, try, fail some more, and keep trying…and failing.

Now don't get me wrong, go ahead and try some organizational ideas, but don't be surprised or discouraged if it doesn't work for you. You're OK; God made you relaxed and organizationally-challenged.

Instead of feeling discouraged, enjoy the wonderful gift He has given you. And if you are the organized type, enjoy the gift God has given you…but don't be too hard on those of us who don't have your gift (we have our own).

~ A note to your husband: Dad, if your wife is one of those who is NOT naturally organized, love her unorganized-self just the way she is. Don't say critical comments and lower your expectations. You be the organized one in your home.

OK, I gotta go…do something.

Be real.

PS - If you're just sitting around trying to decide if you're organized enough and want something fun to do, read my Top 10 Things Not to Say to Your Wife in the Last Week of Pregnancy which you can find on my website.

A Tip from Abe

Hey Mom,

We're packing up 'the Beast' and planning to head out on a threeeee-week cruise, a three-week cruise (images of Gilligan's Island should flash through your head).

Because of time, I'm going to make this short. In fact, I'm going to give you a dad-tip from my son Abe. Let me set the story. A week ago I was minding my own business on my way to the bathroom to take care of...business. As I walked through the bathroom door, I was greeted by an explosion of little ½- inch-wide sticky notes in a rainbow of colors stuck all around the toilet corner wall.

Each note had three little words on it, I love you. And all were lovingly written and placed there by my son Abe. It was like an outpouring or avalanche of love notes. As I sat...on the throne, surrounded by my son's love I thought, "Who doesn't love to be lavished with love notes?"

Afterwards, I found Abe and returned the love, and since then, every time I walk into the bathroom, I am greeted by the notes (although they're starting to fall off).

So here's an Abe-tip for you, Mom: pick up one of those little variety packs of 1/2" x 2" sticky notes (I think they must be page highlighters). Write I Love You on each one and then stick the daylights out of your husband's dresser, son's desk, family bathroom mirror...or the space surrounding the toilet.

I'm telling you, THEY will feel as loved by their mom/wife as I felt loved by my son Abe.

Be real.

JANUARY 28

Wrongperspectivitis

I've got good news and bad news for you. The good news is that we had our baby last Tuesday morning. It was a boy...a big boy. As far as Wilson's go, he was the biggest yet, weighing in at 9lbs 8 oz. It was not an easy delivery and the contractions almost stopped by the end. In fact, my wife was about pushed out, and I was beginning to wonder if I could help things along by squeezing her like a bottle of ketchup...or catsup.

Anyway, everyone is doing great and this big boy of ours may go down as the quietest baby too. That's the good news!

The bad news is you might have a touch of 'wrongperspectivitis.' It tends to be an epidemic this time of year amongst homeschoolers, but don't be alarmed, I've seen worse.

Here are some of the symptoms: your children fuss a lot during school hours, you think your kids are dumb, lazy, complaining monsters…I mean, little darlings. The only time you smile is during summer vacation and two weeks at Christmas. You have less joy than a turnip and constantly compare your children and yourself with other homeschooling families (homeschool envy).

Yep, you've got it all right.

So, here's the cure. You have to change your perspective. Quit using the 'world's' measuring stick and start using God's. Believe it or not, God made you smart enough to figure out what that is – you don't need any 'experts.' So, figure out what that is and stick to it…no matter what! Quit looking around at how other families are doing and start enjoying your own. Stop measuring your success by your activities and achievements and how others will look on them.

I'm telling you, 'wrongperspectivitis' will kill you and sap every ounce of joy from your being.

Take a good spoonful of the truth, but don't call me in the morning!

Be real.

JANUARY 29

Cabin Fever

Hey Mom,

It's funny (in a morbid sort of way) that the topic of cabin fever should come up, because we have it here at the Wilson house. Maybe it's because we just had a baby or because the ground has been snow-covered for a couple of months now or that it's supposed to be warmer today. Whatever the reason, we'd like to load up the Familyman Mobile and go somewhere warm like… southern Indiana.

Now you may find yourself living in the tropical location of Kentucky and still be feeling the effects of cabin fever. It happens to all of us around this time of year. We're beginning to run out of steam after five months of homeschooling and have caught the faintest glimpse of the light at the end of the tunnel (and what a glorious light it is).

If we were in traditional school, we'd just have to gut it out, BUT we're not. We're home educators…LIFE educators. We can do what we want, when we want to do it. If we want to take a day or two off to play games, go shopping, do a little spring cleaning, or head to McDonald's for lunch, we can do that.

In fact, our family will be better off if we do, and so will yours.

So, if you're feeling the effects of cabin fever and have contemplated eating your children, then do something different for a day or two. In your best official voice announce, "We're doing something different today...something fun." Then do it...and don't feel guilty about it.

Be real.

PS – Need more convincing? Last week I was at a coffee shop and saw a bunch of obviously not homeschooled kids and asked them if they had school today. "No," they answered, "it's teacher workday, today." You tell me, what in Andrew Pudewa's name is teacher workday? If you ask me it sounds like a fancy name for cabin fever.

JANUARY 30

Thar She Writes!

Hey Mom,

I'm feeling a little woozy as I write. I spent a good chunk of the night sleeping on the floor next to my son Caleb (2) who threw up every fifteen minutes like Old Faithful. I'd pat his back, clean up, fall onto the floor, and just about doze off, when, "Thar she blows!"

Anyway, I'm hoping the feeling in my gut is all in my head. So I'm not sure if my thoughts will be very coherent regarding the topic at hand.

Actually, my thoughts on inspiring kids to write are pretty simple:

1) Don't use writing as a punishment.

"If you don't clean your room, you'll have to write a paper on why cleanliness is next to godliness."

You don't want to associate writing with punishment.

2) Make writing fun. Have them write about things that interest them. Let boys write about wars, sword fights, and bloodshed. Have your girls write skits about dolls, tea parties, kittens, and feelings.

3) If they cry while writing...take a break for a while.

Lastly, I don't think this is a point, but realize that some of your kids are going to be writers and some are NOT. My daughter Katherine can write better than I can. She didn't learn it; she was just made that way. My son Sam draws. Writing pains him, so we don't overly force it. That's just the way it is.

Don't believe the lie that says everyone needs to be able to write poetry and novel-length papers or they won't lead productive lives. Some people never learn to write super well...and that's OK.

There's just too much pressure on parents that all our kids have to master everything. The truth is they won't. And like I often say, that's OK.

Thar she blows!!! Gotta run.

Be real.

PS –My wife wanted me to let you know that Andrew Pudewa's writing stuff (www.writing-edu.com) has worked great for us. Tell him Todd sent you!

JANUARY 31

Say Cheese!!!

Hey Mom,

Let me take you back in time to when I was a boy living in a brick house in a small town in Indiana. Like the Walton's "Goodnight John Boy" routine, we had a bedtime ritual that still rings in my heart.

"Good night, Mom. Love you and like you, and see you in the morning."

"Good night, Dad. Love you and like you, and see you in the morning."

It might seem redundant to the casual observer, but it spoke of two distinct truths: loving and liking. And our kids need to know both.

The first one is a given: parents have to love their kids. Ask your children and they'll nod their heads and say, "Oh, yeah, I know you love me."

BUT then ask them (if you're brave enough) if they think you like them. You might be surprised by their answer. Because if you're like me, then you often prove to them all day long by your comments, frowns, and your "don't bother me now I'm typing an email" that you don't like them. Ouch. I think I just did that 4 seconds ago.

Guilty? Then how about showing your children today that you LIKE them. The best way to do that is SMILE. A smile conveys that 'I like you.'

So when your daughter changes her clothes for the third time BEFORE lunch…smile. When your toddler messes up the schoolroom…smile. When your teenager says something to irritate you…smile. When your husband says he's going to watch the game tonight…smile.

I guarantee if you smile at them…they will feel LIKED.

On your mark, get set, SMILE.

Be real.

Take it From a Dirt-Jar

Hey Mom,

Here's the long and the short of it. A day at our house is much like a day at your house, although you probably don't believe me. You're convinced that YOUR house is the only one that is filled with bad attitudes, yelling, and pigpen messes.

You assume that every other family starts the day before sunrise, spends an hour in family worship, and eats a good, hot, home-cooked breakfast together before the children happily do their chores, with school beginning promptly at 7 AM.

You really believe that every other homeschool family basks in the glow of learning and being together all day, that the children share joyfully and are several grade levels above their peers, and that each of them has mastered the Cello.

The truth is…all of our houses are pretty similar in different ways. No one has arrived; in fact, there are days where I feel like we haven't even shown up at the starting line.

As hard as we'll try today to please God in all that we do, I'm just about sure the kids will argue, or I'll blow my cool, snip at my wife, ignore my children, or act about as ungodly as I DON'T want to be. I wish it were different…and someday it will be (when I die!), but I draw comfort from knowing we're all in the same boat together.

We're just plain old dirt-jars (that's what the Bible says) so that when we do have a good day, exhibit a good attitude, or experience self-control, we can say, "That was totally God because it didn't come from me." (2 Corinthians 4:7)

So from one dirt-jar to another, keep praying, trying, loving, and asking forgiveness from those you hurt, and take comfort in knowing that you're not alone and that one day…things will be different.

Be real.

FEBRUARY 2

On Your Mark, Get Set, Convention!

Hey Mom,

Should you go to a Homeschool Convention this year? Does a one-legged duck swim in a circle? Of course you should go. As a dad who goes around speaking at conventions all over the country, I believe there is no better place to feel encouraged, challenged, and part of something big.

Where else can you go and be surrounded by people just like you and look at and handle a hundred different homeschool possibilities?

Mom, I know I don't need to convince you. Usually it's the husband who can be the sticking point.

So let me talk to him for just a second: Dad, your wife needs her batteries recharged. Now you might think otherwise, but you're wrong. In fact, ALL homeschooling moms need encouragement and refreshment in this journey, and a homeschool convention does just that.

So, Dad, can I put the pressure on you to take the bull by the horns and plan to go to the convention nearest you? Don't want to plan it all out? Then just tell your wife, "Honey let's go to a convention this year."

I know it's not the most exciting thing for a guy, but it's not all about you. Sometimes you have to do what she'd like to do. She may say she doesn't need to go...but don't accept that answer. Insist not only that she go but also that you accompany her. Go all out if you can. Stay in a hotel, eat out, stroll the aisles, and make it a weekend to remember.

Who knows? Maybe I'll see you there. You can view my convention schedule on my website.

Be real.

FEBRUARY 3

Balancing M and H

Hey Mom,

Why do you moms always talk about balancing ministry and home as though they are two different, and at odds, entities? The truth is: your home-school IS your ministry...or less schoolishly put, your HOME IS your ministry.

As a former pastor, let me apologize for all the well-meaning pastors, teachers, and Christians who have made you feel guilty if you're not involved in 'real' ministries like the church choir, Sunday school, women's Bible studies, or the nursery.

Not to downplay those important ministries, but your ministry of caring for the needs of your husband and family are just as important.

My fear is that the guilt can be so great that you might neglect your most important ministry (training your children) for one that can be done by someone else. In fact, I would say that it might be time to say NO to some of those 'ministries' you've been involved in so you can devote your time to your REAL ministry.

Just tell them, "Todd told me to say no."

~ A note to your husbands: Let me restate that there is a lot of pressure on our wives to be busy outside the home. It's up to you to be her muscle and take the heat for some of her "no" decisions.

When I was a pastor, I once was called on the carpet by the senior pastor because my wife didn't attend a women's meeting. I politely said, "I told her she doesn't have to go. She is busy ministering to our family and that's a full-time ministry."

You know what? He was OK with that...but even if he wasn't, I would have stood my ground.

Be real.

FEBRUARY 4

Don't Call it a Fieldtrip

Hey Mom,

Want to hear a sad story? The only fieldtrips I experienced in all of my growing up years were trips to the Wonder Bread Factory, the zoo, the state museum, and as a senior in high school, a day in Chicago doing...something. That's it.

In contrast, my children have been to civil war battlefields, national monuments, museums of every variety, historical sites, and hometowns of famous Americans...all because they are homeschooled.

I can remember standing in line to tour a lighthouse on Anastasia Island near St. Augustine, Florida a couple of years ago. There were just a few people behind us because it was in late spring and 'real' schools were still in session.

As is often asked, the lady behind the counter said, "So, no school today?"

"Oh, we homeschool," I answered a little reluctantly. "Our kids get to SEE what most kids just read about."

The words were barely out of my mouth before a lady behind me spoke up.

"I'm a public school teacher," she said boldly as I prepared to be blasted, "and I think what you're doing is WONDERFUL."

I smiled, thankful that she hadn't blasted me and that she encouraged us in the direction we had chosen to go. A few minutes later, we stood atop the St. Augustine Lighthouse stunned by the view and the history we were experiencing.

Now we don't record our fieldtrips, make the kids write reports, or have them take a test on what they saw...in fact, we don't even call them fieldtrips. It somehow desecrates the good name of fun and family outing and stifles learning. We just experience the moment and enjoy it with the people we love most...and buy a few souvenirs.

I'm telling you, that's a lot better than a trip to the Wonder Bread Factory.

Be real.

Easy and Hard Creation Science

Hey Mom,

There are two kinds of creation science: the easy kind and the hard kind. We've been teaching the easy kind even before our kids could talk.

"Oh, look at the pretty flower. Doesn't it smell good? God made that flower."

When they get a year or two older it goes like this: "Oh, look at the pretty flower. Doesn't it smell good? Who made that flower?"

Without hesitation the child answers, "Gawd."

"That's right," we say and then march down "the list."

"Who made the grass?"

"Gawd."

"Who made the clouds?"

"Gawd."

And on it goes. That's the easy kind. It's not about a certain curriculum or textbook (even though there are some good ones); it's about teaching your children about God and all of His creation.

The hard kind of creation science is...harder. It doesn't involve flowers, dinosaurs, and nebula so much as it involves RVs. We're heading out TODAY for a three-month homeschool convention tour. As I type this, my RV is in the shop having expensive, inconvenient things done to it. I had planned to be loading today, but I can't because it's not here...but there.

Here's where REAL creation science takes place because teaching creation science is more than teaching our children ABOUT God and His creation; it also involves modeling the realization that GOD is in CONTROL of His creation.

So when my RV isn't working, I say, "God is in control, and He knows what's best."

When it snows, and I'd rather have sunshine and warmth, I say, "This is the day that God wanted us to have...let's enjoy it and make it a good one."

When the car doesn't start, a tree falls on the garage, or I run over the mailbox with my big RV (like I did yesterday), I say and believe, "God's in charge and this is part of his plan...somehow. Let's thank him right now."

That's REAL creation science...and what our children need us to teach them every day. It 'ain't easy, but you can do it.

Be real.

Keep Laughing

Hey Mom,

For the last several years, I've earned a big chunk of my living by looking at the hilarious side of homeschooling. I poke fun at our seriousness, peculiarities, and unique struggles. I talk about them, write about them, and have even immortalized them in a few volumes of homeschooling cartoons.

My sole purpose in doing this is to remind homeschoolers that they are not alone. The ugly truth is that you think you're the only one who has ever hid in the closet to have a good cry, threatened your children with REAL school, or done some absurdly weird behavior in order to MAKE your children ENJOY school.

The truth is: you are not alone. You are normal. Your children are normal, your marriage is normal, and your struggles, failures, and peculiarities are NORMAL.

And the natural, herbal, healing response when faced with such normal behavior is to…laugh!

And of course…Be real.

PS – If it's been a while since you've had a good laugh, get all four volumes of The Official Book of Homeschooling Cartoons. You can find them on our website store: familymanweb.com.

The Trotting Gourmet

Hey Mom,

Okay, giving advice on meal planning is a first for me, but I'm up for the challenge.

So, here is the Familyman's Guide to No-Guilt Meal Planning.

1. If your dog won't lick the plates afterwards, then don't serve it.
2. Sugar is not poison.
3. Just because it comes in a box, plastic package, or a can, does not mean it's evil.
4. Macaroni and Cheese served with hot dogs is the perfect meal.
5. If you want to serve macaroni and cheese and hot dogs twice in one week...that's OK.

6. If cooking something from scratch makes you cry or causes great emotional distress, then don't cook from scratch (see rule 3).

7. Teach your daughters to cook and then make them do it...for school.

8. Serve Twinkies for dessert to your gourmet friends the next time they come over. If you are a natural-only foods eater, stop reading this email, get in your car, run to the store, buy a box of Twinkies, and serve them for dessert tonight to your family (they're going to love you).

9. If you like Frosted Flakes for breakfast, whatever you do, don't hide the box in the back of the pantry. Consider displaying it on top of your refrigerator or mantle to let people know.

10. Remember Jesus' words, "It is not what goes into a man (woman or child) that makes him unclean but what comes out (of his mouth)." See rule 8.

11. Avoid articles, books, or people that discuss the spiritual qualities of eating only what you can pick from your front yard.

12. If you enjoy gourmet cooking, eating organically, and grinding your own...whatever, enjoy it...just keep it to yourself. Oh, and don't write mean letters to me.

13. And last but not least...BE REAL!

Bon Appétit!

FEBRUARY 8

Send Them Outside

Hey Mom,

Three homeschool conventions down and only ten to go. Tell you what, we're looking forward to some warm weather and meeting even more great homeschoolers this weekend in Albaxur...Albquaque...Alboqwark...that place in New Mexico.

One of the great things about traveling around in the Familyman Mobile is that we get a change of scenery. Not that I ever get tired of all that Indiana has to offer, but it is nice to see mountains, cactus, and the ocean from time to time, which brings me to this topic: studying the great outdoors.

In the olden days, studying the great outdoors was just part of life. Kids played outside and dads and moms answered the questions that playing outside generated.

But homeschooling ruined that. Now we feel as though we need to sanctify playtime by 'schoolifying' it. We justify outside time by throwing in some instruction so that we can mark it down on our permanent record.

It's too bad. Outside used to be so fun and children learned so much. Now I'm afraid kids learn less and enjoy it less.

So my encouragement is this: on the next sunny afternoon, let the kids go outside, play until they're worn out, and allow learning to take place all by itself. Don't try to schoolify it, mark it down, or make them write a paper on it.

Be real.

FEBRUARY 9

An Understanding Mom

Hey Mom,

We spent the weekend in Greenville, SC and had a great time...other than locking our keys in our van TWICE and accidentally breaking one window trying to get in.

We didn't take the Familyman Mobile this time. I forgot how difficult it is driving a bunch of miles in a non-bathroom containing vehicle. In the RV when the kids need to 'go' they just get up and 'go.'

In a regular van you have to find a gas station and wait until everyone gets out and gets back in, ONLY to hear 15 miles down the road, "Daddy, I have to go to the bathroom."

I did better for a change. Normally, I make sure that everyone knows how upset I am to be stopping...but not on this trip.

As I drove, I thought: why do we get mad at those we love for things that seem so petty? Is it because our kids and wives get in the way of our agenda? Or because we can't take 10 minutes out of our lives...or are we just jerks?

Later when we pulled into our driveway everyone went inside to plop into bed. I had to make MY stop at the bathroom when I heard my son, Abe (11) yell down from upstairs, "Dad, can Cal (5) sleep in my bed?"

"Sure, Abe," I snapped..."I'll move him when I'm done." Why is that boy so afraid? I asked myself.

When I finally got upstairs, Abe was crying, apologizing, and explaining his fear. I'm such a jerk. I held him tightly for a whole minute, reassured him everything was OK, and that I understood.

Sometimes Mom, we've stopped trying to understand. We forget what it was like to be 8-years-old (or 18-years-old), to have a small bladder, to be short and unable to reach something, to be weak and not able to open something, to want to go somewhere and not able to drive...or to be afraid of the dark.

So my fellow parent, next time you're tooling down the road and hear, "I gotta go," or "Can we stop there?" REMEMBER what it was like to be 'them', and say, "We'll stop at the next exit."

I gotta go myself.

Be real.

Make it a Date

Hey Mom,

Hot-dog! Now this is a topic I can wrap my arms around. If there is anything lacking in the typical homeschool family, it is the fact that husband/wife dating has been nudged out of its seat at the family table and been replaced by duty, business, and...homeschooling.

As my old buddy the Apostle Paul used to say, "May it never be."

Husband/wife dating is not just important; it is vital. I know you're worn out by your daily responsibilities, but Valentine's Day is the perfect time to re-ignite those passions and remind your husband just why you said, "I do." You know what? I bet you could use a little reminding yourself.

So here's what you should do:

As soon as you finish reading this, stand up and announce, "We're doing something different today for school."

Then gather up all the red, pink, and white construction paper you can find and have the kids spend an hour cutting out hearts of varying sizes. Next, write every love phrase you can think of on those hearts. Use family favorites, Bible verses about love, and even silly thoughts. Then stick them up on every surface in your home, string them together and hang them from the doorways, and hide them for your husband to find.

Now, back to the date thing. Get on the phone right now and see if you can find someone to watch the kids (maybe even trade with a friend...you watch their kids on Friday while they go out and then switch for Saturday).

Next, think about what you might wear on that date. I know it's a couple days away...but you used to think about it before you were married. Write out a list of 10 questions to ask your husband to talk about on your date. Nothing too serious, just "do you remember when" questions.

Finally, once the plans have been made, email or write a note to your man letting him know about the date and that you'll be looking forward to the night...wink, wink.

Oh, I know it sounds like a lot of effort...but it is worth it, and it just might jumpstart your homeschool-induced, sluggish marriage and make it ZING!!!

Happy Valentine's Day!

Fun Things to Do For Valentine's Day

Hey Mom,

Here's the secret about fun things to do for Valentine's Day...they're not always fun.

It sometimes seems like something that starts out as a fun idea...turns sour. In my head, I imagine a day filled with red construction paper valentine cutouts and a house filled with love. I imagine a romantic candlelight dinner on a white linen tablecloth as my wife and I get lost in each other's eyes...and then I wake up to the reality of kids who are bickering over who got to hang the valentine decorations last year and how somebody doesn't like what we're having for dinner and why they would have rather had the candy someone else got instead.

Oh no, Valentine's Day isn't always fun...but it is so important. It's the one day each year that is set apart to let those in our lives know how important they are to us. And while a valentine scrooge might insist that we should be showing love all 365 days a year...I know some would kill to be shown it on at least this day.

So Moms, go all out! Declare a school vacation, decorate with red hearts, make a special pink and white cake, buy those wonderful heart-shaped candies, and tell that family of yours how much you love them. It may not be fun... but it is important.

Be real.

FEBRUARY 12

All You Need is LOVE...

Hey Mom,

Can't you just feel the love in the air? Of course, if you're a typical home-schooling mom...sometimes the love gets lost in all the...the...homeschooling.

It's kind of sad really. You started this homeschooling journey thinking everyday would be filled with love and learning (not the love OF learning). You imagined yourselves reading books, laughing, and being together. But something changed. You went from laughing to talking really LOUD.

It's understandable. The lies begin to creep in through the cracks in the walls the day you start homeschooling. Whispers of "you aren't doing enough...the kids are behind...you should be doing more" reach your heart, and you start getting LOUDER.

I was just reading some pathetically sad stories of homeschooled children who left their families, homeschooling, and in many cases walked away from God. They left because their homes were filled with fear instead of love and they were pushed to look and act a certain way.

I guess I should be hard on their parents, but I can't seem to bring myself to that. I feel sorry for them instead. They were after all just doing what they thought was best…even though they bought into a LIE from the pit of Hell.

Jesus didn't ask them to do what they did…but some homeschool/family 'experts' DID. The experts scared the parents and then offered simple solutions to complex issues. Parents traded loving their children for loving their children's behavior and progress…and it didn't work. In fact, in so many instances it turned out terrible.

So here's my Valentine's Homeschooling advice: LOVE YOUR SPOUSE AND CHILDREN…NOT their behavior or progress. Spend less time being LOUD and laugh more and expect less.

That's amore!!!

Be real.

FEBRUARY 13

I Love this Day

Hey Mom,

To be honest, I'm a fairly recent convert to being a Valentine's Day lover (if you count 20 years as recent). Growing up, it seemed like one of those holidays where my mom fixed a nice dinner and placed our favorite candy on our plate. There were no presents involved…no decorations, Valentine's tree, Valentine's music, or TV specials.

Then one V-day my new wife and I traveled to the middle of nowhere Wisconsin with some friends for the weekend. We stayed at their parents and were with them for their family Valentine's dinner, and they had decorations. Nothing elaborate; just a bunch of red hearts cut from construction paper with 'love phrases' and Bible verses written on them. I was hooked.

How cool that this family celebrated God's love for them and their love for each other. Since then, we've done the same thing. In fact, right now I'm surrounded by those same red valentines with our own phrases of love written upon them. On the big V-day, we'll have a nice meal and place our kids' favorite treat at their plate, and we'll let them know how much they are loved by God and by us.

I love Valentine's Day. Just a simple holiday without the pressures of Christmas, devoted to saying to those you sometimes overlook, "I love you so much."

Be real.

Happy Valentine's Day

Hey Mom,

I have a few old school memories tucked in the back of my head: the smell of chalk dust, white paste, and mimeograph paper. The feeling of nervousness on the first day of school, the asbestoses looking pipes in my middle school (even though it wasn't called middle school at the time). I remember Christmas parties and hot summer days without air-conditioning. One distinct memory is of classroom Valentine's Day parties.

In those days we made Valentine's Day Mailboxes to receive our dime store Valentine's Day cards. We'd decorate the boxes and then watch the cards come pouring in, hoping that there would be lots of suckers stuck to the cards. Man, that was fun.

Sometimes homeschoolers miss out on those memories because...well, you know why.

You know Mom, today would be a great day to do a little Valentine-ing. Instead of the regular show today, load up the kids and go buy some of those cheap Valentine's Day cards or have the kids make their own. Then write little notes on them and give them to some of your special friends and relatives.

While your children are doing that, make sure you write a few of your own, telling each of your children (and your husband) how much you love them.

I'd just about bet the farm that forty years from now your children will remember making those little cards in your home just like I remember doing at White River Elementary School.

Happy Valentine's Day.

Two Thumbs Up for Math

Hey Mom,

I won't even pretend to be a math curriculum expert. I barely get by with counting. What I will tell you though is what has worked for our family. Like many homeschoolers, we've tried a myriad of math curriculums...or curricula, in search of some easy, foolproof, holy grail of math.

Unfortunately, it's all a math-myth, and there is no one-size-fits-all, magic math program. BUT, even after having said that, we tried and are very pleased with Teaching Textbooks*. Both of my older boys have used it now. It's the first program after 8 years of homeschooling that they've actually liked, and imagine this, even finished their level for this year (which is almost unheard of in our family).

In fact, my sons, Ben and Sam, give Teaching Textbooks two big thumbs up. My daughter will start the 6th grade program next year and can hardly wait. I'll also give a little plug for the creators of the program: two Harvard graduate brothers that we affectionately call the Algebra Brothers. We've known them since they first started and have been pleased, not only by their product, but also by their testimony, philosophy, and knowledge of the educational field.

So from this math-challenged dad, that's my recommendation.

Be real.

PS -I originally wrote this almost six years ago and we're still thrilled with Teaching Textbooks.

FEBRUARY 16

Don't Retire!!

Hey Mom,

It seems like just a few years ago that we began this homeschooling journey. We started with two little boys and high hopes. We got a wooden table, some books, a plan, and set off on this great adventure we call homeschooling. Oh, it wasn't as easy as we thought and there were times that we thought they'd never get it...and you know what happened? They both graduated. Just like that it's over. At least for them. We still have a seven-year-old so the way I calculate it we'll be homeschooling....FOREVER, plus a year or two.

That thought makes me feel old, especially when I was reminded earlier this week that some of those people who started about the same time as we did are done. Finished. Complete. Their kids have graduated, and they've got the freedom gleam in their eye.

That makes me even "sadder" because they're still needed by so many other homeschoolers. In fact, their encouragement to other homeschooling moms may be more valuable now that their kids are gone. But retired homeschooling moms are jumping ship. They stop going to homeschool conventions, support group meetings, and mentoring young homeschooling moms.

That's what my sister, Wendy said to us last summer. She's been home-schooling for five or six years and told my wife, "All my mentors have left...I feel like I'm all alone with no one to encourage me in what I believe."

That's why I'm writing to you while you're still homeschooling, because the day will soon come when you'll be done. You'll pack up the books and quit subscribing to homeschool magazines. You'll toss the state convention flyer in the trash and quit visiting homeschool blogs. When that time comes I hope you hear my voice ring loud in your head. DON'T RETIRE! THEY NEED YOU NOW MORE THAN EVER!!!!!

Those other homeschool moms need you to:

1. Remember what it was like to homeschool and to be real with them. Tell those moms your struggles and fears and how you locked yourself in the bathroom and pretended to be dead just so they would leave you alone. Tell them that these are the best days and that one day soon they're going to miss all the chaos and homeschool clutter.

2. Remind them about what really matters (and what doesn't). Several years ago I was in church and overheard a new homeschooling mom ask a hyper-academic homeschool mom for advice. I listened intently to what she was going to say and was surprised when she said, "I guess I would just enjoy your children more." You tell those moms the same.

3. Remind them to make their marriage a priority. My wife and I talked last night about how all these homeschooling couples are struggling. Homeschooling can suck up marriages if it goes unchecked. You tell those moms to love their husbands.

4. Stay involved. Go to the support group meetings for them. Go along with the girls to the homeschool convention (maybe even pay for someone else's admission). Renew your homeschool magazine subscriptions so you'll know what's going on. Keep visiting the homeschool blogs and share your perspective. Pick a young homeschooling mom to have lunch with once a month.

I know it would be easier to drop out and move on…BUT DON'T RETIRE!!!! THEY NEED YOU!!!

Be real.

FEBRUARY 17

Graduating Preschoolers

Hey Mom,

I'm not sure I have any great ideas to help you homeschool with preschoolers in the house that don't involve duct tape and a cage, but I will say, don't wish these days away.

One day you will wish you had these difficult days back. I hear that from moms whose kids are all grown up. They long for the silly giggles, busy little hands, and tireless chatterboxes that once filled their days…days that pass too quickly.

So my fellow parent of preschoolers, enjoy these days of chaos and unending messes…because one day you'll wish you had.

Be real.

PS - Need s song to back up this truth? Listen to "Don't Blink" by Kenny Chesney.

FEBRUARY 18

Classic Shmassic

Hey Mom,

Classical Education? Hmmm. If you want to know about classical education, I'm afraid you're talking to the wrong guy. In fact, I probably know more about the eating habits of the cuttlefish* than I know about classical education, and that 'ain't saying much.

Classical Education sounds smart though and it wouldn't take much to convince this simple minded dad that classical education is better say than…a regular education.

That's the thing about us parents; we're saps for a fancy title. We just naturally assume a cool, 'smart' sounding anything must be better. So we abandon our old way of doing something in lieu of our new classical 'something or other.'

Now, again I won't pretend to know anything about classical education, but I will say if after you look at it and don't like it…don't do it. In fact don't let anyone convince you do it. Or if you've already started it and hate it…STOP. You're smart enough to figure out what is best for your child.

Of course on the other hand if you look at and like the classical education model…go for it…just don't tell anyone else, "You have to do this!!!"

Be real.

PS - The name cuttlefish is sometimes erroneously applied to the squid. About 100 species of cuttlefish are known, widely distributed in the seas of the Tropic and Temperate zones. Cuttlefish are the most incredible looking creatures. A cuttlefish has ten arms and a chalky internal shell. One pair of arms is longer than the rest and is used to capture prey. Along with squid and octopus, cuttlefish propel themselves through the water at great speed by jetting water from the mantle cavity through a siphon. Cuttlefish have some economic importance, not only for their flesh, which is eaten in many countries, but also for the "bone" of their internal shell and for the ink they secrete to cloud the water and elude their enemies.

Vacation Learning?

Hey Mom,

Oh man, learning AND vacation?!!! What is the homeschooling world coming to? Learning and vacation go together like a peanut butter and meatloaf sandwich.

Now don't get me wrong. I'm all for learning while on vacation. I'm just against trying to force our kids to learn while on vacation. Vacation is a hallowed institution that shouldn't be tainted by trying to get our children to learn something.

They will learn on their own. They'll learn that there is a time to rest, recreate, and enjoy. They'll learn about all kinds of stuff like how to shuck corn on the cob, how to get along with others, and how to spit watermelon seeds. They'll learn by digging in the dirt, playing outside, and being with friends and grandparents.

That's the beauty of vacation, but I'm afraid many homeschool moms mar its beauty by trying to turn it into something it is not…school.

What I'm about to say will be hard for some of you schooloholic parents to swallow, but it needs to be said. When the time comes, you need to take a summer vacation.

That's right! You need to start around Memorial Day and go all the way through August. You need to put the books, the schedule, and the school agenda away and put on your summer fun hat instead.

You need to enjoy your children as children NOT as students, and your children need to experience you as their mother NOT as their teacher.

I know that some of you are feeling an aneurysm coming on at the mere thought of taking a vacation…but trust me on this one. You and your children NEED a vacation.

So talk to your husband and start planning a vacation away from life. Feeling broke? Plan it anyway. You may not be able to go to a tropical island, but it's amazing what you can do for 'not much money.'

Be real.

Just Let Him

Hey Mom,

It's a drizzly, rainy day as I write this from a truck stop near Toledo, OH. Other than the almost-nightly severe thunderstorms and tornado warnings, we had a great time at the state homeschool convention in Des Moines, IA...at which many of you informed me that it means "River of Monks."

OK, now onto the topic at hand—the importance of homeschooling fathers. Let me say that not only do I think homeschooling fathers are important, but I think they are the KEY to successful homeschooling. If that's so, then the question to ask is how do you get one more involved?

Glad you asked.

Are you ready for this? Whenever he involves himself in any way...LET HIM. Don't tell him how he could do it better, point out his shortcomings, or correct him. If you do, he won't want to involve himself again. Instead, when he involves himself in any way, let him do it HIS WAY and then thank him.

If you do that, I GUARANTEE he will do it again—end of topic.

Be real.

FEBRUARY 21

You're a Trailblazer

Hey Mom,

Right now, we're at Sandy Cove*, a spectacular camp facility near the headwaters of the Chesapeake. I'm speaking at Homeschool Family Week where 600 homeschoolers have gathered to play, worship, and encourage each other in the most demanding/rewarding task on the planet...homeschooling/parenting.

This fits perfectly with the topic at hand...homeschool trailblazers. Often we think of the homeschool pioneers as those who homeschooled 30 years ago in curtain-drawn rooms, boldly doing what few dared to do. While that is true, I'm constantly reminded how just about everyone who homeschools is a trailblazer.

Just this week, I've talked to some trailblazers who are the only home-schooling family in their mega church, trailblazers whose family just can't seem to figure them out, and a family who lives in China Town in New York City who doesn't even know of another homeschooling family anywhere nearby.

Trailblazers…all of them. Did I say them? I mean all of YOU.

You're blazing trails through still-hostile territory for others to follow. You're dealing with in-laws, neighbors, and church members so that your children won't have to.

And for that, I salute you.

Well done trailblazers…keep up the good work and…

Be real.

PS - Want a great homeschooling friendly summer vacation? Check out these two great places: Sandy Cove Ministries at sandycove.org (look for the homeschool week) and Harvey Cedars Bible Conference at hcbible.org.

FEBRUARY 22

A Few of Our Favorite Things

Hey Mom,

Semi-Tranquility Base here: the Wilson family has landed. After traversing the country speaking at state homeschooling conventions and meeting lots of moms and dads, we pulled into our driveway and have begun the long process of unpacking and getting life under control.

One of the cool things about our travel season is being reminded that all of us parents face the same issues. We work hard at training our children, fail often, and try some more. I'm so encouraged to hear your REAL stories, because somehow it's comforting to know we're all in the same boat (although sometimes it feels like it's sinking fast), which leads me to share with you the Wilson's favorite science resources (notice the seamless transition). Let me just list them.

1. Life – bugs, slugs, and grubs.
2. Books – Not the textbook kind, but those living books that bring science to life, like Carry on Mr. Bowditch, Pagoo, and My Side of the Mountain.
3. Audios – My children love to listen to stories about normal people who discovered amazing things.
4. Magazines – Much of our science book learning comes from the science magazines that we stash in our bathroom. The kids love to leaf through them whether they can read or not. Some of our favorites: Answers, Zoo books, and Nature's Friend.

Be real.

There are History Books and Then There Are HISTORY BOOKS

Hey Mom,

I love history, but I'll confess that after completing the best public education had to offer, about all I knew was that World War II came AFTER World War I. I was a TV kid after all. And if it wasn't featured on the Wonderful World of Disney or mentioned on Happy Days or Laverne and Shirley, I didn't know about it.

My love of history was ignited when I began to study the Bible but was fanned as we began to read to our children. Ask them about history, and they can tell you about all kinds of Civil War generals, ancient civilizations, and obscure facts in history. I attribute 95% of all the history they know from reading good 'story' books…we don't do history textbooks (although we love Diana Waring's resources*). The other 5% of history comes from audio CDs that they've been listening to since they were little critters.

If you want a great list of history books, visit Sonlight Curriculum, stop by Books Bloom, or start with the Little House on the Prairie series.

I'm telling you, it's all about reading good 'story' books. It's not about memorizing dates or being tested. It's about immersing your children in a well-told historical tale and experiencing it.

Now with all that said, some of your children will not get history. They just won't care for it. My oldest daughter has been reading since she was tiny. She loves stories about horses and relationships between girls and kittens, but cares diddly about history, although she's visited the battlefields of Gettysburg and Chickamauga, the site of the Johnstown flood, and Edison's Menlo Park. AND THAT'S OK. Some get it, others don't. The important thing is to cultivate your child's strengths.

Be real.

** Sonlight.com is a great resource and one of our all-time favorites. The folks at Books bloom.com don't get any better. You can get some great history resources at Dianawaring.com.*

Each is a Gift

Hey Mom,

Actually my wife should be writing this because she's the reading curriculum expert. I CAN read…but don't know much about teaching it. We've used two different methods: Sing, Spell, Read, and Write and Teach Your Children to Read in 100 Easy Lessons.

But let me tell you, it's not so much about the curriculum as it is about the child. I know my wife decided to teach my oldest daughter to read with the 100 Easy Lessons. Katherine got it on lesson six. It just made sense to her, and it wasn't long before she was reading chapter books with incredible fluency.

Now my son right after her has struggled. In fact, I'm not sure he would get it after using the curriculum How to Teach your Child to Read in 10,000 HARD Lessons. It just doesn't make sense to him. Oh, he understands that the letters make sounds and has mastered that, but when you put them together… well, that's another story.

So what's the difference? Did Katherine become a great reader because the curriculum was so awesome and my wife was such a great teacher? No. She's a great reader because God made her that way.

What about her brother? Does he struggle because the curriculum stinks or my wife has forgotten how to teach? NO. He struggles with that subject because that's the way God made him (he's a wiz at math by the way).

My job as a parent (and your job as well) is to love my child just the way God made him/her. Instead, we get frustrated and our children might just think, "Mom would like me more if I read better."

I know that's not the truth. You love your child as much as I do mine…but I'm afraid that's what we sometimes portray.

So Mom and Dad, got a good reader? Enjoy the gift. Got a slow reader? ENJOY THE GIFT as well.

Be real.

FEBRUARY 25

Our Favorite things

Hey Mom,

Favorite things about homeschooling…hmmm…favorite things…favorite things. (Queue the music.)

School in my PJs and short simple school days
Hot steaming coffee and basking in sunrays
Children that miss out on lots of 'bad' things
These are a few of my favorite things
Oom pah pah…oom pah pah
Mountains of good books and time for their hobbies
Learning to be godly daddies and mommies
Chores and routines that help keep our house clean
These are a few of my favorite things
Babies and toddlers and growing teenagers
All in the same house without social dangers
Living and learning although the phone rings
These are a few of my favorite things
When the kids scream
When I act mean
When I'm feeling sad

I simply remember my favorite things and then I don't feeeeeeelllll sooo baaaad.

The hills are alive with the sound of REALNESS!

FEBRUARY 26

Mind Reader

Hey Mom,

Howdy from Shippensburg, PA. The last couple of days have been good; we visited Harper's Ferry National Park and the Antietam Battlefield – sight of the bloodiest day of the Civil War.

Seeing the old photos of dead men piled high in Bloody Lane and then watching my kids run and play in the same deeply worn lane is a little sobering. It's been 150 years since those sons and fathers died. Each one of those bloated and decaying bodies had stories, unrealized dreams, and unspoken words of love, as well as regretted words.

As I walked to Lowes with my sons Abe (10), Cal (5), and Jed (3) this evening, I noticed an old guy sitting in his truck in the Wal-mart parking lot. Although he wasn't dead and bloated yet, he was quite old as he sat watching my sons and I weave through the maze of cars.

Actually, I felt more like I was walking two dogs, tangled as they chased each other around me like a maypole. When I looked up and saw the old guy in the truck, I had to check my face to see if I was smiling or growling.

At that moment, we caught each other's eye. I smiled and nodded; he just stared blankly at us, but it was what he THOUGHT that caught my attention.

Oh, yeah, I have that power to read the thoughts of other dads.

"I miss those days," was all he thought, "a lot."

As I crossed the parking lot, I thought about his…thoughts and knew one day I too would miss these days of chaos, exhaustion, homeschooling and walks across the parking lot with giggling boys.

And so will you.

Be real.

FEBRUARY 27

Don't Teach a Fish to Climb

Hey Mom,

I was just in my son Sam's room looking over his shoulder as he sketched a story board drawing on his computer. He's enrolled in Animation Mentor*, a program designed to train the next wave of Pixar and Disney animators.

I stood amazed, not by his ability or the nice things his teacher said about his work, but that this was the same kid who was born a shocking shade of yellow, whose head slumped to one side, and who would write his words like they were in a mirror.

I guess what amazed me then and does even as I type this is the truth that every one of God's creations is a masterpiece. But when we judge everyone by the same standard only a few…measure up.

I think that's what smart guy Albert Einstein meant when he said, "Everybody is a genius. But if you judge a fish by its ability to climb a tree, it will live its whole life believing that it is stupid."

My other children don't have Sam's artistic abilities. One is an incredible communicator, another is an inventor, one is a writer, one a builder, another is relational…and a couple of little boys are just plain fun. But they are all geniuses, gifted by the Creator for some important role they are to play now and in the future. ALL of them.

The thing about us homeschooling parents is that we like to use the same standard for everyone. We like those who do well in math (and reward them with an A), those who are entrepreneurs, play instruments, excel in sports, or do something applaudable. We've forgotten that it is ALL applaudable. They are geniuses!!

Not only do we spend much of our time feeling uncertain about our children's ungenius-like qualities but we doom our children to failure in our eyes. Like Einstein's illustration we spend all our energies trying to teach fish to climb trees...somehow believing that is more noble and worthy.

The beauty of homeschooling (and parenting) is that we can relax, knowing that our children will excel in what they were created to excel in. They may not make much money, have fancy houses or cars, but they will be happy doing what God created them to do, IF we allow them to swim (if they're fish).

So...if you have an art kid let him do art. If you have a math kid, let him do math, if you have a relational kid, let him...relate. Let each of them explore the areas of their giftedness and spend as little time as possible on their non-gifted areas.

Stop listening to the experts and start listening to the genius inside of you who knows what your children need to excel. And if you're struggling to see the genius in your child, then back off and observe him more. It's in there and will come out if you give him a safe place to express it.

And then as, or when, they do their thing give them a standing ovation filled with smiles and applause for being a genius.

Be real.

**Animation Mentor is an incredible online resource for training future animators. It's not cheap or easy...but it is awesome.*

FEBRUARY 28

Home Alone

Hey Mom,

Greetings...from the lovely Wal-Mart parking lot in Fredericksburg, PA. Just finished up the huge Pennsylvania State Homeschooling Convention (CHAP) and met so many homeschool moms just like you.

Right now, we're restocking groceries, and my wife left me alone with four RV savages who are a little restless in the tight confines.

It's the joy of parenting...yeah. I can't even imagine how difficult parenting would be if I had to do it by myself...let alone try to homeschool. In fact, I'll make the suggestion that the idiom – 'busier than a one-armed paperhanger' be replaced by – 'busier than a single parent homeschooler.'

If you've found yourself in this situation, my hat of admiration goes off to you. I know you don't feel very admirable. After talking to many single parent homeschooling moms, I know that most of them feel like failures. I know you often get "great" advice that you've got too much on your plate, have no business homeschooling your children, or that your children NEED to be in school.

Well, let me just say that the Greek word for that kind of advice is: BALONEY!!

Even as a single parent, you're perfect for homeschooling your children. In fact, your children might even need you to homeschool more than a two-parent home. I won't even pretend to give you any advice, because you're doing just fine without my wisdom. So, let me just say, "Keep on!!"

Mom, if you're not a single homeschooling mom but know of one…remember that she needs your help, not your advice. She needs you to baby-sit so she can gather her thoughts or go out for coffee to vent. She needs you to invite her children over to play, to pray for her, and to encourage her often. Sounds like a great New Year's plan.

Well, I need to go, a few of my RV savages need a little…um, attention.

Be real.

MARCH 1

They Copy You

Hey Mom,

After a quick Google search, I discovered that the term Home Economics was coined in 1899. I'm guessing that some public school officials decided that school needed to be more like home. I assume the thinking went along these lines:

"Ladies and gentlemen…academics are not enough. Our young women need to learn the valuable skills of preparing meals and managing a home. I suggest that we teach homemaking skills and call it something institutional like…home economics. Ooo, we could even shorten it to Home Ec. All in favor say, "Aye.""

Since then, public and private schools have not only been teaching Home Ec, but in recent times they have also modeled THEIR schools after what we already do in our homes.

They let their students build things with wood and metal and call it "industrial arts." They have turned finger painting into "art class." They call playing, "gym" and "recess." They plant gardens, go on nature walks, and teach children how to get along with each other.

In short, they KNOW that the best place to teach children is in the HOME and have spent the last 100 years now trying to make their schools more like it.

In light of that, why do we homeschoolers try to make OUR homes like THEIR schools?? We need to stop and do what we do best. So, Mom and Dad, let's teach our children to cook, clean, and care for the needs of our home and those who live in it…but please, PLEASE don't call it Home Ec. It's just home.

Be real.

MARCH 2

They Are Special and Have Needs

Hey Mom,

I have special needs children. In fact, ALL my children are special needs children. First, there's Ben who really needs me to listen to him talk…because he talks a lot. Then there's Sam who likes to tease but who needs me to know when it's time to stop teasing and be understanding. Katherine needs me to be extra gentle during these 'changing' years.

Ike needs lots of one-on-one attention. Abe needs snuggling and closeness. Maggie Rose needs me to help her use self-control. Cal needs me to read books to him and Jed needs me to smile at him.

Now before I get an angry note from some well-meaning mother who insists that I'm making light of, or minimizing, special needs children, let me say that I am not doing that at all. I know some of you have children who demand incredible sacrifice and labor on your part. I know you lie awake at night wondering if you can make it through another day. I'm certainly NOT trying to equate my 'special needs' kids with your 'special needs' kids.

Yes, they have special needs, but as I've already pointed out, all children do to some extent. Amazingly, God has given you the abilities to meet those special needs and has given your children the mom and dad just right for them. You don't have to feel inadequate or apologize for their lack of progress, or label them as a "special needs" child.

All you have to do is love, train, and prepare them for THEIR future. Oh, yeah, and one more thing…

Be real.

MARCH 3

Let Them Fly

Hey Mom,

My daughter Katherine likes horses…it's an eleven-year-old girl thing. Now we didn't go out and buy her a horse, cowboy boots, or a belt buckle the size of a dinner plate, but we did supply her with a good stack of horse books, a horse curriculum (go figure), and even gave her horseback riding lessons as a gift.

Our purpose in doing these things isn't so that she'll become a rodeo queen or a ranch hand, but in hopes that it will help her discover the many gifts that God has given her.

That's the great thing about homeschooling; it allows parents to cultivate the interests of each child…because EVERY child has distinct interests. Some like bugs, others like numbers. Some like to draw, play house, talk with others, organize, go on adventures, take apart mechanical devices, or cook.

As parents, we should be watching for these interests to use as vehicles to help train our children. A child who likes bugs may not grow up to be an entomologist, but he or she might learn to love reading by looking at bug books, or become a chemist from learning about bug killers, or study to be a theologian because of being awed by the incredible diversity of God's creation. All these are possibilities that can take root from an interest in multi-legged insects.

Sadly, sometimes homeschooling gets in the way of cultivating our children's interests. Instead, we become consumed with getting through the curriculum. We feel the need to cover the stuff that everyone else covers, using the resources that experts tell us are best, and in so doing, we inadvertently KILL the interests of our children and may even miss the gifts that God has given them.

So, today, step back from the "packaged" curriculum and watch for where your child's interests might take them instead.

Be real.

MARCH 4

What is Curricular?

Hey Mom,

Let me get right to the point:

1) Not meaning to sound like a broken record, but since we educate our children at home, we don't have curricular activities (official school stuff) and

EXTRAcurricular activities (unofficial school stuff)…we do life, where it's ALL school stuff.

That means extracurricular stuff is just as important as curricular stuff. Playing outside is just as important as 'learning' inside. It's all important. Now on to my next thought.

2) At the risk of sounding overdramatic, let me say, extracurricular activities outside the home can kill families. By extracurricular activities, I'm talking about lessons, clubs, and sports activities for which you have to load up the minivan, haul your children all over the place, and keep a detailed calendar just so you know where you're supposed to be at any given moment.

Somehow there is a great pressure placed on homeschool families to make up for the lack of non real-school activities by filling our children's lives with extracurricular activities…and it's killing us.

We spend most of our time running from activity to activity until we hardly land at home anymore. We are homeschoolers who are never home. We began this journey to spend more time as a family, and now we spend LESS time as a family.

So what should an overly busy homeschooling family do?

I'm not going to tell you…God made you smart enough to figure it out. But I will say this: Don't be swept away just because everyone else is doing 'it'. IF you feel like it's too much…then say NO. If you feel like it's not enough… then say YES.

Take the extracurricular activity bull by the horns and do what is best for your family (no matter what anyone else might think).

~ A note to your husband: Dad, be 'da dad and take the lead. Your wife needs you to make the tough decisions because…. they're tough and that's what dads do.

A note to you, Mom: if your lead dog leads…follow.

Be real.

MARCH 5

From My Quiet Office

Hey Mom,

From my wife's point of view, teaching multiple ages is probably one of the hardest things about homeschooling…especially when you have a truckload of kids. I know she often feels like she doesn't have enough time to devote to each individual child. From what I can gather from some of the phone calls that she receives from other stressed out moms, apparently she's not alone.

BUT from my perspective…the one that sits in a nice, quiet office in the basement, that's the BEST part of homeschooling. In fact, I think it's the best way to learn…being surrounded by a bunch of other family members. Why?

Because your children are learning a whole bunch more skills than just math and English.

They are learning how to function as a family, that life doesn't revolve around them, that sometimes they have to wait or help others, and that they have to work as a team to accomplish anything.

Those are vital skills that need to be mastered. By teaching a bunch of children at the same time under the same roof...they will master those skills.

So I'm not going to give you any advice on how to devote time to each individual child...because you may not be able to do a lot of that. But let me say, that's OK.

So keep up the good work...while I go back to my nice, quiet office.

Be real.

MARCH 6

The Show's Over

Hey Mom,

We've been running crazy the last several days trying to get our big RV packed for a couple months of travel. Everything that needed fixed is fixed, the trailer is packed with all our books, and most of the clothes are put away. All I need to do is finish this article and...a MILLION other things and then we'll be ready to hit the road.

What's interesting to me is that no matter where I travel, homeschooling parents are all the same. They may dress differently and vary from hyper-conservative to liberal, but they're all basically the same—parents who are trying to do the best they can to raise children who love God.

The other thing they have in common is that it is hard for them to be REAL. It just seems from my perspective that homeschooling moms are trying so hard to look like they have it all together...yet they're really dying inside.

I talked to one of these moms this past weekend. She was trying to hold it together, by smiling, but the tears streamed down her face. "I'm working so hard to make it look good," she said wiping the tears from her cheeks, "and we're having a terrible year...because I'm so concerned about what people think."

I told her to quit worrying about her in-laws, friends, and other homeschooling friends and just be real and enjoy her children who are growing up fast.

Mom, I'm telling you that too. Quit trying to look like you have it all together and be REAL. There is nothing as lethal to a healthy family as playing the 'I've Got it all Together' game. I know a family who plays that game like a seasoned veteran. The kids look great...always dress impeccably, and the parents smile and give the right, Biblical answers.

But as they've hung around us (a very real family that tells it like it is), I'm shocked by what they've begun to share about their lives (not that I'm shocked by the facts, but by the freedom they feel with us). And guess what? I can tell from their smiles and laughter that it feels GOOD!!!

I'm telling you, Mom, if you feel shackled and worn out by family, you need to be REAL. Stop playing the game of trying to look good for others, and let a few others see the real you and the ugly truth. Believe me on this one… you'll never be the same again.

Be real.

MARCH 7

Don't Trust That Thing

Hey Mom,

Let me just jump in and say that the computer is a great tool for homeschooling families. We use it for typing, piano, math, and grammar. The computer allows children to learn at their own pace and get hands on instruction… sometimes from a person who is a whole lot smarter than us.

Let me jump in again and say that the computer is dangerous and should NOT be trusted. I constantly have parents write me and share horrible stories of how their sons and daughters have been caught in its snare.

These are some of the lessons I have learned from them: never allow your children unsupervised time on an INTERNET-connected computer. Don't ever assume that your son or daughter is just doing online school. Don't ever assume that they won't go poking around sites they shouldn't be looking at. Don't ever assume that it won't creep into your house.

Make sure you have controls, filters, guards, and passwords on your computer. One dad told me how his son would sneak down at night and get on the INTERNET while they were asleep.

How does something like that start? Just a little bit at a time. It begins by doing a research paper and stumbling across something 'bad.' The first time or two they resist…but later on, they might just take a 'click.' The next thing you know, they're in over their head.

I'm telling you, Mom, the computer that is hooked up to the INTERET is a possible pathway to death.

I know it sounds like I'm making a big deal over nothing, but when you hear horror story after horror story it changes your perspective.

Yes, use the computer…but be careful. Don't assume that it's safe…because it is not. Take precautions, train your children to flee temptation, and view your computer like a potential family destroyer.

Be real…and be AWARE!

MARCH 8

You May Quote Me

Hey Mom,

I was asked to give some of my favorite homeschool quotes so here they are:

(I'm not sure if these qualify as 'homeschooling' quotes but these are a few of my favorite quotes...but I bet some homeschooling parent out there can apply them to homeschooling...probably.)

"Live fast, love hard, and don't let anybody else use your comb!" ~ The Fonz

"I don't step on toes, Little John, I step on necks!" ~ Chuck Norris

"Courage is being scared to death and saddling up anyway." ~ John Wayne

"Today you are you, that is truer than true. There is no one alive that is youer than you." ~ Dr. Seuss

"What women want: to be loved, to be listened to, to be desired, to be respected, to be needed, to be trusted, and sometimes, just to be held. What men want: Tickets for the World Series." ~ Dave Barry

(As I read this one I like to say it in my Jimmy Stewart voice) "Years ago my mother used to say to me, she'd say, "In this world, Elwood, you must be – she always called me Elwood – "In this world, Elwood, you must be oh so smart or oh so pleasant." Well, for years I was smart...I recommend pleasant...you may quote me." ~ Jimmy Stewart as Elwood P. Dowd in "Harvey"

"If it's easy, it ain't good, and if it's good, it ain't easy." ~ The Familyman (you gotta like that guy)

Oh, and my last favorite quote... "Be real."

MARCH 9

Embrace the Mess

Hey Mom,

If you know me, then you already know that I'm a slob, although I do like things picked up and put away around the old Wilson home. And we've tried just about everything to bring our little pigs into line.

We've created chore charts, assigned cleaning jobs, pick up several times a day, and spend a chunk of Friday on an overall cleaning. The result: our house is still a pit.

We just can't keep up with eight children making messes faster than eight pigs in a pod.

Now my wife would love to de-clutter our house. The only obstacle in that little operation is...me.

I like my clutter, although I prefer the words "memory holders." Not that all clutter holds a memory. In fact, I love it when she weeds out McDonald's Happy Meal toys, outgrown clothes, and unused bread makers. BUT when she tries to get rid of the Steak 'N Shake hats from last Christmas, a scribbled page that Maggie drew for me, or a pair of my favorite, old, broken sandals, I have to put my foot down.

"You can't throw that away! Ike drew that for me when we were at Denny's in Pittsburgh," I protest. "And Sam made that rocket out of toilet paper rolls when he was 8... I loved those old sandals, that sandwich bag of hair, Ike's black pirate tooth! You can't just throw those things AWAY!!!"

So, we live in clutter, much to my wife's chagrin, surrounded by the reminders that what we have invested our lives in...matters.

Be real...and embrace the clutter.

MARCH 10

Bye-Bye Old Friend

Hey Mom,

On the Technology front I have officially given up my wonderfully, handy smart phone in favor of a hard to use, unglamorous...dad-phone. I use to have the world at my finger tips, with email, Facebook, maps, and the World Wide Web...now my only feature is a clock.

I'll be honest, the first week was hard. I went through smart phone withdrawals...but now, I'm doing OK. In fact, I went a couple of days without touching my cell phone, because what's the use...I didn't need to make any calls, and I can look at the clock on the wall for the time.

And here-in is the payoff for getting rid of my iPhone buddy. My phone was sucking my 'dad-attention' away from my family. I know some moms and dads are able to follow their self-imposed limits...but I knew the only way I would do it is if I eliminated the temptress.

I've seen the value already. Now when I sit in the van waiting for my wife, I talk to my kids instead of checking my email. When I sit on the couch, I listen to my daughter ramble on about her Christmas list instead of checking my Facebook page. When I go to the bathroom, I go there because I have to GO, not as an excuse to check my phone.

I'm telling you, I've eliminated one of the parent-attention suckers. There are others out there, but I can cross this big one off the list. Mom, don't get me wrong, I'm not telling you to do the same thing...but if you feel like your smart phone is sucking your mom (or wife)-attention, THEN DO THE SAME!!!!!

Be real...the time is 8:01.

PS - My wife started by taking Facebook off her phone. That might not be a bad idea for you too.

MARCH 11

The Scary Word

Hey Mom,

The words 'High School' strike fear into the hearts of most homeschoolers. It's somewhat comparable to the Bermuda Triangle...a mysterious place that forebodes doom and unexplainable death.

Even our non-homeschooling friends and relatives question us differently when our children hit a certain age and wonder if we should be altering our course. They are mildly tolerant of our homeschooling in the elementary years... after all, we are the parents and can surely guide our kids through the waters of A, B, C's and beginner's math.

But as we approach the 'Triangle', they say things like, "What are your plans now that Charlie is going into high school? You're certainly not going to try teaching him in high school, are you?"

Even if we ignore their skepticism, their words poison our minds causing us to doubt and fear the unknown waters of the High School Triangle. To add injury to insult, even other homeschoolers, homeschool experts, and curriculum dealers reinforce the LIE that homeschooling during the high school years is almost beyond the reach of mere mortal homeschoolers.

They don't mean to (at least I don't think they do), but they scare us with the constant reminder that we'd better be prepared for the high school years if we have any hope of survival.

Mom, let me remind you of the truth: You are the best teacher for your children during the elementary years AND during the high school years.

God made you smart enough to know what's best for your children during the elementary years as well as the high school years. Matter of fact, I believe that the best time to homeschool is during the high school years.

Hey, I remember my high school years...I learned a lot, but little of it had anything to do with school, and almost all of it I wish I hadn't learned.

So quit listening to the doomsayers, keep your course, and be confident as you sail through the high school triangle. Sure it will be hard at times...but the good things always are. And for goodness sake, don't forget to...

Be real.

MARCH 12

I Sez So

Hey Mom,

The question that plagues modern homeschoolers, in the same way that men and women in the middle ages wondered if the world was flat, is: are we making any progress and are my kids really learning anything? I say 'modern homeschoolers' because I don't think the pioneer homeschoolers asked that question.

For them, it wasn't about whether their children knew enough but about 'what' they knew. They used God's standard in the Bible as their standard. In the last couple of decades, we've changed that standard.

Now the standard used is the level of academics a boy or girl should be at by age 8, 12, or 17. We look towards the 'experts' who say a child should be reading chapter books by age seven, doing algebra by 9th grade, and taking Chemistry in 11th grade.

"Sez who?" sez me.

It certainly isn't God. The truth is that some children don't read until they're ten, struggle to learn algebra, or never make it to Chemistry. And that's OK!

Your children are learning! They will be well prepared for whatever it is God created them for. That doesn't give us license to blow off school; instead, it gives us grace to enjoy our children at whatever level they are.

I think it was a homeschooling mom who introduced me to one of my new favorite quotes.

"Everybody is a genius. But, if you judge a fish by its ability to climb a tree, it will spend its whole life believing that it is stupid." –Albert Einstein

It's not just good...it's TRUE. So believe it, and…

Be real.

MARCH 13

You Are. . . Believe Me

Hey Mom,

I hate when I hear some mom bemoan the fact she should be more intentional in her parenting. She came to that conclusion because she admired someone else's intentional parenting or because some parenting expert told her she should be.

Truth is, if you homeschool, then you are intentional in your parenting. It would sure be a lot easier to let the kids get on the magic golden bus and disappear for eight hours each day. But you didn't choose that because you didn't think it was best for your children. You prayed, weighed your options, and decided that it would be better for your children to learn at home.

That's really what intentional parenting is: not doing what is easiest in the moment, but doing what's best for your children's future. You've already got the homeschooling thing down, so let's look at a couple of other areas to consider.

To make it easier, let's start in the future and work backwards. Imagine 30 years from now. Your children are grown and have families of their own. What do you picture in your mind? Is your son sitting in front of the TV watching sporting event after sporting event while his family does their own thing?

If you don't want him to have that habit in the future, then you have to intentionally create different habits now. Is that easy? Not if you're like me and were weaned on the milk of network television. But intentional parenting says I don't care how hard it is now...I have my eye on the future.

How about another area? Look into the future. Do you see your daughter sitting at her computer chatting away with friends she's never met while neglecting her family's needs and her relationships with the real people who live in her house? If you don't want that for her in the future, then you will need to limit her texting/facebooking time now…and yours.

Would it be easier to just let your kids do what everyone else is doing? Yes, but that is not intentional parenting. There are a hundred other areas in which you need to consider and take the high road.

One more before I go...and it's for your husband. Imagine your grown son working late into the evening to build his career while his children long for their daddy to come home and his wife's heart has grown cold and empty.

My fellow dad, if you don't want that for your sons...then you must model something different. Because if you work too much...your boys will work too much.

Intentional parenting ain't easy...but it is worth it in the end.

Be real.

MARCH 14

Hi Ho Hi Ho, It's Off to the Convention We Go

Hey Mom,

Greetings from a Home Depot parking lot in lovely Evansville, IN. After a rough start, we're on the homeschool convention tour and the Familyman Mobile is running smoothly.

The great thing about homeschool conventions is that they allow worn out, about-to-toss-in-the-towel homeschoolers to see that they're not alone. You get to browse through the latest and greatest curriculum and homeschool helps available and have your batteries recharged by some top-notch speakers.

Also, can I encourage you to remember that most of the vendors that fill the hall make their living by selling their wares? I've talked to several who have been around a long time but are barely scraping by right now. They view their businesses as ministries, but if they can't make a profit, then they can't continue doing what they're doing.

So let me encourage you to buy your products from the vendors at the conventions. I KNOW you can save some money by looking at their products at conventions and then go buy them cheaper online. But that doesn't help them out. And really, we all need each other in this great adventure.

Ok, just one more bit of homeschool convention advice. Remember that you are smart enough to know what's best for your children. It is a foolish person who does not seek the counsel of others, but a bigger fool tries to follow it all. Translation: don't feel like you have to heed the advice of all the homeschooling 'experts'. Go ahead and listen, but if it doesn't fit your style, your (& your child's) bent, or your family's learning style…toss it.

Be on the lookout for the Familyman Mobile and…

Be real.

MARCH 15

Feel the Fear

Hey Mom,

I'm convinced that 'family fun' is the glue stick of the family. Of course, one of the drawbacks of family fun is that it's not always fun...that is, for the mom and dad. Or maybe I should say that the IDEA of family fun doesn't always sound fun. In fact, sometimes it sounds inconvenient, messy, or like a big pain in the neck.

But here's the key to family fun success: feel the fear and do it anyway. It's really just a matter of doing what you know is important, whether it sounds fun or not. For example: January is a good time to go roller-skating. Kids like roller-skating, and for a small fee (watch for specials), your family can go roller-skating. So, even if roller skating sounds like torture, you say, "Hey kids, tonight we're going roller skating as a family."

Your children will laugh, try to knock you down, challenge you to a race, and want to hold your hand during the 'couples' skate.' AND to top it all off, you'll ALL have a great time and your children will remember nights like that forever.

It's really that simple and it works with...
...bowling
...bike rides
...pillow fights
...movie nights
...swimming parties
...tea parties
...long games of Monopoly
...Etc.

All you gotta do is...grit your teeth, open your mouth, and say, "Tonight, we're going to _________."

Feel the fear and do it anyway!

MARCH 16

Love Isn't Easy

Hey Mom,

Loving the unlovable can be broken down into two camps: those who live outside your home and those who live inside your home. The first group is sometimes hard to love; after all, they're dirty, smelly, and ...different. But the second group is about ten times harder to love because they're so daily.

I'm not sure why it's so hard to love those sometimes-unlovable people in our house, but it is. We can't escape them. We wake up and they're grumpy, we eat lunch and they're grumpy, we gather for dinner and they're grumpy, and they go to bed grumpy.

We pray and ask God to help us love them unconditionally and then hope that they will be supernaturally transformed during the night.

"Good morning, Honey," we say cheerfully to said unlovable.

"What's good about it?" they respond gloomily.

Here we go again.

We're tempted to inwardly think, That's it. I'm done trying...I just can't be nice to you. But that's exactly when God whispers back, "Wives, love your husbands...Husbands love your wives...Parents love your children...Love your neighbors...Love your enemies...Love those who persecute you...Love those who mess up your house, wake up grumpy, and fall in the 'unlovable-camp'.

So, Mom, tighten your belt, roll up your sleeves and keep praying for endurance, patience, and for the ability to love unconditionally. Don't just pray for their change...but also for yours.

Usually, when an unlovable is being unlovable, they need extra attention and grace. I know that's the last thing you WANT to give them…but it's what they need.

And remember this: sometimes you belong to the group of unlovables.

It ain't easy, but then again, love never is.

Be real.

MARCH 17

Making EACH Child Feel Special

Hey Mom,

"Spending time with EACH child" is an interesting topic and one that can leave you feeling a little more depressed after reading about it than when you began, especially if you have a bunch of children. Because the truth is, it gets harder to spend one on one time with each child the more children you have.

We have eight children, and the thought of having to take each child out for a daddy-date or a mommy-date sounds overwhelming and practically impossible. I know for a fact that my wife sometimes feels weighted down by this area. She's fallen under the impression that for anything to be special to a child, it has to be one on one.

I'm not sure that is true or even good for a child. Maybe it's possible for a child to feel special even when surrounded by all the other children in a family. Maybe it's even better. And that is doable.

For those of us with more than a couple children, we can make it a point to hold one of our children on our lap and talk about the day, read a book to one of our youngest, or work on a project with our oldest. We can watch a family video and snuggle up to one child in particular, go out to eat and let child "D" sit next to us at the table, or go roller skating as a family and hold hands with one of our sons or daughters as we make our way around the rink.

If you think about it, maybe it's good to train our children that they can be special without having to be away from everyone else.

It's not that I'm against spending time with a child one on one. There are times when I have to speak somewhere, and I take one of my children with me. It's fun to talk, work, and eat together. And my wife takes one child along with her when she goes grocery shopping each week. They rotate, and she buys them a special food treat when they go. The kids love it.

Although we do these things and you might implement them as well, you should not feel guilty because you just can't seem to get them alone for one on one time very often. Instead, try making them feel special within a family context. I bet you could even do that today.

Be real.

Love Another Family

Hey Mom,

As you read this, my family has just landed in Hawaii. Yep, we've covered 6,000 miles, played every time-occupying game imaginable, and had to say, "Excuse me" a thousand times as we made our way to the bathroom on the airplane. But now, we're here...and exhausted.

But it's Hawaii and and it's warm.

OK, now on to the topic of families loving other families. To be honest, sometimes I'd be happy if we could master the topic of our family loving each other, but I know part of living out the gospel is loving others. So as we work at loving each other, we also work at loving others. Maybe that's the best way to learn both.

Now, while we can't always run out and physically help another family, we try to do what we can right from our own home. One of the ways we do that is by praying each morning as a family for the needs of others. We talk about needs around us and then pray around our family circle for those people. Today, we prayed for an uncle who is selling his business, a family who lost a child, a couple of families in our church who need work, and a couple of homeschool families that are getting ready for the homeschool convention trail.

Does that make a difference? You bet. But we don't let it stop there. Sometimes we talk about how we can help meet needs. We've sent money, care packages, and done other special things to let others know God is in control and will care for all their needs.

We want our children to see God work through us so that they'll want God to work through them in the future.

I know one family who made it their family project to bless one other family (or person) each week. One time they delivered a six-pack of Orange Crush (a guy's favorite drink) and attached a verse of encouragement to each bottle when he was going through a stressful time. WOW! That's so cool...and something your family could do too.

Be real.

The Lombardi Principle

Hey Mom,

I'm sure about every motivational speaker, conference leader, and back woods preacher has used the illustration about football coach and legend Vince Lombardi to make a point about going back to the basics.

Standing before his team at the first practice of the season he held a football as he began his opening pep talk. The veteran coach held the football high and said, "Gentlemen, this is a football."

Since then the story has been told and retold in all kind of venues…and maybe for the first time is about to be applied to homeschooling.

My suspicion is that Coach Lombardi knew that sometimes even the best player forgets what matters and what it's all about. I know homeschooling moms do. You can't blame them really, there's so much expert advice being tossed about. This expert says this; this blogger says that, and this Facebook article says yet another thing.

Mom, picture me standing in front of a smelly locker-room filled with homeschooling moms with eager faces hoping for some new nugget of truth to make this the best 'season' ever. Up front I stand wearing 1950's black rimmed glasses, a white short sleeved shirt, and a thin black tie. I clear my throat.

"Homeschooling Mom," I pause for dramatic effect and everyone holds their breath for what is about to be said, "home is the best place for your kids."

The room sighs at the obvious, thinking there should be more, but that's it. The thing about this simple truth is that we've forgotten it. You'd think it would be pretty obvious for HOMEschoolers, after all we're HOME educators. But most of us have forgotten it nonetheless.

It wasn't always so. Back in the early days (say from creation on) parents knew that truth. That's where all the important training and battles took place. That was the place where children were born, raised, and taught, and where they lived and died.

It was the place where important lessons were taught and learned each day, 24/7/365. Lessons like how to trust God, love each other, and everything else they would need for life. And then something happened…someone said, "Home is a good place to sleep and eat, but it's not a good place to learn. What we need to do is get children out of their homes and into a place where REAL learning takes place." No longer did real learning take place 365 days of the year, now it only took place 180 days of the year.

The early modern days of homeschooling was an exodus from that kind of thinking. But since then we've slid back into that 'home is bad' mindset. We've bought into the lie that REAL learning takes place 180 days out of the year instead of the truth of 365 days (if you 'count it' you believe it). Even my wife said to me as we lay in bed one night, "I feel like school was a waste today. No one learned a thing."

In the darkness I reminded her of the truth that our kids learned more after the books were closed than they did during 'school' anyway. That's because home is a place of constant learning. In it, they learn about sharing, loving, forgiveness, trusting, and family.

In fact, has anyone but me noticed how traditional schools are copying US? They plant gardens, take field trips into the woods, talk about being polite, how to share, and getting along with others. They try to copy HOME, because, whether they admit it or not, they know HOME is the best place for kids.

Can I bring it down to you? The truth is your HOME is the best place for YOUR kids. If you feel like throwing in the homeschooling towel, cling to this truth. In Dorothy Gail fashion repeat after me, "There's no place like home. There's no place like home. There's no place like home." (You can click your heals if you want to).

To do a great job of homeschooling you don't have to get your kids OUT of your home to learn…you need to KEEP them home.

Be real.

MARCH 20

When They Show Up

Hey Mom,

Aloha! As I write this, I'm in my cold basement office, but as you read this, I'm living the life in warm Hawaii. I don't know right now if I'm happy or miserable because as you know, sometimes it's at those places where you should be the happiest that you act the worst.

I know this is especially true for dads and moms...or to be more specific, this dad. I'm hoping we're having the time of our life...but I know that much of that depends on me and how I respond to all the 'tense' situations (man, I hate being the responsible one sometimes).

Anyway, while we've been in the Aloha State we've gotten plenty of homeschooling done. Oh yeah, we've learned all kinds of stuff about loving one another through sunburn, bad attitudes, and varying agendas. We haven't touched a book, but we've covered plenty of important stuff.

Even, Jed and Cal, our one and two-year-olds have been involved in heavy-duty schooling. That's the beauty and horror of homeschooling; it starts at birth and continues as long as they live in my house (and really beyond that).

Every day we train them in forgiveness, obedience, and trusting God. They don't get it the first time around, but hopefully by the end they will have gotten it. Now, don't get me wrong, I'm not talking about pre-school (I don't think there is any such thing...all of life is school).

Although I meet and talk to a lot of stressed-out parents of three-years-olds who are buried under a mountain of guilt, I don't like the idea of pre-school or of starting too early. In fact, I believe one shouldn't start any earlier than the child is ready to start and even then, I think it should be mostly playing, creating, and more playing.

Homeschoolers have made a big mistake by buying into the "get them started early" philosophy and are paying the price through premature burnout in their children and in themselves.

So if you have a pre-school aged child, enjoy him/her. Let him play and be a child. If you've been guilty of pushing too hard, too young; repent and make it right. Put away the books and bring out the Play-Doh.

Maoli (Be real).

MARCH 21

Going Green

Hey Mom,

I am not a tree hugger, animal rights activist, or climate-change nut. I do not wear clothing made from recycled paper, drive a hybrid car, or have a windmill on the roof of my house. I'm not sure I believe all the hype that scientists pump out, public radio preaches, and that Al Gore got an Oscar for.

However, the Familyman did go green a few years ago.

I was feeling a little guilty about all the trash our large family contributes to the landfill each week. In fact, on a normal week, I was taking between 4 and 5 garbage cans out to the curb on Thursday mornings.

"I've decided we're going to recycle," I announced one day to my wife's chagrin.

So we bought a few containers, labeled them appropriately, and began to save our glass, metal, plastic, and cardboard. Since then, I have reduced our trash contribution tremendously. I now haul 1-2 trash cans out to the curb each week.

On the downside, our back entry is now piled high with boxes, cans, and plastic milk jugs. I have to load them into the van every week and take them to the recycling bins in town, but no one can accuse this large family of hurting the environment because we recycle.

I feel better now and would be able to look Al Gore in the eye without a hint of guilt. In fact, I may even sell our diesel RV and consider traveling around the country on bicycles...NAW!!!!!

Be real and go green.

MARCH 22

Don't be a BToG

Hey Mom,

I feel fat. Some have called me stocky...but I like to refer to myself as a big tub of guts (BToG). In my pre-BToG youth, I used to look at overweight people and think, all they need to do is quit eating and lose some weight. Now, I know just how hard, sometimes overwhelming, and unobtainable that seems... but we owe it to those we live with to get healthier.

That's really why maintaining a healthy weight is important—so we can be around for our families for a long time. About 15 years ago, I was in a terrible car wreck. Both my feet, ankles, knees and legs were crushed and my face smashed flat. Since that time, my feet and legs always hurt, but I'm sure my feet and legs would feel a lot better if they didn't have to haul around a BToG. I really want to be able to walk and be active with my children and wife for a lot more years, but I fear that if I don't get some extra weight off, that might not happen.

Now, I know that some of you reading this eat healthy, exercise, and are thin and trim. Let me just say to you...I hate you.

But for the rest of us BToGs, I'm telling you we need to get to work... forgetting all the weight-loss failures of the past, the broken, healthy-eating promises we've made, and forge ahead.

I'm not going to tell you HOW to accomplish what you'd like to accomplish, except that you should talk it over with your spouse, get an accountability partner, set a REALISTIC goal, and try, try again.

BtoGs, let do it.

Be real.

PS - FYI - Since then I' lost about 30 pounds and have kept it off. I'm not pushing a program, but Body for Life is what my wife and I follow. It seems reasonable (even though we don't follow it religiously) and has been doable.

But They're Already Doing It

Hey Mom,

Well, we're up to our knees in the homeschool convention creek. We've got four under our belt and a bunch more to go. We were in Peoria, IL this past weekend and have a couple weeks to get our RV ready before we hit the road for over a month.

I've already walked up and down the aisles of curriculum vendors, eaten their free candy, and listened to their spiels. There's some good stuff out there and it can benefit you greatly...but sometimes it feels a little 'artificial.'

Not that that's always bad, but if you think about it for just a moment, walking around your yard, your house, and your world is like walking down an all-natural homeschool vendor hall.

Not only is everything free, but also it is often more effective at teaching and training our children in what's most important.

For example, my wife has been pondering the usefulness of a writing program for my oldest daughter Katherine. The thing is Kat already writes all the time. She emails cousins and friends, writes letters to grandparents, keeps a journal when we travel, and writes stories about horses and girls named Kristen…all because she likes to.

One is natural and one is artificial. One is already working and one makes parents feel like it works, satisfying the need to 'check it off the list.'

So...one day while I was talking to my wife I said, "Why are we having Kat use this writing program when she writes ALL the time?"

My wife started to give me all the 'right' reasons for using a writing program and then stopped.

We decided to forget artificial writing programs with her and go all-natural. For our other kids, we might not do that. But there are natural ways of learning everywhere. They might include playing board games or cards, gathering bugs, or going to places that most people just read about.

One is easy to check off...but the other works.

Be real.

PS - My daughter also used or heard good things about these writing programs: Learn to Write the Novel Way, The Power in Your Hands, and The One Year Adventure Novel. She published her first novel, The Stolen Princess, when she was a junior.

Mom-Guilt

Hey Mom,

It's kind of quiet at my house right now. For some reason, I got up early this morning, and I'm all alone as I type this. Usually some of my kids beat me up. Speaking of beating up, we had a pillow fight last night. I didn't want to at all, but my daughter Katherine guilted me into it.

She and I were sitting around talking when we started to tease each other… about stuff. I must have said something that crossed the line of good teasing because she retaliated with, "Well, maybe I should tell everyone that my dad is the Familyman, but he doesn't do all the stuff he tells other parents to do."

It was a hard blow and made me defensive, but before I could defend myself she said something about never having pillow fights anymore. As she said the words, some kind of unseen alarm must have sounded in the realm of kiddom because Ike bounded around the corner and blurted, "Can we have a pillow fight tonight?!!!!!"

In spite of the anti-familyman conversation we just had, I said, "No." But then as guilt pulsed through my veins, I rethought my answer and said, "Yes, we can."

Like a shot, he raced upstairs to spread the word and a few minutes later, armed to the hilt with non-brain damaging pillows, we slugged the begebers out of each other. That, my fellow dad, is what memories are made up of and the glue that holds us together…and it can all be yours if the guilt is just right.

Parent-guilt is powerful stuff. If you let it, it will push you into planning family trips, taking the youngest with you to the grocery store, staying up late watching a movie with your oldest, forking over the money to buy that 'toy', or bashing each other over the head with a pillow. That parent-guilt gets us to where the good stuff lives.

But if you ignore it…and insist on getting school done, its power diminishes until you no longer feel its prod and you miss out on all that it pushes you toward.

So, Mom, feeling any mommy-guilt? Act accordingly.

Be real.

Let it Happen

Hey Mom,

I'm convinced that 'talking' is the vehicle that God created for us to train our children in godliness, life, and all that matters. Just look at His command to that rag-tag bunch of Hebrews in the wilderness in Deuteronomy 6:7.

"These words, which I am commanding you today, shall be on your heart.

You shall teach them diligently to your sons and shall talk of them when you sit in your house and when you walk by the way and when you lie down and when you rise up."

I'm afraid the homeschooling movement has botched the whole thing up. We don't think that 'talking' when we get up, go to bed, and go about daily life is enough. We think we need to curriculumize it and restrict it to 180 days of official school.

Nowadays, we don't have time to talk to our kids because we're too busy teaching them. We miss those teachable moments at bedtime because we're so tired and want them in bed...NOW. We don't have time to talk around the breakfast table or while sitting on the couch because we have to begin our school schedule.

We're so busy schooling...that we have forgotten about the power of just talking.

So here's what you...and I need to do: we need to postpone our curriculum and set our agenda aside, and sit on the couch or around the table and talk about spring, Easter, and summer fun. Don't force the conversation by asking probing questions...just let it happen.

And happen it will.

Be real.

To Test or Not to Test

Hey Mom,

Don't even get me started on testing. I took tests as a kid and I got mostly A's, but I learned very little. That's because tests have little to do with learning. They were put in place because the number of students was too large for a single teacher to monitor their progress so they invented 'tests'.

You already know how your kids are doing. Why do you need to test, unless it's just to make YOU feel better? If your child gets an A, you feel good. If they get a D, you feel bad. But that has little to do with what they know... and you already know what they know.

So for what it's worth from this educationally-challenged rebel...leave the testing to those who don't know, and instead enjoy your position of knowing.

~ A note to your husband: Dad, can we talk for a minute? Your job is to encourage your wife in the homeschooling job she is doing. When you say things like, "Do you think we ought to have the kids tested?" your wife hears, "Honey, you're obviously doing a terrible job of educating our children. We need to find out if they're as stupid as I think they are."

That's not encouraging. So don't do it.

Be real.

MARCH 27

Homeschooling Through the Tough Times (Translated: No you don't have to put them in school just because they're driving you nuts)

Hey Mom,

Tough times? TOUGH TIMES??? It's all tough times, whether school is in session (and it always is) or whether you're taking a vacation through the summer months (which you should be). Instead of shrinking back, caving in, or throwing in the towel because it is 'tough', you should get great comfort BECAUSE it is tough.

Life truth #2 – The good stuff is tough.

Life truth #3 – The easy stuff isn't good.

So instead of wishing it away or thinking I'll put them in 'school' next year, suck it up, dig in your toes, look toughness in the eye and say, "I'm sticking it out, embracing the toughness, and going to enjoy it...because it is GOOD and it is worth it."

Any questions?

Be real.

PS –Life truth #1 – You are loved by God more than you deserve, understand, or can even appreciate.

Homeschooling with Heart...and Without It

Hey Mom,

When I think about 'heart', I think about a Yankee's baseball coach giving the pep-talk of a lifetime. His team stinks...but he knows it's about something inside. Cue the music...

Coach: [Spoken]

See boys, that's what I'm talking about. Baseball is only one-half skill, the other half is something else.....something bigger!

[Begins to sing]

You've gotta have....Heart! All you really need is heart!

When the odds are sayin' you'll never win, that's when the grin should start!

You've gotta have hope! Musn't sit around and mope.

Nuthin' half as bad as it may appear, wait'll next year and hope.

When your luck is battin' zero, get your chin up off the floor. Mister, you can be a hero. You can open any door. There's nothin' to it, but to do it.

You've gotta have heart! Miles and miles and miles of heart! Oh, it's fine to be a genius of course! But keep that ol' horse before the cart! First you've got to have heart!!!!

SCRATCHHHHHHH!!!! (Think needle pulled from the record player.)

You know that may work for a bunch of sweaty, tobacco-chewing ball players, but the truth is sometimes as parents and homeschoolers we don't have heart...not even inches and inches of heart. That's where God comes in and lifts you up when you don't think you can even muster a smile.

So instead of trying to pep you up, let me just say, "Enjoy the day, your children, and the fact that God loves you more than anything...even when you don't have heart."

Be real.

MARCH 29

The David and Goliath Test

Hey Mom,

OK, this is one of those curriculum article, thingys. I'm not even going to pretend to know anything about curricula, although my wife could write a book about them. But I will say this: God made you and your husband smart enough to figure out which (if any) curriculum is best for your family.

In fact, I like to take the David and Goliath test regarding curriculum. Remember how in one point of the story David ends up in King Saul's presence? The King says, "OK, if you're going to face a giant, then at least wear my armor."

David was smart enough to try it on but wise enough to take it off. I guess it just didn't fit well. Instead, he did the dumbest thing in the world and went off to face the giant with some rocks from a creek.

But that's my advice. Check out the ads. Listen to the curriculum salesmen and your friends, and read the write ups in the homeschool magazines and websites. Try them on, but if they don't fit you or your family…leave them behind. And don't feel guilty about it. You do it the way that seems best for you and forget about what anyone else says.

Then go face the giant.

Oh yeah, and be real.

MARCH 30

Lesson Planning

Hey Mom,

I'm sure you're all dying to know what the Familyman has to say about lesson planning. Well, I have nothing to say…so I enlisted the help of Debbie, my very wise wife, on the subject, and here's what she said:

"Like most women, when I started homeschooling our first child, I developed lesson plans and a schedule and got to work. But, I soon felt frustrated by delays, interruptions, and problems, because it meant I didn't complete my lesson plan for that day or even worse that I wasn't able to stay on schedule.

One day, I heard a speaker suggest that instead of having the school day planned out minute by minute or adhering to a written schedule, I could implement a "do the next thing" schedule. So, instead of having times listed, I just have a general order or routine. That freed me from being a slave to my schedule and allowed me to bend with the day, no matter what it brought.

Some days it means letting the baby be the lesson plan. There are days when a sick or fussy baby makes it too hard to "teach" anything. Those are good times for the lesson plan to become learning how to care for a sibling or help mom instead of any "official" school subject. Actually, those are the most important lesson plans in the long run…the ones that rise to the top when you're living life daily.

So, if lesson planning has you weighted down, stop planning lessons. If you really need that structure but are frustrated when you don't accomplish it, then have a "do the next thing" lesson plan instead. And, if all you and your children accomplish on any given day is taking care of a sick child or helping your husband, friend, or neighbor on an important task, then that is the lesson plan that God deemed best for your day. Allow Him to direct it, even though you plan it."

Man, she's smart...and she's as real as they get.

Do the same.

MARCH 31

Record Keeping Ideas

Hey Mom,

The way I understand it, records should be kept in a dry, cool location. Apparently, warmth tends to warp the records and cause them to wobble when they're placed on the turntable.

That's the great thing about records; they always play. I mean CDs are unpredictable. You treat them with kid gloves, are careful not to breathe on them, and they skip, jump all over, or cannot be read by the CD player.

I have records that have sat in my basement for twenty years, and they still play just as well now as they did back then. In fact, scratches make the music sound better.

I mean there is no better sound than the melodic notes of a John Denver or Karen Carpenter record album, or the thrill of placing the needle on the edge, and the sadness of the quiet silence as it reaches the end, slips into the smooth end zone, and then rises gently from the record to return to the arm holder.

Magic.

Hold on a minute, my wife wants something...what? What do you mean this topic is not about record keeping but about keeping school records?

What do I know about school records? I'm a free spirited dad who can't be expected to know anything about record keeping. In fact, the only kind of records I keep are drawings of turtles by three-year-olds, notes left by ten-year-olds, lost teeth, old pop bottles, and other important stuff that serve as reminders of what I've spent my life on.

Actually, recently I decided to make a transcript for my children of what really matters.* That's record keeping.

Be real...and let your kids hear the sweet music of a real record player.

** Here it is: OFFICIAL SCHOOL TRANSCRIPT FOR MY CHILD*
FULL NAME: Ben
ADDRESS: 123 Main Street, Anywhere, AK 56879
PHONE NUMBER: 555-555-5555
EMAIL ADDRESS: email@email.com
DATE OF BIRTH: 07/13/92
- Spent 7,300 mornings together
- 630 spontaneous heartfelt talks
- 36,421 everyday conversations about nothing
- 176 heartfelt apologies
- 2,126 not-so-heartfelt apologies
- 18,000 meal prayers together
- Many moments he saw me at my worst
- Saw me at those rare times when I laughed so hard I could barely breathe
- Watched 100's of episodes of Andy Griffith, Dick Van Dyke, and Hazel
- Watched the snow fall in the middle f the day and wished it would never stop
- Watched the kids play outside in the early spring dressed in a superman cape/ shorts/and winter boots
- Sat outside in the sun and talked
- Dropped in on our older kids just to talk about the night before or the day's plans
- Had lunch at McDonalds and splurged on McFlurries...the big ones
- Baked cookies in the middle of the day
- Worked side by side getting ready for company
- Took flowers to an old person
- Wrapped gifts and listened to Christmas music
- Experienced the mundane and the sacred together and realized it was the same
-Redeemed 16,380 hours because we chose to educate our kids at HOME

APRIL 1

Bible Memory

Hey Mom,

Normally, I read the topic at hand and jump right in. The words flow and thoughts are clear...but this time I didn't jump right in after I read the topic of Bible memory. In fact, I felt a dread come over me that I rarely feel...except when this topic comes up.

It's not that I'm against Bible memory, just the opposite is true. I believe in Bible memory, in its power and purpose. It's just that I'm a loser-dad and fail to make it a priority in my family.

Yes, we've memorized lots of Bible verses and at times memorized large sections of scripture. It's just that I'm not very good at memorizing and...my good intentions often get pushed aside because of life.

My wife is better than me and includes scripture memory as part of the school day (she uses Awana material). She can memorize like crazy.

Normally, I give advice like, "If you don't like it, then don't do it; you decide what's best for your kids, or you don't need to feel guilty." But I'm not going to say that on this topic. Maybe you and I need to a feel a little guilt.

Mom, you and I need to have our children memorize scripture, not so we can say they did it, but because it needs to be in their hearts. It pays such huge dividends especially in this increasingly secular and ungodly mosh of 'whatever you believe best.'

You can skip grammar, science, and history, but don't skip the Bible. If you're feeling loser-ish like me, shake it off and scrawl down a short Bible verse and have the kids memorize it starting today.

Let's do it.

Be real.

APRIL 2

A Penny for My Thoughts

Hey Mom,

I think allowances are a great idea...although we don't do allowances at our house. It isn't like we made a conscious decision NOT to give allowances; we just never purposed TO give allowances.

I think allowances can be used to teach children HOW to save, give, and spend in a way that pleases God and can be a great training tool for the future.

Now even though we don't give allowances, we DO allow our children to earn money. We certainly don't pay them for family duties...like washing the dishes, cleaning the house, or cutting the grass. They do those things because they're on Team Wilson and we all work together as a team.

But sometimes we PAY them for doing something 'special'. It might be for babysitting, doing a job we don't have time for, or assembling products for Familyman Ministries.

That way it allows them to have some money to give, save, and spend as well as teaching them the VALUE of money...because when you have to work for something, you feel its value. Allowances don't always do that.

My kids may not have the regular income of an allowance, but that's OK because I want them to know that if they really need something, their father will supply it. Then one day down the road they'll remember that if they really need something their heavenly FATHER will supply it too.

That concludes all my wisdom concerning things financial.

Be real.

APRIL 3

Peepaw and Moompa

Hey Mom,

Grandparents are a wellspring of experience and love. They offer so much to grandchildren as well as their own children...but sometimes they can drive you nuts. That's the rub.

Most grandparents lived in a different time...when the only people who homeschooled were camped out in hills and hollows making babies and moonshine. So when you grew up and did normal things differently, they freaked out.

Grandparents often say discouraging remarks and seem judgmental. The easiest thing to do is withdraw and keep your family to yourself...but that would be the wrong thing to do.

Like I said, grandparents are too valuable a resource to not make the effort to keep things right. They may never see eye to eye with you, but that doesn't mean that you should keep them at arm's length. Instead, you just need to say to yourself, "The relationship is more important than our differences."

You need to let things slide off your back and not be bothered when they act exactly like you think they'll act. You're not just doing it for yourself, your children, or even your parents (although you'll all benefit from being together); you're doing it because God said to honor your father and mother.

Because I'm telling you, if you're withholding yourselves from your parents or in-laws, you're not honoring your parents.

Besides when you do that, you're teaching your children NOT to honor you one day. If you withhold yourselves from your parents, I can just about guarantee that one day when your children are all grown up, they will do the same.

I know things might be bad...but you should take the first step to make things right.

Be real.

APRIL 4

He's All Boy

Hey Mom,

Boy: a noise with dirt on it…that likes to 'rassle and shoot things

Yep, I think that pretty much sums up the male species. And I'm proud to not only be the father of six of the critters but also to be one. I think boys are born dangerous. They like to climb high, run fast, and spend the majority of their early years pretending to kill things.

I know that tendency can drive you womenfolk crazy. You don't have any pirate in you, but for every male, there's a little bit of pirate in them. It's unfortunate that we train most of that out of them by the time they leave our homes.

We tell them to be careful, get their ducks in a row, be responsible, and not to be so dangerous.

Now, I'm not advocating the macho, lumberjack kind of men who can only do manly things, but I am saying we modern homeschooling Christians have been training our boys to be 'safe.'

We're not meant to be safe. God the father was not safe, Jesus was anything but safe, and your boys aren't meant to be either. We need to train them to trust dangerously, love dangerously, give dangerously, and work dangerously.

When the world looks at them spending more time with their families than they do at work, leaving comfort to tell people about Jesus, or giving during a time when they should be saving…they will say, "They're just plain dangerous."

So feminine moms, the next time your sons step out the door, don't forget to remind them to, "Be dangerous!"

Be real.

PS – We've produced a CD for parents called Raising Dangerous Sons. It's a great resource and loads of fun to listen to. You'll find it on our website.

APRIL 5

My Princess in Pink

Hey Mom,

Several years back my wife asked if I'd like to run to the Super Hardware Mart for her. It was like asking a bass fisherman if he'd mind picking up a few things at a bait shop. I imagined strolling down aisles of shiny new plumbing fixtures, freshly milled lumber, and expensive power tools. Heaven.

"Can you take Katherine with you?" she asked.

"Sure," I answered, thinking this would be a good father daughter outing. Besides if I protested too much, she might ask me to take all four kids, and then any thoughts of strolling would get flushed down the toilet.

I made a few measurements, adding them to my wife's list. While I measured, Debbie took our three-year-old daughter upstairs to comb her perpetually fly away hair and change her clothes into more appropriate Super Hardware Mart clothing—don't ask me, it's a girl thing.

Five minutes later I heard a clicking sound descending the stairway, and a moment later Katherine rounded the corner wearing a flowing, pink, princess gown and a lovely pink bow in her neatly combed hair. What caught my attention, and the source of the clicking, were the shoes on her cute little feet.

Made entirely of hard pink plastic, they were open toed with several purple and green straps holding her feet in place. The kicker was that they were at least twelve and a half sizes too big. How she kept them on her feet was a miracle in itself and can only be attributed to the odd way she lifted her feet.

Taken aback, but not daunted, I said to my little Kat who wore a smile that said, "Don't I look Beautiful Daddy?"

"Wow, you look pretty."

"It's my princess dress," she said.

"You're going to wear that?" I asked.

"Uh huh," she said, unaware that most people we would encounter might not be dressed that way.

"Well, don't you think it would be easier if you wore your own shoes instead of those?" I asked pointing to the pink plastic ones.

"I want to wear these," she insisted. "I can walk good in them."

I wasn't sure about that last statement, but I thought, what the hay. If my daughter wants to be a princess at a Super Hardware Mart, who am I to stand in the way? Besides I've gone to McDonalds with Batman, Taco Bell with Zorro, and some other place with a pirate...or was that a spaceman? How much different could this be?

With the list in hand and the princess in her car seat, we drove to the store chatting along the way. Somewhere en route, my usually talkative Kat got awfully quiet. I was just about to ask her what was wrong when she spoke.

"Daddy," she said with insecurity in her voice, "will people laugh at me in my princess clothes?"

My heart swelled.

"No," I answered, "they won't laugh; they'll think you look like a beautiful princess."

She didn't answer, but I could feel the warmth of her smile and knew her uneasiness was washed away by my words of reassurance.

About that time we pulled into the mammoth parking lot, and I casually said to my pink princess, "Katherine, you can walk to the store entrance but then you'll need to ride in a cart."

"But I want to walk in the store," she protested.

Yeah, but it's a big store, and we have a lot of things on our list," I countered.

"That's OK," she said cheerily, "I can walk that far."

"OK," I said.

Stepping from the van, I felt self-conscious holding the hand of a three-year-old princess wearing a flowing pink gown and plastic shoes that clicked and clacked on the pavement. Heads turned toward the plastic sound and smiled when they saw her. My eyes met theirs, and I smiled a smile that said, "She wanted to wear this...ha ha..." I was wrong. This was different than taking Batman to McDonalds, Zorro to Taco Bell, and a pirate...or spaceman to that other place.

Katherine walked proudly, if somewhat slowly, in her pink plastic shoes. We walked through the automatic doors, and to her horror I had the nerve to offer a cart for her highness. She of course refused, and together we walked slowly down most of the aisles clicking as we went. People of all ages turned and smiled adoringly at the little princess and her dad.

There was even a hardened contractor or two whose tanned faces lit up as we crossed their paths. In the caulking section I offered to let her ride in the cart, and it was then that she confided in me.

"I like to hear my shoes on the floor," she said.

Maybe it was her childlike innocence that caused a tidal wave of love and adoration to sweep over me, or maybe it was just because she was my girl. But all of a sudden, I forgot about the shiny power tools, glorious building supplies, and the embarrassment of walking down a Super Hardware Mart with a little girl in a flowing princess outfit.

By the time we reached the nail aisle, I felt like a King escorting his lovely daughter, proud to have the whole world looking on. And to think I almost ruined it. Had I told Katherine, when she first appeared, "Now, you march right back upstairs and change your clothes; you can't go out looking like that," I would have missed that life defining moment. Because leaving the Super Hardware Mart, I knew that no matter how many years pass she would always be my little princess...even long after she outgrows her flowing pink gown and pink plastic shoes that clicked as she walked.

Be real.

APRIL 6

Closer Than a Brother

Hey Mom,

Let me begin by saying, there are friends and then there are friends. I think you ought to have all kinds of friends: church friends, neighborhood friends, childhood friends, acquaintances, and especially homeschooling friends. BUT the most important kind of friend to have is a 'like-minded' friend...especially if you homeschool.

A like-minded friend is someone who is on the same homeschooling page as you are and who homeschools for the same reason you do. Let's say you homeschool because you're most concerned about the character in your children (you'd like them to read...but that's not the main reason you've chosen to educate your children at home).

Now, say you go over to a homeschool friend's home whose main reason to homeschool is for academics. While you're there she talks about scholastics, testing, academic achievement, and her rigorous schedule.

How do you feel when you get in your full-sized van and drive away? Yep, like a big, fat zero—a failure.

I'm not saying you should avoid those friends, but I am suggesting that you find a like-minded friend who homeschools for the same reason you homeschool and then stick to her like gum on a shoe.

I guarantee that when you leave from spending time with THAT friend you will feel energized, encouraged, and ready to keep running the homeschool race set before you. And before I forget, make sure you find a friend with whom you can...

Be real.

APRIL 7

The Chief Purpose of Mom

Hey Mom,

Well, after two weeks on the road, today is the first time we had to be towed. The distance towed was only 1.8 miles, and technically, they pulled us...but it still counts

Up till now, things have gone swimmingly. Of course we almost froze to death in Duluth, but Monday we were able to enjoy a little fun at the Mall of

America in St. Paul, MN. That's when I discovered and codified the East Minster Shortest Dad Catechism – The chief purpose of a mom is to wave and smile.

I discovered it as my sons Cal and Jed drove around a little track at the Mall of America. And then I did it again when Maggie rode the Ferris Wheel, when Jed road the Carousel…when Ben and Sam rode the Brain Freeze…and when Ike stood on a gangplank four stories above the floor.

I waved and smiled as only a parent can do…with gusto. I know they all liked seeing the pleasure in my face as I watched them and waved. Then it hit me; that's what I'm supposed to do—what we're all supposed to do.

Yeah, I know we have important stuff to teach our children, but I think what they really want is for us to wave and smile at them, not just when they go around a theme park ride, but also when they ride their first bike, swing high, get their driver's license and first job, share a dream, walk down the aisle, buy their first house, have a child…or anything else in which they look to their mom and dad for approval.

That's when we should wave and smile…cheering them on. Sadly, we moms and dads don't do it as often as we should. But we need to.

So find a reason to wave and smile…today, even in the midst of home-schooling.

Be real.

APRIL 8

What Have I Learned?

Hey Mom,

I've been sitting in front of my computer for a good ten minutes trying to think of something funny to write about that I've learned as a homeschool parent. I was thinking about a Top 10 list or something clever…but I just don't feel funny right now. I feel busy and bothered by all the little annoyances that need my attention: our wireless isn't working, our RV needs some attention, the siding on our house needs to be finished, and most off my kids are asking me to help them fold and cut paper snowflakes.

Let me repeat: I don't feel 'funny.'

So maybe that's what I've learned as a homeschool parent that I hadn't anticipated when we began this journey. I think both my wife and I envisioned something a little more Norman Rockwell-ish. Happy parents teaching happy children…while a turkey bakes in the oven.

It sure doesn't look like that very often. More often than not it looks like… today. I used to think that was bad…now I know that it is 'normal.' It's normal to be busy and bothered. It's normal to be surrounded by children who have no idea that you're trying to get something accomplished. It's normal to feel overwhelmed and underappreciated.

I think sometimes homeschooling magnifies all those feelings and even that's normal.

So to sum it all up in a non-funny way, I used to think homeschooling would be 'easy' and good. Now I know homeschooling is 'hard' and good. BUT IT IS STILL GOOD.

Be real.

APRIL 9

The Family Mission Statement

Hey Mom,

I hope this doesn't come as a shock to you, but I don't think I have the gumption to write or keep a family mission statement. Truth is most husbands don't. What happens is that wives like that kind of thing so they write one up and then act crazy for about five days trying to enforce it…driving everyone around them nuts and then give up in frustration.

That said, I do think we need some kind of plan or code that our families live by. I know the Bible works and it is sufficient…but there is a lot there, so how could we boil it down to a few simple things that would provide purpose and a code of conduct for our homes and family relationships?

(Time passes while I try to think…and then more time)

OK, here's the best I can do for our family mission statement: Wilson's don't ever stop trying.

We fail, fall, and stumble. We ask forgiveness, seek God, and love others. We will not brush it under the carpet or hope it all goes away. We will deal with things…sooner or later. We will take our punch and get mad at each other, but we will NOT give up or quit trying.

Other than that we will always strive to…

Be real.

A New Perspective

Hey Mom,

I'm going to share a little phrase that I often use with my wife when she's struggling to keep things in perspective. I usually offer it up when she's telling me how one of our children isn't reading at the level they're 'supposed' to be, she wasn't able to squeeze math in because they played a game, or she's wondering if she should be covering molecular biology.

That's when I pull out my special phrase and say kind of loudly, "Who cares?"

Now by saying 'who cares' I'm NOT saying her thoughts and feelings aren't important, but I am saying, "Who cares that our child isn't reading at the level some expert sets...who cares that she wasn't able to get math in because she did something more important...WHO CARES if she skips molecular whatever?!"

I usually look her in the eye and say, "You're doing a good job, our kids are getting a good education, and they WILL be prepared for life...and WHO CARES about what anyone else thinks or says."

Now, my wife usually counters with reasons why the experts may be right or how other children we know are so much further ahead. But I have an answer for that as well.

"Who cares?!! We are not them and you're doing a good job, our kids are getting a good education, and they WILL be prepared for life."

~ A note to your husband: Now I know that may be hard for some of your wives to swallow, that's why your role is so important, Dad. You need to be the voice standing firm in the homeschool wilderness. So when your wife shares that she feels like she should be doing more, doubts her results, and wonders if the experts are right, then you need to whip out the phrase.

Listen to her feelings, put your arms around her, and then loudly say, "WHO CARES?! You're doing a good job, our kids are getting a good education, and they WILL be prepared for life."

Now that's the truth!

Be real.

APRIL 11

Oh, the Whining!!!

Hey Mom,

Whining is to parenting like…Lex Luther is to Superman-the arch nemesis. Even parenting gurus Gary and Anne Marie Ezzo talk about whining like it is the one foe that is tough to beat.

Now I could tell you to be 100% consistent, don't allow it or give into it, and always make it counterproductive, but you've been told all that before. I could share a few verses about doing everything without complaining or arguing or offer a few 'tricks' you can do to try to eliminate it…but the arch nemesis is not always beaten so easily.

So let me just encourage you to not give up…and to remember that one day the whining kids will be gone and "you're gonna miss them*." That's what the song I heard at Subway yesterday reminded me of. I found it on the Internet so you can hear it too.

So don't give up, and enjoy your children who will soon be all grown up and gone…leaving you alone in a quiet, whining-free house. Let the whining be the music of your home…yeah, it doesn't work with me either.

Be real.

**"You're Gonna Miss This" by Trace Adkins*

APRIL 12

Homeschooling and Pregnant

Hey Mom,

First, a little disclosure: I've never homeschooled while pregnant. However, my wife has done that plenty of times and has lived through it, and so will you.

The way I see it, the trick is to adjust. Let me just say that again…adjust. That's hard for a lot of you. You set your schedule and then come heck or high water, you plow through. You even feel guilty when you miss half a day because your entire family was admitted to the hospital for swine flu.

You actually believe you can continue homeschooling, just like when you aren't pregnant…but you can't. That's the beauty of homeschooling. It bends and flexes around life. It not only adjusts for naps and days of overwhelmedness, but it also adjusts for snowy days, sunny days, and days when you just need a break…and guilt never accompanies it.

So if you're pregnant…which you sometimes are, you need to adjust. Homeschool when you can, and when you can't, let your kids do what they can on their own, let life be their teacher, or ask your husband to help out.

~ A note to your husband: Dad, you should pitch in and offer BEFORE she even has a chance to ask.

Actually, the way I see it, you womenfolk make a pretty big deal out of all that pregnancy and child birth stuff. I mean, how hard can it really be? ;)

Be real.

APRIL 13

Todd on Toddlers

Hey Mom,

I don't have time to write about toddlers right now because I'm up to my eyeballs in…toddlers. Last night, my brother and sister-in-law, along with their eight children came up to go skiing with my family.

I just so happen to be the only one who was seriously injured in a car wreck and have no business whooshing down a hill strapped to two sticks of wood. So being the good husband and father that I am, I insisted that they leave the four youngest behind in my care.

So right now, I have four children (under 4 years of age) playing Play-doh at the kitchen table while I write this. I just looked over at them…and it's not pretty. There is Play-doh all over the floor, but they're fairly quiet which is a nice break from the arguing.

There's just something about two four-year-olds that both think they're the Alfa male.

"It's my ball."

"No, I had it first."

"I'm four!"

"I'm four too."

"Uncle Todd, look at what I can do."

"Dad, I can do it too…Dad, you're NOT looking!!!!"

So that's why I can't write about toddlers right now…I had all kinds of good ideas for training them I was going to share. But I can't.

It's suddenly quiet…I gotta go check on the little darlings to make sure they're not in trouble, or playing doctor, and then sweep up the Play-doh and clean up the Lincoln Logs. Maybe I'll put in a long-play video for…I don't know…the rest of the day.

As my Dad used to say, "You can have kids or you can have a clean house… but you can't have both."

Enjoy your toddlers and if you're past that age, offer to watch someone else's for an hour or two to give that mom a break.

Be real.

APRIL 14

Preschoolers on the Launching Pad

Hey Mom,

This is a little embarrassing, but I'm not exactly sure what a preschooler is. I mean at our house, school (or training) begins about 10 seconds after birth. The baby learns all kinds of things in those early days like how to hold his head up and where to look for food. Later, he discovers faces, learns to smile, and even sits up.

Once he's graduated to walking, he learns even more, like how to interact with brothers and sisters, how to obey his parents, and how to sit on a lap during church—important stuff.

I guess what the topic is trying to get at though is doing actual school work…before kindergarten and calling it pre-school. My advice is…DON'T.

As I travel around the country, I meet many mothers who come up to me and share how exhausted and overwhelmed they are from teaching their child. Many times I ask, "How old is your oldest?"

"Four," they respond, like I might have some helpful tips on how to teach algebra more effectively. Now I don't always say this, but sometimes I say, "Why are you making your four-year-old do school? Four-year-olds don't need to get a leg up on the competition. They're learning plenty on their own. Who cares that a five-year-old can read or a six-year-old can multiply?"

I would be pleased if I could get my children to throw away the wrapper from a bag of fruit snacks they just woofed down.

Too many moms are killing themselves and destroying the love of learning in their children because they feel the pressure to 'do' pre-school. Don't. Let me say it again…don't. Let's not even use that word. Maybe a better word would be 'little student-lings', early learners or…young children.

Even if your young child shows an interest in learning…don't ruin it by turning it into official, "sit down" school. Just let them learn at their own pace. If they show no interest in book learnin', that's fine. Enjoy them as they enjoy life, which is the very best pre-school…and school for that matter.

I've got to run. I heard a crash in the family room where my 'little student-lings' are learning the basics of architecture (building a fort) and design (creating a mess).

Be real.

APRIL 15

Let Tweens Be Tweens

Hey Mom,

Here's my advice for the 'tween' years: Don't rush them through. Although some might be going through changes, my experience has been that tweens are NOT yet teens. They still live most of their life in childhood.

Boys still play with Legos, make forts, and do battle with homemade swords. Girls play with dolls, have tea parties, and talk about riding horses named, Blackie. They're great years, but the temptation is to rush them through and do away with the childlike things and move on to 'teenager' things.

Don't do that. Let them be children…because their childhood time is running out. That's the great thing about homeschooling, it allows you and them to enjoy the tween years. In a regular school setting, peers and others push them through prematurely, causing them to skip these valuable and wonderful pre-teen years.

In fact, I don't really like the word 'tween'. It forces our children into an 'other than child' role. After all, that's all an eleven-year-old is…a child.

So, when your big, gangly twelve-year-old son is building Legos on the floor, smile. When your eleven-year-old daughter wants to wear a prairie dress to church, don't tell her, "You're too old for that." Let her. The time will come all too quickly when Legos, Playmobil, and prairie dresses will be left on shelves and replaced by cell phones, iPods, and fashionable clothes.

The teen years are wonderful, too, and you're children will get there soon enough…just don't rush them.

Be real.

APRIL 16

The Terrific Teens

Hey Mom,

The way I see it, there are two types of homeschool teens: homebodies and need-a-little-more-than-homebodies. The first type rarely complains about being bored and takes to homeschooling like a fish to water. We don't need to worry about those kids in this article.

The second type often sighs in boredom and asks, "Do we have anything on today?" They like to go and do…and the more friends involved the better. I talk to many parents who solve that dilemma by putting their teens in 'real school.' That might solve THAT problem (& add a whole host of new problems)…but it doesn't mean that it is best. What you want to do is train your children to love their home and count their family members as their best friends because one day they'll have a home of their own and need to spend their time with their family, not be 'hanging out' with the guys or gals.

At the same time though, you don't what to frustrate and provoke to anger your need-a-little-more-than-homebodies. So I think there are some guidelines to follow to ensure their happiness, not only for the present but also for the future.

1 – Don't assume that your children know what is best. Just because they want to go to real school, hang out with friends, be in every sport, and have the freedom to choose what they want doesn't mean they should be allowed to do those things. You're the parent, and you must do what you think is best no matter what.

2 – Acknowledge and accept that your child might need a little more. Don't discount his bent and say, "Tough toenails. We homeschool, and we just can't be everywhere."

3 – Just because your child needs a little more doesn't necessarily mean he needs 'a lot' more. In fact, I'd go so far as to say that 'a lot' isn't good for anyone. It begins a dependence on being surrounded by others. I heard a secular expert on the radio discussing how this generation doesn't want to be left alone. Our kids are always texting, emailing, talking, and hanging together. Even as a non-believer, he acknowledged that it was not good.

If you're like your child, then you know what I'm talking about because you sometimes feel discontent with being at home too. You want to help your child learn contentedness.

4 – Do what you can to fill 'some' of those needs. If you're a homebody this might be tough. I know I am one, but one of my children needs a little bit more. Thankfully, I have a wife who works hard to meet 'some' of those needs. She plans volleyball nights, invites families over, runs errands with him, and offers things at home to enjoy as a family.

You'll probably find that the child still isn't satisfied…and wants more. Don't feel guilted into providing it. You've got your eye on the future. You're training your children to be satisfied with their family. Give them a little, not a lot.

5 – Make your home so much fun that they'll want to be there. Some families just look miserable most of the time, and I can imagine that their children eye all of the fun that everyone else seems to be having and want to jump ship.

I know it isn't easy…but just keep at it. We're all in the same boat.

Be real.

APRIL 17

My Little Sis

Hey Mom,

I feel sad when I hear of a mom who is second guessing her homeschooling-self, but I feel really sad when it's someone I'm related to…who isn't my wife. Actually, I'm referring to my little sister who has been homeschooling for several years now.

She was talking to my wife not too long ago and shared how she felt discouraged by the fact that so many of her homeschooling friends have quit. She went on to tell how she feels weighed down by all the things she 'should be doing', lists and ideas that others place upon her and that she has begun to make her own.

When my wife tried to encourage her with the truth that homeschooling is worth it and best, she responded by saying, "Oh, I know it's worth it. I believe in it…I just don't think I can do it…prepare them well enough…"

That saddens me, not just because she feels that way, but because I know you sometimes feel the same. The truth is, Mom, your kids are going to be OK. They are going to know enough, be better equipped to deal with what matters (all that happens in a home), be able to get into college if they desire to, and live happily ever after.

Believe it or not, YOU are better equipped to train YOUR children for life than anyone else is. You may feel otherwise…but it's a LIE.

So get back in there and love your kids, get rid of the school curriculum that is making life ugly, plug away, enjoy your role as a homeschooling mom… and quit telling yourself you're not doing a good enough job.

Be real.

APRIL 18

Springtime = Mess

Hey Mom,

Oooo, I saw my first Robin of the season yesterday afternoon. I'd been hearing its distinctive call for the last couple of weeks but had yet to see one. There's just something 'hopeful' about that little bird. I know that spring can't be far away.

Maybe even more 'hopeful' are all the scooters, bikes, swords, and garage junk that my children have dragged out into the yard as they've been enjoying the warmer weather. Tell you the truth, I hate the mess, and I know it about drives my wife nutty, but I know that our messy days are numbered.

It's only a matter of a few short years before my junky yard will be neat, tidy, and pristinely landscaped, AND I know I'm going to hate all that tidiness WAY more than I hate the messiness.

So…my fellow junk-hating parent…it's springtime…enjoy the mess while it lasts!!!!!

Be real.

APRIL 19

Homeschool Conventions

Hey Mom,

Growing up near Indianapolis, IN, April signaled the start of the greatest spectacle in auto racing (the Indy 500). Now, March/April signals the start of the homeschool convention season. A few days ago we uncovered the Familyman Mobile and are readying it for our time on the road.

I don't know if you've ever been to a big homeschool convention, but if you haven't, you've missed out on a great resource. I know for some homeschool moms it's better than going to Disney World.

Not only can you get hands-on time with just about every kind of homeschool material imaginable, get pumped up by great speakers (check out the Familyman), but you get to rub shoulders with hundreds or thousands of homeschoolers.

Some veteran homeschoolers state, "I don't need that anymore."

Baloney!!!! You sure do. In fact, you may need it even more. And even if you don't, there might be some homeschooler there who NEEDS YOU. I can't tell you how many times my wife has been encouraged (and has encouraged) by another mother who happened to be in the nursing mother's room, sitting at a concession table, or standing in the same booth as my wife.

So...GO!!!! Find a baby-sitter and go!! I haven't even talked about the possibility of some much needed 'date-time' with your spouse which reminds me, Dad, you need to take the lead and insist that you and your wife attend an upcoming convention.

By the way, if I happen to be at your convention, make sure you stop by and say, "Hey."

Be real.

Homeschooling and Facetube

Hey Mom,

I'm just going to wade in and say that while the INTERNET has made homeschooling and life easier, it has also made it much more dangerous. Like white water rafting, it can be a lot of fun, but people who are not careful, DIE. I can't tell you how many emails I've gotten from moms and dads who have crashed their lives on the rocks by assuming that they were safe.

Can I speak frankly about Facebook? (I can hear the collective gasp of all you Facebooking fans...as in fanatics.) Ever since being introduced to Facebook, I've had a growing concern about the dangers lurking in the Facebook waters. From the moment I was persuaded to become a member, I saw the dangers of reconnecting with old buddies and flames from a simpler, happier time. I noticed pictures of innocent, Facebook teens that I knew posting alluring photos of themselves. I think they meant it in fun...but I thought then as I do now... they're wading into dangerous waters.

Then I started hearing reports of teens that ran off with older teens, women who ran off with men, and men who ran off with women, all of whom met or re-connected on Facebook. In fact, just last week a homeschooling Dad wrote me and shared about how he had an innocent contact (or four) with an old girlfriend on Facebook. His wife found out and was devastated, feeling betrayed by her man. He told her as he told me that it was stupid but nothing more than an innocent mistake. Well, something intrigued him about making the reconnection, and even if he didn't realize it, he was headed towards the rocks. Praise God that his wife interrupted the 'innocent' emails.

How many more innocent stories of shipwrecked marriages and families do we need to hear before we say, "Maybe all this fun stuff isn't worth the worth the price of admission?" Here's the clincher. I'm not just talking about our children on Facebook; I'm talking about YOU, Mom. I would just about bet that some of you've had a contact with someone that you felt a little awkward about, yet also felt a rush like rafting down the canyon. That awkwardness was God warning you that you were wading into deep, dangerous waters.

There are some reading this who by next year will have done something that will alter their lives forever in this 'fun' place to connect with people. And if that happens, then their homeschooling efforts will be wasted. Now, I'm not going to tell you what you need to do, but if you need to pull your raft out of the water, DO IT! If you need to gather your children and say, "Things are going to change", Do IT! Dad, if you value your marriage and family, you may need to take the raft by the horns and DO IT!!!!!

But if you don't, then don't say you weren't warned that there are some turbulent waters up ahead!

Be real.

Difference Between 'Does' and 'Doesn't' Matter

Hey Mom,

I'm running a little bit behind this week as we get ready to hit the road. Actually, I spent the better part of yesterday changing the oil in the RV (25 quarts and a filter the size of a howitzer shell), installed a new scratch and dent A/C unit, and finally located the RIGHT air filter that has been a filtering-fiasco until yesterday.

Today, I'm heading up to Utica, Mi to speak and then Saturday we have the big field day in our little town. I'm telling you, there's nothing quite like the sight of 15 four-year olds running the 20-yard dash. The last couple of years my Maggie Rose has been like the Usain Bolt of the six- to eight-year-olds.

Now don't go blabbing what I'm about to say to my kids, but the truth is…I think field day is a pain. Not only is it supposed to be cold & rainy on Saturday, but I have so much I need to get done that day. But here's what any dad worth his salt knows…some things matter and some things don't.

For a refresher, here is the 'don't' list - RV maintenance, yard work, business odds and ends, hitting a white ball into a little hole, the big game on TV, email, political junkie behavior, or hanging with the guys.

Here's the 'matters' list - Field days in the rain, the errand your child wants you to run, the project you said you would do for them, watching your kids while your wife goes to lunch with a friend, finishing that job for your wife, a tea party with your daughters, jumping in a pile of leaves, fall festivals with the family, and tucking your children into bed at night.

So, I don't know what you've got planned this weekend…but do the stuff that matters.

Be real.

PE Resources

Let me just list some of the indispensable resources that I think of when it comes to PE:

-The yard
-A ball
-Their imagination

That's all you need for a healthy PE program. About the only other thing you need to do is unplug the TV, computer, and gaming devices. Then stand back and watch them physically exercise. Any questions?

Now if you live in Florida or Texas, then let me point out my favorite Florida guy and founder of the world's greatest Homeschool Phys. Ed program (known as the SAINTS), Rick Andreassen*. It's an incredible program led by an incredible guy.

For those of you who don't live in Texas or Florida, stick with a ball, the yard, and your imagination. And don't let folks bully you into thinking you have to do something extra to be able to 'count it' as PE. It all counts, but if it will make you feel any better, get a pair of polyester coaching shorts and a whistle and wear them around the house.

Be real.

**www.saintsofflorida.com*

APRIL 23

Go Ahead and Brag

Hey Mom,

I don't mean to brag, but...I am the proud parent of extremely gifted children. I mean one of my kids is great with children, one can pick up bugs and snakes without flinching, one smiles almost constantly, and yet another one can burp his ABC's. That's the cool thing about children; they're ALL gifted. After all, that's how God delivers them...as gifts, endowing each child with a specific gift designed to build up the body of Christ.

Now, I don't buy for one moment the notion that only the ones who are good at math, science, or some other academic discipline are the gifted ones. Yes, they are gifted, but no more so than the child who can draw, cook, work on cars, build, or is just plain kind. I get a little tired of the parents who humbly say, "Oh, it's nothing I've done...but I just praise God that my child is in the 99.9th percentile in academics." Oh, give me a break. Have we been duped by the world for so long that we measure our children in percentiles?

How I long to hear from the parent, "I just praise God because my child is in the 4th percentile."

Truth is 99.9% and 4% are both gifts from God and both should elicit praise to HIM.

So, I know you don't mean to brag...but all your children are gifted too. Your job is to tailor their education to best fan those gifts.

That's what homeschooling is all about. And the greatest resource for training a gifted child is...the home.

Be real.

APRIL 24

Games Teach

Hey Mom,

Greetings from Tulsa, OK. We're sitting in the parking lot of a neighborhood park as the rain comes down. We've been on the road for a whole three days, and I feel grumpy. Why does this always happen? They get to me…and I let them and then I'm the bad guy. Tonight we're celebrating Ike's birthday, and I'm going to try real hard not to ruin it. I'm going to be fun…right after I apologize to everyone.

Anyway, that doesn't have a thing to do with teaching with games. The way I look at games is that games were made to be fun and since having fun with your children has enough value of its own, don't feel like you have to validate it by making sure they're learnin' something.

In fact, maybe we just need to play games with our children because it is fun and valuable even if it teaches them nothing…except that family is fun.

That's about as good as I can do right now…in my condition. Maybe I need to go play a game.

Be real.

APRIL 25

Homeschool Groups

Hey Mom,

Boy, it's been fun meeting so many of you homeschooling moms on the road. And last week's Old Schoolhouse Expo* was a blast. Talk about fast-paced and energized. If you weren't able to listen, then you missed a great night…and a great online conference. I'm not sure if you can listen to it as an archive…but I sure hope you can.

Today, we're 'fieldtripping' the Space and Rocket Center in Huntsville, AL. Then, it's off to the CHEWV homeschool conference in West Virginia.

Now as far as homeschool groups go, I'm hardly an authority (seems to be a pattern with me concerning many of these topics). I'd just like to say, "Don't go-it alone." You need an encourager as much as you need to be one. You're part of the homeschool body of Christ, and you have a part to play.

Sadly, many moms feel alone. In fact, we were visiting a church in Nashville this last Sunday when a homeschool mom came up to us and said she didn't know of another homeschooler in the 2,000 person church. Within minutes, my wife introduced her to another homeschooler in the church we had met and she told her there were a bunch of homeschoolers at the church…and even a couple of homeschool groups that met there. There was even a homeschool family Sunday school class.

So I guess you just might have to ask around. But make sure you do. And make sure you find a group that is like-minded with your reasons for homeschooling because there is nothing more discouraging than being surrounded by homeschoolers who homeschool for totally different reasons than you do (ex. academic vs. character/spiritual reasons).

To wrap up my thoughts on homeschool groups…I'm for 'em as long as they're not running you ragged. Just be sure it's a REAL group.

Be real.

**The Old School House Expo - www.schoolhouseexpo.com*

APRIL 26

This is Too Simple

Hey Mom,

I'm going to share with you the holy grail of how to get your husband more involved in your life, your children's life and your family. I can see you nodding your head in disbelief, but I'm serious. What I'm going to share with you has the power to transform your life, your marriage, and especially your family.

Actually, it's not all that difficult in theory. In fact, it all boils down to one very simple principle. I could be putting myself out of business by sharing it with you, because it's that simple. Are you ready for it?

Here it is: Whenever your husband involves himself in any way...LET HIM.

That's it.

You see, most of the time when a husband tries to help out, he gets told that he did it wrong, whether it's loading the dishwasher, dressing the toddler, or picking something up for you at the store.

Consider this scenario for example: Your husband sees you struggling and feels guilty about the huge burden that you shoulder alone so he decides to try and help. Hoping to surprise you, he straightens up the kitchen before he goes to bed so you can start the day with a spic and span kitchen.

Thinking he has done something good, he excitedly waits for you to see the room the next morning. But instead of being appreciative, you complain that he messed things all up by putting stuff where it doesn't belong. You put the mixing bowls where the pans should be...where are my measuring cups...I can't find anything.

Now, guess what goes on in your husband's head when he gets that kind of response?

He makes a mental note never to do that again. And he doesn't.

We pull out. We quit leading, quit offering to help, and sit on the couch and watch TV instead. It's easier...and safer.

So here's what you need to do. Whenever your husband involves himself in any way, shape, or form...LET HIM.

Mom, I'm telling you, as I have told thousands of other moms that this will work. Try it this week and see for yourself. He may not do it your way, but that doesn't matter. The important thing is that he will become more involved in your family, you and your children will reap the benefits, and he will love you more because you believe in him.

So go on, let him.

Be real.

APRIL 27

Come on Over

Hey Mom,

Instead of discussing "Reaching Out to Families" in this article, I thought we could modify it slightly and discuss "Inviting Another Family Over." Not only is it just plain fun, but it can also be a tool for encouraging another family that is struggling…because it's my belief that all families are struggling (in some way or another).

When we have a family over, the kids enjoy time just hanging out with each other, and my wife and I are encouraged by talking with other parents who are facing many (if not all) of the same issues we face. They also have kids who have attitudes, are married to spouses that are sometimes hard to get along with, or are wrestling through church issues, family issues, or financial issues. It's GREAT to talk with other parents facing similar issues—not only for us but for them as well.

And although it may seem like a pain sometimes to go to all the effort necessary to make it happen, we're always glad we did…and you will be too.

So, how about getting off this computer and getting on the horn to invite a family over who could use a little encouragement from a bunch of REAL people who are just like them?!

Be real…and take along some bug spray.

APRIL 28

A Homeschooling Legend

Hey Mom,

I know a homeschool pioneer who is as tough as the trail is dusty. When all else chose the road more traveled, she chose an unmapped path filled with what-ifs and uncertainty. She assumed responsibility for her choices, prayed like crazy, and spent most of her time wondering if she made the right choice.

But even in the midst of uncertainty and constant dangers, she pressed on. She got up each morning, pulled on her boots, herded her young'ns, and hit the trail. She's a hero…a homeschooling legend. And she is…

YOU.

Yes, others have gone before, blazing homeschooling trails and winning freedoms, but you blaze trails every day. What you do today leads the way for so many others who will follow…it might be your child, a young mother at church, or a neighbor who knows no other home educator except you.

So…imagine me holding a rose bud out to you in honor as I say with deep appreciation, "For all your hard work in blazing the homeschooling trail for those who will follow—this bud's for you."

Keep being real.

29

Elmer Fudd Needed a Mom

Hey Mom,

Let me tell you a story. Twenty years ago I took a bunch of twenty-something's to King's Island near Cincinnati. On the way home, I drove and Johnny sat next to me in the shotgun seat. Now I should tell you Johnny had a speech problem…he couldn't say the "R" sound so his 'R's" sounded like "W's."

We were driving along and I asked the question, "So Johnny, what do you like to do for fun?"

I couldn't see his face, but out of the darkness he said, "I like to weed."

Caught off guard by his odd hobby, I said, "You like to WEED?"

"I like to weed," he clarified.

But it didn't clarify anything. "You like to WEED!!?" I asked again because I just couldn't understand why anyone in their right mind would like to weed.

"I like WEEDing," he said once again.

I didn't get it. "Weeding? You like weeding?!!!" It was like a bad dream, but then it dawned on me… "Oh, RRREADing…you like to read!"

I thought on the way home how sad it was that no one ever corrected a correctable speech problem when he was young dooming him to awkwardness and silence for fear of betraying his handicap.

I'm no speech expert, but I will say that we do our children a great disservice if we allow correctable speech problems to go uncorrected. If your child is hard to understand or says words incorrectly, then either you need to work to change it or you need to get a specialist to help correct it. But whatever you do…CORRECT it. Take it from Johnny and…

Be weel.

APRIL 30

Don't Make Me Sing

The following view expressed in this short article by Todd is not necessarily the view of Familyman Ministries and they should in no way be held liable or responsible for what is about to be said…although they should have known better.

Hey Mom,

To all of you moms who worry, fret, and are appalled by your seventh grader's terrible handwriting, let me just say, "Let it go!!!"

My friend Bill is a highly educated, successful engineer who is gainfully employed, has raised a great family, and plays a vital role in our church, BUT… Bill has not-so-great handwriting.

My brother, bless his soul, has a vital ministry with Campus Crusade for Christ in a college town and has about the worse handwriting of anyone I've seen…including his college-educated wife's (whose handwriting skills are not much better).

My mother taught me how to write my cursive letters nice and straight… and no one cares. I hardly have to write anything now-a-days except to fill out a form or sign up for free windows down at the county fair. And you know what? I can't even remember how to write in cursive anymore…especially the letters Z and Q.

If you think that what I'm suggesting has gone too far..."Let it go!!!!"

The absolute truth is…handwriting doesn't really matter. We live in a day and age where hardly anyone writes with pen and ink anymore. We use keyboards and cell phones for most everything. Yet, I know many moms who are in constant turmoil because their teenager's writing looks like scribbles and scratches on paper.

"Let it GO!!!!!!!!!!"

I know there are many other experts who would tell you otherwise, but this semi-non-expert dad is telling you to LET IT GO!!!

Don't make me break out into song! Let it GO!!!

Be real.

MAY 1

Just a Mom

Hey Mom,

Just a mom. That's what I would like on my tombstone. No, not the mom part…but the phrase, Just a dad. No apology, no explanation, no justification, no tongue in cheek defense…just three wonderful words. Just a dad.

Listen here, Mom. Relish those three words. Don't define them, defend them, or justify them…just bask in them. Especially today.

Happy Mother's Month.

PS – How's that for short and sweet?

MAY 2

Do the Math

Hey Mom,

You know I'm not a math guy. I can pretty much add, subtract, and multiply, but I can't count back change, no matter how easy everyone says it is and my younger children (who ARE math guys) can add numbers in their heads way faster than me.

Ironically, I took every math course my high school offered and took an advanced calculus class in college where we worked with imaginary numbers and equations that took up more space than this entire email newsletter.

Even still…I'm not a math guy and couldn't solve a simple algebra equation today to save my life. You know why? Because I'm not a math guy.

You know why your child struggles with math? He's not a math kid. You can work him like a dog, have him try every math curriculum known to modern man, and guess what…he still won't be a math kid…AND that's OK.

Know what we do? We teach basic math (everyone needs to know how to do that stuff) and then for the math kids, we give them more math...for the non-math kids we give them less. That's the beauty of homeschooling: you can teach towards each child's giftedness, eliminating advanced math courses that you don't deem necessary even though some needle-nosed math expert says they need advanced math.

Don't believe me? Do the math.

Be real.

MAY 3

Reading Happens

Hey Mom,

I'm sure there have been volumes written about how to instill a love of reading in your children. I'm sure they have some good things to say and plenty of solid advice, but in this age of 'we want a formula for everything,' I'm going to share a fool-proof formula for instilling the love of reading in your children. Brace yourself for this.

Here it is: Don't let your children watch TV or play video games.

There you go. I have spoken.

OK, I can tell you need a little more explanation. Here's the deal. If you put TV and video games (VG) head to head with reading, TV/VG will win. You can entice them with exciting books but the TV/VG will win out. Always.

That's the reason I'm not much of a reader. I didn't need to read; I had TV.

My children are readers. They read when they get up, during free time, and in their beds. Why? Because they have nothing to watch or play.

Now, if I give my book-loving children a choice between reading a good book and watching a mediocre video, guess which one they'll choose? Right, the video. That's the power of TV/VG. Now don't get me wrong, we let our kids play and watch...but not all the time. They only play video games two hours out of the week and TV is an evening activity.

So, if you want your children to be readers, unplug the TV/VG and they will become readers. Guaranteed.

It's that simple...and it's that hard.

Be real.

Teaching Boys

Hey Mom,

My advice when teaching boys is…don't get in their way. Boys were made to learn, but sometimes we (parents/teachers) kill real learning by insisting on 'fake' learning.

For example: Before the weekend, my sons Ike and Abe asked if they could build a lemonade stand. I thought, "Yuk" but said, "Sure," thinking they'd never get far with their idea.

Well, by the end of the day Friday they had built the stand and were ready to rock and roll. Fortunately, we were gone over the weekend, and I thought that would put a kibosh on their lemonade stand.

But when we pulled in our driveway after being gone, the sight of their stand reignited their entrepreneurial passion. Monday afternoon, the partners gathered supplies, made signs, and moved the stand out by the road.

All along the way I felt like saying, "Come on guys; just go do something else," but I didn't. I decided to let them do whatever they wanted to do as long as it didn't require my help.

Right after lunch the two brothers opened shop and within minutes had their first customer. By the end of the day, they had sold-out of product, made $7, and were talking about expanding their line to include cookies.

My fellow parent that is worth a whole week's worth of 'fake' learning. They learned way more than they will learn today while sitting at a desk working through story problems such as, "If Joe has a lemonade stand and sells…"

So to reiterate my advice on teaching sons…don't get in their way.

Be real.

God is Bigger Than Grandparents

Hey Mom,

The relationship between a grandparent and grandchild is vital, but in homeschooling circles sometimes grandparents are looked upon as the bad guys...the un-doers...the ENEMY. In fear, homeschooling parents limit their child's exposure to grandparents and grill them afterwards by asking, "What did they say...show you...expose you to????!!!

In all fairness, parents are not the only ones who 'have issues'. Grandparents look at homeschooling parents like cult followers and assume that we think that we're better than them.

Who loses when this happens? EVERYONE. Not only does the grandchild miss out on a potential meaningful relationship, but grandparents and parents miss out on the deeper relationships as well. So it's up to you, mom and dad, to keep the relationship in tact...to allow your children to be sharpened and deepened by a relationship with their grandparents.* It's up to you to do whatever you need to do to allow your home-educated children to influence and love their grandparents and in so doing, honor your parents.

I'm not sure how you do that and still protect your child from every outside influence that they may be exposed to, but I know God is bigger than that. He established the multigenerational idea way before other Christian leaders coined the phrase. We all need each other.

Be real.

**This is assuming that they are not engaged in immoral or sinful acts.*

MAY 6

Your Big Reward

Hey Mom,

Well, we're almost to the big day...the day on which the entire world honors you mothers for all you do. For all the labor pains, sleepless nights, dirty bottoms, runny noses, and endless days of monotony of homeschooling, you get...a flower in a cup. That's right. For all your sacrifices, you'll probably be handed a wilted marigold in a Styrofoam cup at church.

If you're lucky, you might get a quickly made card, a grunt of appreciation from your teenager, an "I was going to do something for you...honestly," from your husband, or lunch out at Pizza Hut.

Believe me, the day will come when your children WILL rise up and...call you (probably collect) and tell you how much you mean to them, but that might take a couple of decades. And your husband, well take it from me...he's a man. He appreciates all you do so much, but sometimes it gets lost in the translation.

So let me be the one to say, you ARE spending your life on what is best, Mom. Every one of the many sacrifices you have made and WILL make as a mother is infinitely worth it. And even if everyone overlooks you on your special day and all you get is a flower in a cup; don't ever doubt your worth.

Also, because at least one mom didn't appreciate me saying early on that I don't do poetry 'cuz I'm a man...let me just close with a little poem.

Roses are red, asphalt is gray,
I hope you have a great Mother's day!

Be real!

PS – Be thankful you're not a dad...we don't even get the flower in the cup.

MAY 7

It's Not That Hard

Hey Mom,

We sometimes use the phrase 'relaxed homeschooler' as if it's some strange or new thought, idea, or concept. In typical homeschool fashion, we try to work out a relaxed system, curriculum, or chart in order to...relax.

We've made something so simple too complicated. A veteran homeschooling mom at our church said it best.

She's one of those super homeschoolers, and the white marker board that hangs in her schoolroom looks like it should be mounted in a college lecture hall. Talk about brainiac.

Anyway, I overheard her talking about giving advice to a new homeschooling mom, and I thought, "This should be rich...it'll probably have something to do with brain drills, molecular biology, and turbo-charged learning." I was almost shocked when instead she said, "I told her if I were to do it all over again, I would enjoy my children more."

That was it. Nothing about academics, testing, or curriculum choices.

"I would enjoy my children more."

That, my fellow homeschooler, is relaxed homeschooling. All you do is make a conscious effort to worry less about the schooling and more about the relationships with your children.

Don't gasp in horror...that's the way God designed it. Now, go and do it.

Be real.

MAY 8

Labels Don't Make it Good

Hey Mom,

To be honest I'm not even sure what a classical education is (they obviously didn't have much of a screening process to be a homeschooling speaker). In my head I picture marble busts of Aristotle, Socrates and a bunch of dead guys. To me, classical is just another label. For some reason we homeschoolers love labels.

But I don't think we were created to live by labels. Labels are safe, in the box, categorical, and easy to check off. Life is anything but that. It is dangerous, unpredictable, and not so easy to measure. But you were created for life.

So here's my late night, twelfth hour, almost past my deadline advice: forget the labels and do life.

And of course... be real.

PS - What I am about to say is NOT a slam against the classical learning style. After all I don't know much about it. All I know is what I see in some who try to hold to it. Those moms begin proud, struggle to keep up, and feel like failures afterwards. My two cents: it sure puts a lot of pressure on parents. OK I'm done.

MAY 9

Spitting Mad

Hey Mom,

Sometimes I get so mad at homeschoolers I could just spit. To clarify, it's not all homeschoolers...it's just the over-achieving kind, the kind that LOVE the school part of homeschooling.

It's not that they're so bad or anything, it's just that they don't know when to stop. They say things like, "My kids do math every day for two hours...my fifth grader is doing advanced calculus this year...I've been working through Latin roots with my preschooler."

And it's not that what they do or don't do...say or don't say is bad, it's just the way it makes everyone around them feel...is bad.

No wonder we have homeschooling moms ripping out their hair in handfuls and dropping out of homeschooling like old people at a dance marathon. We've allowed people who love the SCHOOL part of homeschooling to lead the way. The problem is that the vast majority of homeschooling moms don't love the SCHOOL part. They feel inadequate, unmotivated, and ungifted in certain areas.

As leaders, we've perpetuated that kind of wrong thinking. We should have said from the beginning that SCHOOL is just part of homeschooling. The biggest part is the HOME part.

And while some might actually believe that not everyone is qualified to homeschool, the TRUTH is every parent is qualified to homeschool their children. They may not want to…but they are qualified to do so if they feel so led.

So here's the deal, over-achieving mom, if you like the school part –great!!! Just don't rattle off all you or your children's accomplishments to everyone… and don't think that it's the norm. It's really the 'ab-norm'.

And if you're part of the group of homeschoolers who are committed but don't necessarily love the teaching part, you're doing just fine. Keep plugging away, loving your children, and refusing to compare yourself against the other over-achieving homeschoolers.

Be real.

MAY 10

You 'da Mom!!

Hey Mom,

Mom, don't you ever let anyone…I mean ANYONE (including yourself) make you feel guilty for being a mom as though there might be a higher calling or service. As a church, we've forgotten that one of the highest calling is mothering.

You don't need to apologize for being one, rename it, or pretend like it's a temporary gig until the kids grow up. Our daughters don't need to be ashamed to have 'homemaker' as their ambition, pushed into choosing something 'marketable,' or looked on as 'undecided' when they don't want to go to college.

As mothers and homeschoolers you serve others every day. You nail your life to the cross, give up your desires, drop into bed exhausted from serving your family, and serve God daily by serving your often ungrateful children and husband.

I believe with all my heart that God's message to you is, "Well done."

The only thing I would add to that is don't be like Martha who was distracted by her serving (Luke 10:38-42). She missed out on the relationship part…the part that mattered. Sometimes homeschooling moms are guilty of that.

Have a Happy Mother's Day.

When Dough Runs Low

Hey Mom,

This is a great topic, and now you get to learn something new about me: I'm not a financial guy. I just don't do money. Usually when the topic comes up, my feet start to itch. My wife, on the other hand, has had our checkbook balanced to the penny ever since we were first married. She's amazing in this area; I'm not.

So, I don't have any financial savvy advice to offer, but I do have some advice.

1. Turn off the TV, stop reading the newspaper, or surfing the web. Economy experts will poison your mind with their doom and gloom predictions.

2. Never forget that God is in control and that your Father will provide all your needs. I promise and so does HE.

3. Don't shield your children from financial difficulties. Involve them instead. This is school at its best. They need to see you live out your faith because they're going to go through financial difficulties one day as well. Also, be sure to teach your children how to handle money. Make personal finance a required subject in your homeschool. If you need help in this area, check out Dave Ramsey's resources (www.DaveRamsey.com).

4. Although the world tells you to spend and conservatives tell you to save, God tells you to GIVE. Look for someone that you can bless, either with your time...or with your money. God loves a cheerful giver.

5. Be honest. There is a difference between financial difficulties and things just being tighter than they used to be. If things are just tight...don't put off vacations and family stuff just because your pile is a little smaller. Enjoy your family today and don't wait for things to get better...because they might not.

6. Don't pretend to have it all together. If you're in trouble, let the body of Christ know so that they have the opportunity to help.

Be real.

Building Character

Hey Mom,

I'm having a little trouble composing an article right at the moment. My wife is in doing laundry at a corner Laundromat in downtown Orlando while most of the kids and I wait in the RV watching an old I Love Lucy DVD.

So…about building character….if only it were as easy as building a picnic table, a bird house, or a shed. Somehow, Christian parents have exchanged the idea of instilling character (which is a slow, laborious process that is demonstrated by the parent and 'caught' by the child) for building character (which is a quick, follow the lesson plan, and do-what-I-say-not-what-I-do kind of thing).

But the truth is that character must be modeled for our children to catch it. Not to minimize teaching Biblical truth or good, character-based curriculum… but the single greatest teacher is example. In fact, one smart dead guy once said, "Example isn't the main thing, it's the ONLY thing."

Deuteronomy 6 says it perfectly: "And these words, which I am commanding you today, shall be on YOUR HEART (first); and (then) you shall teach them diligently to your children." (Verses 6-7).

So if you want to 'build' character in your children, begin with our own character and it will be instilled in them.

Be real.

My New History Thought

Hey Mom,

This is my brand new thought about history that I just 'thunk' after reading about President Obama's omission of 'endowed by our creator' as he quoted part of the Constitution.

History is vital. It may be ignored, forgotten, or re-interpreted...but like truth, it cannot be altered. It must be shared with our children or they run the risk of 'forgetting' what God has done throughout history, in our country, and for the redemption of man. So, whether we learn from history or not...it is. And that makes it important.

Now don't get me wrong. I'm not saying everyone needs to be a history expert. I have some kids who know more history than 99% of the population (including me) and others who could care less. They have their own interests and I would frustrate them by trying to make them all history kids. With that said I still believe our children need to know history.

It may be as simple as knowing the history of our family and how God took care of us when the RV didn't start, someone sent a money gift at just the right time, or how we prayed to find Ike's wallet and boom God made it happen. Those things are history.

That's why the Israelites made memorials out of rock piles, so that when the children would see those rock piles they'd ask their moms and dads, "Hey what are the rocks for?" Then parents would recount the history of God's provision.

That's powerful stuff. And don't just tell them all the pretty stuff. When you're telling them the story, don't forget to...

Be real.

MAY 14

Our Homeschooling Story

Hey Mom,

We're all sick as dogs as I type this so you might want to use hand sanitizer after reading today's entry.

Anyway, this is our homeschooling story:

A long, long time ago my wife and I were young, naive, and rested. We never really discussed our future kids' schooling options. I guess we both assumed we'd do what the rest of the world does and send our kids to school (public or Christian).

Then we had kids. Nothing changed much until we got to know the little boys and girls in the mid-west conservative town in which we lived. First, there was six-year-old Haley, whose house was used to dry marijuana from the ceiling and sweet, little four-year-old Mary. One day she was over at our house and my wife announced, "I'm going to have a baby." Mary looked up at her in complete matter-of-factness and asked, "Who got you pregnant?"

Oh, and then there was Justin, the six-year-old right next door who wrote the "f" word in big, chalk letters in the alley next to our house. Luckily, our four-year-old couldn't read yet.

That's when I thought, There is no way I'm going to send my children off to spend a large chunk of their day with THOSE kids. Even though we were working hard to reach out to those neighbor kids, we knew our kids shouldn't have to be missionaries before being amply trained to do so. We didn't know much about homeschooling, except that my wife's sister had done it for a couple of years...but I decided we were going to do it.

Since then, our reasons for homeschooling have deepened and stayed the same. Homeschooling is what we do…it's part of our life…inseparable from our parenting and walking with God.

We started homeschooling because we thought it was best and we continue (no matter how much we'd like to quit) because we still believe it is best.

But that's just the beginning of the story…because it continues to be written even as we speak.

Be real and pass the sanitizer.

MAY 15

Keep it simple

Hey Mom,

OK we've been together long enough for you to know that I'm not going to offer any kind of organizational advice…I don't do neat, tidy, or organized. So about the only advice I can add to the topic of keeping it simple is…to keep it simple…today.

For most of you, your life is way beyond simple. If there was a homeschool reality show equivalent to The Hoarders, you'd all be the stars. Somehow, you've managed to fill your day to the brim with all kinds of …stuff.

I'm thinking that a total keep-it-simple makeover might be a little daunting so how about a keep-it-simple-today makeover?

Start by making a mental list of all the things you've got going today (include school subjects, co-ops/meetings, doctor appointments, playing games with your children, reading aloud together, laughing together, snuggling with your husband after the kids are in bed…anything else you can think of).

Now, don't do anything on the list that doesn't really matter. So…you might need to cancel that appointment, skip math for your child who is already ahead, read a book that isn't on the list just for fun, bake cookies just because, or watch a video in the middle of the day.

Need help in knowing what matters today? If you think about doing it and you sigh deeply, then it doesn't really matter. If you think about doing it and smile, then that matters.

Be real.

MAY 16

When You're Weary

Hey Mom,

The question has been asked; when you're weary—where do you get homeschool encouragement? WHEN you're weary? Are you kidding me? You're always weary!!! Weary and homeschooling go together like…road kill and rigamortis. That's why we need each other to make it through in one piece.

That's why the Bible says more than once, "Encourage one another." We need to hear from our spouse, family, and friends: "You can do it…keep up the good work…you're doing such a good job…Oh, I know it's hard, but you can do it!"

Unfortunately, we've taken those encouragement verses as "discourage one another." We don't mean to, but so often we offer our advice when all a friend needs is our understanding. We give non-verbal cues of disapproval when what someone needed was our smile of empathy. We Christian homeschool parents are quick to dole out 'godly instructions' when we should say, "I understand."

Yes, you need to have sources of encouragement for yourself…but there are others very near you who need your word of encouragement TODAY.

~ A note to your husband: Dad, can I speak to you right now? Your wife needs your encouragement today. She's weary, at the end of her rope, and looking for a way out. She needs you to be her knight in shining armor, to shoulder more than your weight in responsibility, to smile in her direction, to thank her for her daily sacrifices, to lift her up in prayer, to remind her of your goals and purpose, to cheer her on, to tell her, "You're doing a great job…you're going to make it…you can do it."

Go do it!!!

Be real.

MAY 17

Homeschooling with heart

Hey Mom,

I think it was in the great Broadway musical "Darn" Yankees that the song goes:

You've gotta have heart
All you really need is heart

When the odds are sayin' you'll never win
That's when the grin should start.

Of course there is no great Broadway musical about homeschooling, and sometimes 'heart' doesn't carry you through. In fact, there are plenty of times where my wife is homeschooling not from heart, but from the conviction that this is the best. BUT sometimes even that isn't enough.

That's when I come to her rescue (or should). I remind her of the truth that she once believed and will believe again...but doesn't believe at that moment because of tiredness, fatigue, discouragement, and walking through the valley of homeschool doubts.

~ A note to your husband: Dad, can I bend your ear one more time? Your wife might try to homeschool with heart...but there are times when her heart is GONE and she needs you to be her heart, her defender, her compass, pointing her back to God's best and to God Himself. She needs you. Maybe we should rewrite the song for our homeschool musical.

"You've gotta have your man
He's so much better than SPAM…" (OK so maybe I shouldn't be writing songs.)

Anyway, Dad, your wife is counting on you. Don't leave her without heart.

Be real.

MAY 18

What Happened to the Fun Part?

Hey Mom,

From where I sit, I don't think the typical homeschool mom has a problem balancing homeschool, housework, and other responsibilities. What I see is that so many homeschoolers have tossed out FUN because it doesn't 'fit in' and gets in the way of schedules, presumed responsibilities, and getting things done.

Kids ask to play games and parents answer, "Not right now, I'm busy."

They'd like to see our smiles…but we're busy getting important things done. We have gotten out of balance. We've made school our number one priority and forgotten the more important aspect of family…and that's enjoying one another.

So, can I encourage you to let a few of those other things 'slide' for a while and concentrate more on the fun part? Everyone will be glad you did.

Be real.

Here's What I Expect

Hey Mom,

Sitting here in front of my computer I've been thinking about the topic of great expectations. In my head, I've been making lists of what I expect from my children, and crossing items out, adding others…crossing them out…and re-listing some that I had crossed out earlier.

I thought about boiling it down to my expectation that they must obey me…but sometimes they fail to meet those expectations. Right now my list contains nothing. I've crossed out everything that was once listed or re-listed and now I sit here staring blankly at my laptop monitor.

What do I expect…what do I expect…what does God expect of them… of me????

GROWTH.

I really expect my children to disobey, fail, blow it…they're children after all. They don't come programmed for learning, obeying, honoring, and godliness. In fact they show up at our doorstep depraved, wrinkled, and selfish.

But I expect my children to GROW in the same way God expects me to grow.

So, when I call them and they don't obey it's my job to help them GROW in obedience. If they can't read now, it's my job to help them grow in reading. I don't get depressed because of their poor behavior (after all they're children), BUT I expect them to GROW in those areas as God expects the same of me.

Be real.

The Hard Child

Hey Mom,

If you have more than one child, then you're bound to have a 'difficult child.' And by difficult, I don't mean 'bad'; I mean one that isn't always 'easy.' Sometimes we forget that there's a difference.

Problems arise when we, the homeschooling parents, take it upon ourselves to 'de-difficult' them. We've followed standards set by experts that say, "At such and such age a child should be doing this in school." We try, they resist, so we try harder…and they resist harder…so WE try even harder until we are in conflict all the time and they hate us.

My advice is to back off and concentrate on the relationship, not the task, subject, or behavior. Do something the child likes to do and get the relationship right. If you need to play games…play games. If you need to read books…read books. If you need to sit down and play a dumb video game…then sit down and play a dumb video game with him.

Once you like each other…you'll find that the difficult child isn't so difficult.

Be real.

MAY 21

After Hours

Hey Mom,

A while back my wife and I were lying in bed after an exhausting day of parenting. I don't remember the whole conversation we had in the dark, but I think it revolved around homeschooling and the feeling my wife had that she wasn't doing enough 'school.'

"You know, Honey," I said, not trying to make light of what she felt, "the real truth is that our kids learn MORE during the non-school hours than they do during the school hours."

My school experience demonstrates that (and yours probably does too). I took all the math, science, and English a kid could take, and to save my life I couldn't solve an algebra problem, define a joule, or diagram a sentence today.

Why is that? Because the natural and best place to learn is not in a classroom memorizing formulas or equations. The best place to learn something and to make it stick is by doing life: by using math in areas of need, by writing because you want to communicate something, and by experimenting and failing.

That kind of learning sticks.

Your children learn by seeing, exploring, and doing the things that interest them. Making one write a report or give a speech about something that doesn't interest him doesn't make it stick any better. He may get an A on the report, but it still might not be 'learned.' It may make you as a parent FEEL better, but it is not a measure of learning.

The things children enjoy, stick…because they were made to stick. Because REAL learning sticks.

So step back a little and watch things stick.

Be real.

MAY 22

A Big Thank You

Hey Mom,

One of the advantages of traveling around the county to state homeschool conventions is that we get to do a little "field tripping" along the way. Yesterday, we had a good one in Charleston, SC. Not only did we visit Fort Sumter (the site where the first shot of the Civil War was fired), but also the boys and I were able to tour the USS Yorktown (a humongous aircraft carrier).

The massive ship was awesome, and we got lost in the labyrinth of below-deck quarters. As I walked, read, learned, and hollered at my boys to quit touching everything, I was touched by the young faces of the soldiers who fought and died for…me.

Then the thought hit me that all these men and women had dads and moms just like me. I hadn't thought of the sacrifice in that way before—that millions of parents worried while their children were put in harm's way, prayed for their safety, and sometimes were delivered the news that their little boy or girl wouldn't be coming home.

Standing on the flight deck of the Yorktown I thought, "Someone needs to thank them…I need to thank them."

So, Mom spend a few minutes imagining what it must be like to spend each day in fear about the 'what ifs' and then imagine the grief of never getting to say, "I love you" to a child who was killed in the line of duty.

Now, email, write, or call a mother or father who has experienced what you can only imagine…and say, "Thank you. I can't imagine what you went through or are going through."

Enjoy Memorial Day weekend with your family and remember,

Be real.

MAY 23

The Vacation Unit Study

Hey Mom,

Last week we had a great time at the Florida state homeschool convention. We met a whole bunch of desperate homeschooling parents who needed some encouragement, sold some books, and had a great time…in FLORIDA!!!

Actually, we've been doing a unit study this whole week on 'vacation.' We looked at the finer points of family unity/disunity, spending, and extravagant love. We taught our children when it's okay to stay up late, spend a little extra, and how to resolve conflict (we did that a lot).

In short, we taught them valuable lessons that they will use for the rest of their lives.

That's the purpose of a unit study: to learn valuable, life-long skills in a complete, natural UNIT of study. It really is the most effective way to learn. It utilizes all the senses and increases retention.

In fact, I really believe unit studies are served up every day in a variety of learning situations that give us the opportunity to teach our children invaluable life skills.

So, I've got to go. Today we're learning something really important… although I'm not sure what it is just yet. I do know that it's up to me to use what God gives us today to train my children for the future.

The bell has rung and class is about to begin.

Be real.

MAY 24

So Your Kids Want to Make a Little Extra Money

Hey Mom,

So, do your kids want to make a little extra money like mine do?

Check out this resource for kids who'd like to make some money. It's called "Better than a Lemonade Stand" by fifteen-year-old Daryl Bernstein.

And, here's a resource for you to read when you are tempted to squash every idea that your kid suggests with sound advice like, "It'll never succeed… you can't make money by doing that…that's not the right way." – It's called Dream Big by the always charming, Todd Wilson.

The hard part isn't for the child but for the parent who likes to have his child do it 'my way.' The key to teaching entrepreneurship is to let them try it, go for it, bomb, and succeed on their own. When they want to sell rocks for $5.00 each…let them. When they want to have a lemonade stand, let them. When they want to offer some service that they dreamed up…let them. Then stand back and watch what God does.

This bigger goal isn't to teach them how to make money…but to not be afraid, to trust God, and to do what God has placed in their heart. And of course to…

Be real.

MAY 25

Family Unity

Hey Mom,

When it comes to family unity, I think Steve Demme, founder of Math U See says it best, "The family that stays together...stays together." He's right. The key to family unity is to be together.

That's not as easy as it sounds when the world seems bent on pulling the family apart. And if that weren't enough, the church and the homeschooling world seem bound and determined to separate families as well.

The logic goes...teenagers learn better and have more fun with teenagers, toddlers learn better and have more fun with other toddlers, and ...parents learn more and have more fun with other parents, without children.

That kind of thinking and living pulls families apart.

The family that stays together...stays together. So fight the urge to be apart and be together. Watch the same video as a family. Go to the same restaurant as a family. Play volleyball as a family with other families. Have a board game night as a family. Do STUFF as a FAMILY!!! It doesn't mean you should never do things separately...but the norm should be as a family.

Want more thoughts on the subject? Then go to Steve's website and listen to his complete 'talk' on the subject. Go to www.thefamilythatstaystogether.org

Be real...together.

MAY 26

Who Said So?

So the question at hand is whether to test or not to test. DON'T DO IT!*

Tests don't measure actual learning and will either leave you and your child feeling like failures or give you a false sense of achievement. You homeschool and your child is progressing just as he should.

If your son is 10 and just now starting to read...great!!! If your daughter can't solve an algebra problem to save her life...that's fine. Some kids can and some kids can't. Standardized tests do nothing but identify those who do well taking standardized tests and those who don't.

Besides 'they' came up with the standard because they were teaching millions of children. It is arbitrary and based on what 'they' think children need to know (or what paid teachers need to teach in order to get paid).

Their standard shouldn't be your standard. It certainly isn't God's standard.

Mom, God made you smart enough to get your child ready for adulthood. Don't use anyone else's educational standards because every child's educational standard is different.

Be diligent, keep plugging, and teach your children while you enjoy them and everything will turn out hunky dory.

I'm not kidding on this one…don't test.

Be real.

PS - If the law makes you test your children (find out for sure…don't assume). Then go ahead and test, but don't show your children their scores…and don't allow yourself to look either.

MAY 27

Building Your Child's Memory

Hey Mom,

Brain drills…that'll build your child's memory, but you have to start early. In fact, if you can begin while they're still in the womb that's even better. Just take any subject, set of facts or historical dates...and drill them over and over until you've driven any love of learning completely from your child's head.

Actually, you can do all that and they still won't remember the facts, unless they were created to remember facts. I'm a case in point. As a child, I would bring home my spelling list on Monday, and my mother would drill me every night until the test on Friday. I always got them right, but to this day I'm the world's worst speller (praise the Lord for spell check and a wife who CAN spell).

Oh, I got good grades for sure…and if that's what makes YOU feel good, drill away. But if you want your children to really learn, then let them enjoy learning the things that are important to them and fit within their gifting; they'll remember those things forever without your drilling. No amount of drilling will make the other things stick.

Kind of makes your life easier, doesn't it? And your child will not only enjoy homeschooling more…but will enjoy YOU more as well.

Be real.

MAY 28

Fun Spring Ideas

Hey Mom,

Greetings from a Walmart parking lot in Louisville, KY. Other than a leaky spot over the shower, the Familyman Mobile is running well. Last weekend we enjoyed the heat in Montgomery, AL, and this weekend we'll be enjoying the bone-chilling cold of Duluth, MN.

Spring is a great time to be on the road. In fact, I think springtime is about the best time of year for families. The weather just screams for moms and dads to do something outdoors with their kids.

You could take the easy way out and just send your kids out on their own or you could go for the gold and do something with your children outside. Need an idea? Here's a few for starts:

-A family bike ride
-The first trip of the season to Dairy Queen
-A family basketball game
-Fly kites
-Plant some flowers
-Clean out the landscape or clear the yard of sticks
-Tune up the bikes
-Take the family to a park with some KFC

That should get you started. The important thing is to do it together.

I gotta go and start the teeth brushing routine.

Be real.

MAY 29

Learning through Stories

Hey Mom,

I'm writing from a hotel in Blue Earth, MN. The Familyman Mobile is sitting in a giant garage waiting for a part to be installed tomorrow.

The story began earlier this morning when we left a blustery Walmart parking lot in Albert Lea, MN. In fact, it looked like a blizzard outside. Yuck.

Anyway, we were on a small detour to see Mount Rushmore while traveling southish to Oklahoma City, OK. Thing were going well, and my wife had just gotten off the phone with her mother. As she shared all the details of a cold and great weekend in Duluth, I heard her say, "Yeah, we had a few problems... but they're minor compared to breaking down."

Three minutes after hanging up...the RV engine stopped. Long story short: we inched our way toward the shop that was 17 miles away, dropped the family off at McD's (since they informed us there was no waiting room), and then stalled permanently 1.8 miles from the shop on a two lane, no shoulder road. The tow truck came, pulled me with a big strap, and figured out the fuel shutoff solenoid was broken.

Now, we're watching HGTV on motel television while feasting on pizza. Hopefully we'll be back on the road by the time you read this.

That's our story, and we learned that God can be trusted...no matter what.

Those are the REAL stories and those are the REAL lessons. In fact, you might be starting one real soon.

Enjoy His story.

MAY 30

Homeschooling in High School

Hey Mom,

There's something about the words 'high school' that sends shivers up the spines of countless homeschooling moms. Somehow high school has become the next level of Homeschool Mario Brothers.

Doomsayers are quick to offer their advice about buckling down, extensive record keeping, and making sure you have all your ducks in a row. Mothers who previously enjoyed their children and homeschooling become scared to death, doubt their efforts, and begin to wonder if they should put their kids in school so they can get a REAL education that will prepare them for college and beyond.

That kind of advice poisons the homeschool mom's mind and generates lies straight from the pit of hell.

Mom, don't believe for one moment that high school is any more difficult OR vital than teaching third grade. The truth is: you are perfectly suited to train and teach your high schooler. God created you to be able to prepare your children for life.

Oh, you may not understand Algebra, Biology, or World History...but it doesn't matter. There are plenty of options available to help you through those subjects. High school is the best time to homeschool, and YOU CAN DO IT.

And don't forget to...

Be real.

JUNE 1

He'll Get It When He Get's It

Hey Mom,

Oh, Martha, Martha...you have so many worries. Yet only one thing really matters...and it ain't reading skills!!!

I don't mean this in a bad way, but the two of you have so much in common. Martha got side-tracked (as do most homeschooling moms). All the stuff she thought mattered and was important was diagnosed by Jesus and cut away in one quick moment.

The same can happen with you, especially when it comes to reading. It all started a few decades ago when some academic nerd announced, "Kids should be reading by 6-years-old." The statement was cast in stone, and from that moment on it became the standard for teachers and parents.

For those parents whose children were created by God to read by six it validated their children's abilities as well as their own. For those parents whose children were not created to read by six years of age, it doomed them and their children to inferiority, frustration, and failure.

Here's the deal, Martha: your child is going to read when he/she is supposed to read. It doesn't matter if they are 3, 6, 9 or 12. The great thing about homeschooling is that you get to be there when they 'get it.'

So forget what Mr. Academic Nerd says and KNOW that your child is going to get it exactly when God designed him to get it...not one minute before or later. Quit worrying, listening to the experts, driving your child like a mule, and...

Be real.

JUNE 2

Shut 'er Down

Hey Mom,

This is the perfect time to give my annual take a summer vacation plea on behalf of children all across the globe. Now you may be the type who does school year round. You work a few weeks and then take a break for a couple of weeks. If that is your pattern and bent that's fine...just be sure you're giving your kids and their mother a break.

But if you're the type who just works all the time and refuses to stop for summer vacation UNTIL the work is done…forget that idea and take a summer vacation, even if the work isn't done.

Nothing personal, but who cares if they don't finish all their work? Do you think for one moment that 'real' school teachers always finish their lesson plans? They don't! And guess what? They don't feel a tinge of guilt for letting their students leave for the summer.

Besides, the first two months of next year's curriculum is mostly review. Your kids will be just fine. In fact, I would bet the farm that both you and they will be better off for taking a couple months of that relaxing elixir called summer vacation.

~A note to your husband: Dad, can I talk to you a minute? I know full well that some of our wives get a little weak in the knees and baulk at doing what they KNOW to be true. That's where you need to flex your fatherly authority and say, "Honey, you've done a great job with the kids and I'm so proud of all that you've done. I know you think you need to do more…but as the head of our house and school I proclaim this school year done." As I've said so many times to the dads around me, "You 'da dad." This is where she needs you most. You can thank me later.

Be real.

JUNE 3

Hogwash

Hey Mom,

What? You don't feel like this past year went very well? You feel like you could have done more? Like you let your kids down? Congratulations!!! That means you're normal. The truth is most homeschooling moms feel like they didn't do a good enough job last year.

In fact, I was talking to a homeschooling mom this past weekend at a homeschooling convention who feels like she blew a lot more than just the past year. As I listened to her, I think she doubted her whole homeschooling career.

She approached me after I spoke on Lies Homeschooling Moms Believe. I wasn't sure what she was saying at first, but the more she talked about other non-homeschooled kids and all the things that they achieved, awards they won, and scholarships they received, she seemed to be saying her children could have been 'something' if only she had done more (read – put them in public school). As she talked, she also mentioned how her son was writing a book and giving a workshop at the convention and he was STILL in high school.

Finally I said, "You are using the wrong standard. You're using THEIR standard, and it doesn't mean anything. Besides, you're telling me you have a son who is writing a book and giving a workshop as we speak." Most parents would call that success and envy you.

The truth is she had done great, but NOT because she had a sharp kid who was speaking and writing. It's because God knew what He was doing when He gave her those particular children to train and teach.

I'm telling you Mom and Dad, if you feel like you didn't good enough this year, it's because you're using the wrong measuring stick. Let me tell you loud and clear, if you taught your children at home…you did a GREAT JOB (even if there are changes or modifications that need to be made)!!! Home is the best place for children to be taught. Don't forget that.

Be real.

JUNE 4

There's Plenty of You

Hey Mom,

If you ever happen to have the pleasure of eating in the same restaurant as my family, you might see one of the saddest sights you've ever witnessed. It's typically at the end of the meal, but it doesn't happen all that often. Usually it begins with the question: "Will you be ordering any dessert tonight?"

Most of the time we say, "No…not tonight."

But every once in awhile we 'splurge' and say: "Yes, we'd like ONE cookie monster dessert…and TEN spoons."

In a world where everyone is supposed to get his own dessert, I'm sure ten Wilson's huddled around a single dessert looks pathetic to some…but to us… it's heaven. And you know what? There's always just enough to go around.

It's the same with moms and dads. You may not be able to give every child everything you'd like…but there's always enough to go around. And that tastes gooooodd.

Be real.

The You're Going to Die Tour

Hey Mom,

It's funny how things change so quickly. One day you're traveling life's highway, making plans, and doing the family thing…the next thing you know, you're dead and in heaven.

Debbie Strayer, the founder of Homeschooling Today, reminded me of that startling and important truth all too recently. In fact, I just got an email reminder from my assistant that I needed to get this article to Debbie in a day or two. She didn't realize that Debbie wasn't there to receive it.

By this time you know the details and maybe feel the hole she left behind. I know her husband, children, and family feel it. The homeschooling community feels it because she cast a large shadow for such a little woman.

It feels all the more sensitive because the homeschooling community is still reeling from the loss of long time homeschool vendor and pioneer, Randy Miller of Miller Pad and Paper. The end of May he was unloading his trailer at the large FPEA homeschool convention and collapsed. A few minutes later he showed up in heaven.

It's interesting to me that one of the most powerful lessons they ever taught me was the one they had no control over. Their exit. It came so suddenly right in the middle of life. They had plans, they had dreams, they had unfinished business. I'm guessing that never in their wildest dreams had they thought, Today might be the day.

They left me with that lesson, and so I'm passing it on to you because you never know, Mom or Dad, when today might be the day. In fact, I've thought about changing the title of my upcoming speaking tour to, "The You're Going to Die Tour."

It's a truth that you need to be reminded of from time to time, before it's too late, and one that adds clarity and perspective to everything…especially family and homeschooling. Maybe you wouldn't get so bent out of shape over the mess the kids left in the yard this afternoon if you knew you were going to die today. Maybe you wouldn't work so hard on all your 'important projects' if you knew you were going to die today. Maybe you wouldn't bring your children to tears over some math problem if you knew you were going to die today.

How would you rearrange your homeschool schedule if you knew this was going to be your last YEAR on earth? How would you view your spouse, if you knew he/she was going to be gone next month? How would you view all your relationships if you knew they were about to be severed by death?

Can't you see the enormity of the last lesson Debbie and Randy left behind? We cannot forget it because we are destined to experience it a whole lot sooner than we'd like. So let me give you the take away advice from my "You're Going to Die" tour.

1. Don't worry about tomorrow. You may be on the verge of losing your house, have a teenager who is running from God, a spouse who is wrapped up in all kinds of distractions, and a middle schooler who doesn't know a verb from a bucketful of hair. Stop worrying about what might happen to them in the future and instead tell them how much you love them today.

2. Remember what matters. Furniture doesn't matter. Lawns don't matter. What's for dinner doesn't matter. Math doesn't matter. Sports don't matter. Your children, spouse, and relationships matter. Always have...always will.

3. If you're not right with someone, make it right. Doesn't matter if they ask forgiveness or have a soft heart towards you...MAKE IT RIGHT anyway.

4. If you need tell someone you love them, say it.

5. Thank God for every single person in your family by name. Do it slowly.

6. Have an ice cream sundae tonight.

With that, have a great day with your spouse, a great week with your children, a great month of homeschooling...because it might be your last.

Be real.

JUNE 6

A Dying Breed?

Hey Mom,

It never dawned on me that homeschool groups MIGHT be considered a dying breed. But of course, I still like the mullet haircut from the 80's and might be missing something.

My thought on homeschool groups is that as long as there are homeschoolers, there will be a need for homeschool groups. Now those groups and how they meet may change and evolve over time, but homeschooling moms will always need encouragement.

If you're trying to 'go it alone'...and I know some of you are, then you're swimming in dangerous waters. You may think you're doing okay, but you were not meant to go it alone. You may not belong to a homeschool support group, but you need someone (besides your husband) to encourage you and for you to encourage.

Actually, I think it was originally called the body of Christ, and they need you as much as you need them.

Oh, yeah, and remind them to...

Be real.

JUNE 7

Keeping Track of Records

Hey Mom,

What is this? Pick topics highlighting Todd's ineptness? The truth is I don't make lists, keep lists, organize, or…keep records. Well, not in the way most homeschooling moms think anyway. Oh, I keep plenty of records, mind you, but not the unimportant ones like how they did on history tests and essays.

I keep important records of growth and maturity like…love notes from my children, scribbles on scraps of paper, lost teeth, pop bottles from special outings, dirt from vacation spots, silly hats from Krispy Kreme donuts, movie ticket stubs, artwork created from mud, sticks, and wood, and 'projects' that they created with their own hands.

All these records litter my office, our house, and the top of my dresser, reminding me of what really matters. In fact, I even have a memory tree out in my yard that God made when he tore the upper half off an old oak tree. On it I nailed items that should be thrown away but I can't seem to part with because of the 'record' of my family's life.

So my advice would be to save the important 'records' and don't sweat the unimportant ones. Works for me.

That concludes my ineptness for today,

Be real.

JUNE 8

The Video Game Struggle

Hey Mom,

Do you feel like you're the only one who struggles with video games? I guess you could look at this question a couple of different ways. 1) Am I the only parent who struggles with children who play too many video games or 2) Am I, myself, the only one who struggles with playing too many video games?

The answer to both questions is the same—are you kidding me??!!! If you have a computer (which most of us do), then you probably struggle with kids who want to play on it more than you think they should. It is so common…and it is dangerous. In fact, this past week I spoke in Houston about this very topic. Afterwards, a clean-cut young man came up to me and said his wife divorced him because he was addicted to an online video game.

Later in the day, a pastor told me he was counseling FIVE different couples at one point in time, in which all of the husbands were addicted to video games. All five ended in divorce. Is it common? Yes. Is it a big deal? You betcha.

It is our job as parents to deal with the 'video beast' so that our children do not grow up and sacrifice real relationships that are HARD for virtual ones that are EASY.

It involves looking into our children's lives and OUR lives as well. It is a commonplace struggle, but it's taking over and killing families (both present and future). Don't just blow it off and say, "It's just the age we live in."

Deal with it. It's not easy, and I wish it would all go away, but it isn't and it won't.

Are you alone? No. Is it hopeless? NEVER!!!!

Be real...and if you still haven't bought my book Taming the Techno-Beast, (which a lot of you haven't), BUY IT NOW!!!

JUNE 9

Vaaacaaaationnnnnnn!!!

Hey Mom,

I'm back in the saddle again...after being on the road for about a month. It feels good to be home again.

Man, we had a great time traveling, meeting so many moms and their families, and relaxing as a family for a week. Mom, I don't know when the last time you spent a little R&R with your family was, but if it's been a while, you should plan some time.

As I sat around the pool watching other parents with their kids, my heart swelled with gratitude for being on the parent-team. There's just nothing better than seeing a grown woman, 75lbs overweight, doing the hoola-hoop with her three-year-old daughter, a balding dad in the pool throwing his son into the air with a giggle and a splash, or a pasty-white dad trying to show a couple of middle-school-aged kids how to play shuffleboard.

In everyday life, parents don't always have time to do that kind of stuff. That's why you should plan a little getaway in the coming months. Somehow, it helps you focus on being mom. Don't have a lot of money? I bet you can find a cheap hotel with an indoor pool on Priceline that you could afford...or better yet can't afford to pass up.

It won't be long before those kids are all grown and gone and you'll wish you could splash around the pool with your kids one more time.

Be real.

You Set the Standard

Hey Mom,

Let me begin this discussion with the fact that I was a TV kid. I was weaned on the static cathode tube of black and white television. My mentors were Captain Kangaroo, Mister Rogers, and Bert and Ernie. I watched in the morning before school, when I got off the school bus, and during the hours before bed.

That said, after I was married and had a couple of young kids, we decided to rein in the tube and cut it out. As a byproduct of that decision our kids…played.

Then, it eventually made its way back into our house…not as a TV but as a video player. We still don't watch TV very often, but we do watch a lot of videos and old TV shows.

Here's the deal: I used to look down my nose in pious righteousness at folks who watched TV and thought more highly of those who threw out their TV. Not anymore. I know that TV can be fun and familyish. It can also be a destructive, lazy habit. But I know this: YOU (and your husband) can decide what's best for your family and not everyone decides the same thing…and that's OK.

Be real.

Let's Go to the Movies

Hey Mom,

Seen any good movies lately? It's funny you should ask. Just last night, my wife and I were sitting on our big couch talking to her sister and husband about movies we had seen and liked. We both are conservative in our choices and are always looking for a good family movie.

So here's a list of some of their favorites…that we plan to view:

-The Scarlet Pimpernel (old version)
-Little Dorrit
-North and South (BBC version)
-Sue Thomas (FBI series)
-What If

Here are some of our favorites besides the normal favorites:

-Toby Tyler (old Disney)
-Summer Magic (old Disney)

-Black Beard's Ghost (old Disney)
-Grey Friar Bobby (old Disney)
-Third Man on the Mountain (old Disney)
-Pollyanna
-Hazel (50's TV series)
-When Calls the Heart (Ooo...I like this one)
-Little House on the Prairie

Now, don't trust our opinion or anyone else's for that matter. You might want to check them out first or at least watch them WITH your family.

Have fun, pass the popcorn, and be real.

JUNE 12

Multiple Grade Levels

Hey Mom,

Homeschool truth number #2 –We believe that life is the best curriculum and home is the greatest classroom.

That means that teaching and learning in multiple grade levels is the best way to learn. Oh, it's not easy (you already knew that) but there is something wonderful about learning WITH brothers and sisters.

Now as is my usual way to get out of addressing the actual topic at hand, I don't have any helpful techniques for teaching a 2nd and 5th grader while a toddler is making messes and a newborn is screaming his lungs out. My wife would probably have some ideas.

All I can do is remind you of the incredible lessons all your children are learning. It's not just about math and reading, but about FAMILY and how to fit in.

That's an incredible lesson considering they're going to spend most of their future life as a family. They'll need to know how to work, rest, and play with others. They'll need to know how to wait until it's their turn (or even go without a turn), how to share their time, attention, and resources, and a whole bunch of other stuff.

In fact, I wonder if WE have so much trouble in OUR homeschool because WE were NOT homeschooled. In a school setting, there is no one you have to wait on. Anyone who is slow is moved down or out. It's all about the ME. Family is all about the THEM or US.

With that said, enjoy the chaos, the interruptions, and seeming lack of progress. They're learning...and so are you.

Be real.

He's 'da Dad

Hey Mom,

As a member of the male species, I'd like to take this pre-Father's Day week to let you non-male readers know what it feels like to be a dad. Actually, I've been thinking about it all week…not because it's the week leading up to Father's Day but because I've been talking to a lot of dads lately...and I am one.

As I talk to dads about their teenagers who are giving them fits, their wives who don't seem to think like them, and the deceptively deadly pull of success that beckons to them every day, I see tiredness in their eyes and hear emotion in their voices.

I listen to them talk and nod my head in understanding until they finish. Then in a gentle but firm voice I say, "Man, I know exactly how you feel, but... you 'da dad. You may feel like giving up, but your family is counting on you. You can't give up on them. Get back in there, because although they may say harsh things...they still need you."

They sigh, stiffen their chin in determination, nod in agreement, and say, "You're right; thanks for the reminder."

Over and over I watch men walk away, determined to give it another shot.

I can't help but think of that old Paul Newman movie, Cool Hand Luke. It's about a guy who winds up in an old Hogan's Hero-like chain gang and repeatedly tries to escape. It's not one I'd recommend seeing, but one scene has been replaying in my mind this past week.

Cocky Paul Newman arrives at the prison camp and is challenged by the biggest guy (probably named Moose, Big Al, or something like that) in jail to a fist fight. Everyone knows Paul will be knocked out cold in the first round but to the surprise of everyone, he just won't go down.

He smiles, gets pounded to the ground, and then staggers up to get knocked down again. Eventually, even the BIG guy feels sorry for him and begs him to stay down...but he won't. You think his dusty and bruised body is incapable of moving at all when he drags himself to a standing position and lifts his hands to defend himself…again.

Ladies, that's your man. He gets pummeled, whomped on, yelled at, and spit on, but...he's too committed (or too stupid) to give up. He loves you, your family, and his role as dad (even though sometimes he doesn't act like it).

Kind of shines a new light on that non-holiday known as Father's Day.

Be real…and love your man.

Father of the . . . WHAT?

Hey Mom,

I've decided to forgo what I had planned to write in lieu of (whatever that means) the news that was just passed to me by a fellow dad. I thought this would be a perfect lead in to Father's Day.

Are you ready for this? It was just announced that The National Father's Day Council selected former President Bill Clinton as the Father of the Year.

The group selected Clinton for his "profound generosity, leadership, and tireless dedication to both his public office and many philanthropic organizations," said Dan Orwig, Chairman of the National Father's Day Committee.

Now, I could respond with a variety of critical comments, but let me forgo those in lieu of (that's 2x's) something more...constructive.

I will say that one's business credentials have nothing to do with fathering, not that most of the world would agree with me.

It seems to me that almost every Father of the Year award I've ever seen given is given to some 'dad' who is successful in business, Hollywood, or some other media. But that should not be the criteria or the arena that determines the Father of the Year award. It's about sacrifice.

So, Dan Orwig, chairman of the National Father's Day Council, here's my criteria for the Father of the Year Award.

The recipient should be relatively unknown, not as successful as his peers, having sacrificed his own ambitions for his family. He should have a wife who smiles a lot, even when no one is looking. His children are far from perfect but they love their dad who is home every night for dinner, involved in their lives, and prays with them as he tucks them into bed.

This man has fingerprints on his dress shirts, handlebar scratches on his car, hasn't played golf in years, and doesn't hang out with the guys. He's been invited to more little girl tea parties than power lunches and can't remember the last time he watched a movie that wasn't animated.

The only important people he knows are Big Bird, Dora the Explorer, and Mr. Rogers. His desk is covered with family pictures and kids' artwork. He tears up when he thinks about his kids growing older. He gives, he sacrifices, and he never quits trying.

And if you ask what he does...he answers, "I'm a dad."

That's my criteria for Father of the Year, Mr. Orwig.

That's what your husband does. Let him know I just selected him as the Father of the Year!

Be real.

Not Getting Any

Hey Mom,

The air is brisk for a June morning, and I smelled just the faintest hint of fall as I walked outside…and I hate it. I'm not ready for summer to be over (and it's only just begun) and school to be starting. I still have stuff to do… adventures to have. I need more time!

But the truth is: I'm not getting any.

I was thinking about that a couple evenings ago. After dinner I told the kids we were going to clean out the basement. Our basement is more like a root cellar: low ceilings, pipes that bump your head, dim lights, and a musty smell. It's dry, just not very glamorous.

To that picture, add 17 years of storage: clothes, coats, spare dressers and chairs, and treasures galore. Believe me, it's time to clean-up and throw out. That's when I was confronted by the time issue.

I was reshuffling, organizing, and stuffing things into crevices when it hit me that some of the stuff was wedding gifts or from our apartment and first house. That wasn't troubling, but then it hit me that my oldest son Ben could need some of it in a few years.

As the thought hit me, it was like a scene from a movie where a sonic wave explodes, rippling across the countryside – HE'S ALMOST THE AGE I WAS…THEN.

I'm not ready for that. I need more time!!!!!!!

But the truth is: I'm not getting any. And neither are you, Mom. Our job is to savor the time today—to enjoy the interruption of young children who want to make messes, to enjoy big kids who don't seem to interact as much as they use to, to enjoy a battle of wills with our almost adult children, and to enjoy every ounce of summer break.

It'll be over soon…and you're not getting any more.

Be real.

JUNE 16

The Best Father's Day Ever

Hey Mom,

This is the topic I've been waiting for. In fact, I almost feel like Joseph – that God sent me here for such a time as this. It's been my dream to make

Father's Day the second most celebrated holiday of the year. I envision the Father's Day tree, fathering carols, and maybe even the 12 days of Father's Day. That's what I dream about happening. More likely, I'll get a few cards that were handmade two minutes before they we're handed to me, and maybe we'll go out to McDonald's and I'll get a Big Mac.

BUT let me give you a heads up about the perfect Father's Day gift for your husband, one that, if applied all year long, will make him a better father, husband, and spiritual leader...and it's NOT a tie.

All you have to do is...hang on his arm and tell him his muscles are big.

That's it. I guarantee that will pump him up and get you the man of your dreams.

Practically, it looks like this:

1) Your husband helps get the kids dressed for church – you resist the urge to redress them and instead say, "Thanks for getting the kids ready. I sure do appreciate your help."

2) During church, you reach over and squeeze his arm and whisper, "You are so strong."

3) After he's had his undisturbed nap, you sit on the edge of the couch and say, "Thanks for working so hard to take care of us."

4) And of course after the kids are in bed...you, uh...um...well, you know. Then tell him, "You're the best."

Do that every once in awhile and not only will you give your husband the best father's day of his life, but he will also become more involved in your life, family life, and homeschooling. Guaranteed.

Be real.

JUNE 17

Learning Music on a Budget

Hey Mom,

Here are my thoughts on the thrilling topic of learning music on a budget. If God wants your kids to learn how to play a musical instrument, then He'll supply the means to do that. So don't sweat it. But here's the deal. I don't think God wants every child to play a musical instrument. Our job as parents is not to bowl through any obstacle to do what WE want for our children but to ask God what HE wants for our children.

Now for those of you who believe God wants your child to play a musical instrument, you have two options: 1) Make sacrifices to pay for the lessons, teachers, and instruments. 2) Let the need be known and wait for God to supply. He will, you know. I've seen it in our lives and in the lives of so many others. But you have to speak up…not so that people will have pity on you but so that the body of Christ can see what the needs of the rest of the body are and act on them.

So let people know that God wants your little Johnny to play the tuba. You'll get offers, advice, and insights. Don't expect free (although that may happen), but if you believe God wants your child to learn the tuba, then you ought to be willing to make some sacrifices in order to see it through.

Be real.

JUNE 18

Enjoying the 'Special' in Special Needs

Hey Mom,

I don't have a lot to say about today's topic...except…love 'that' child.

I know the temptation for any parent of any child is to love the easy-to-love, the easy-to-teach, the smart, the happy, the good student…and the (fill in the blank). Sometimes the ones that don't fit those categories are harder to love or like, especially if you listen to the lies of the 'achievers.'

They're always saying how children should be doing this or that…by now or then. And sometimes special needs kids and (other kids for that matter) don't, and so we begin to see our kids through 'the opposite of rose colored glasses.'

So let me encourage you parents of ALL children, to love your children just the way they are…and stop wishing they'd be something else.

Be real.

JUNE 19

No ifs, ands, or buts

Hey Mom,

It blows me away when I hear homeschooling moms and dads espouse the virtues of public school teachers and the institution in which they work. They measure themselves against 'real' teachers and the 'system' and find themselves on the short side.

After all, their thinking goes, how can 'we' compete with trained, educated teachers and an organization that is devoted to the profession of teaching? They use that 'superior' teacher/school standard as THEIR standard and spend most of their days second guessing their efforts and results.

But here's the TRUTH…the lie-busting truth: YOU, regardless of your training or education are BETTER qualified to train and teach your children than 'the system' is.

Just this past week we met a couple for dinner who feels God's direction in starting something new. The husband, who has spent the last twenty years in the public school system, lamented how poorly the system is suited to teach children. His school received an "F" rating last year which brought about all kinds of ridiculous changes.

"Teachers' hands are tied…kids don't learn…peers punish learners…and teachers aren't able to teach…the system is broken." You could hear the frustration in his voice. He entered the field because he wanted to make a difference but said he no longer can because of how the system has changed. And so, he's trying to find a better way…one away from that system.

To be honest, I wouldn't have thought much more about our conversation had it not been for my wife's comment on the way home.

"Isn't it amazing," my wife said as she had been contemplating the conversation, "how we as homeschoolers are insecure and worried that a school would be doing a better job than we are, and that we often feel like failures in teaching our children, when in reality, it's just the opposite? They're the ones who are struggling and failing."

And so, there you have it—THE TRUTH. You are better equipped to teach your children than 'THEY' are; no ifs, ands, or buts. So start believing it and refuse to dip your thoughts back into the cesspool of doubts and lies that believe, they're better than I am.

You're the best.

Be real.

JUNE 20

Helping Your Reluctant Writer

Hey Mom,

Most all of us have reluctant writers…kids who take to writing like fish take to pudding. I know we've run the whole gamut at our house. I have one daughter who has written several books* and some who can barely write a sentence.

My simple advice to encourage your reluctant writer is to let him write without fear of failure or correction. Have your kids self-correct their own spelling tests, and when you have them write in elementary, don't correct their work, just let them write…and write…without fear. They can learn about grammar when the time comes, but just getting them to write is the important part. Do not let yourself tear it apart with corrections. Leave the misspellings. It's okay.

I believe some of 'our' kids are afraid to write a single sentence because we as parents swoop in to correct their many mistakes. You forgot to put the period at the end of the sentence…you forgot to start with a capital letter, you don't need a comma there…you do need one here…I can barely read your handwriting…you write like a two-year-old…etc.

I'm telling you, I'd be afraid to write if I was treated like that. Just let your kids write without fear of being wrong, and by the way, YOU don't need to be afraid either. I think one of the reasons we drive our kids and kill the love of writing or even school for that matter, is because we don't want them to embarrass us or not be able to get a job because we didn't make them write enough.

I hear story after story of kids who didn't write until they needed to write. And guess what? THEY WROTE…and did fine (some of them even became writers). I saw it happen with one of our kids as well. And if your kids never enjoy writing…that's okay, too.

Just relax and…

Be real.

**A Girl's Guide to Tea Parties, The Stolen Princess, Amira's Secret (Available on our website and on Amazon.)*

JUNE 21

Kid's day

Hey Mom,

I don't about all dads, but this dad had a mighty fine Father's Day…although as far as my kids are concerned, Father's Day was just a warm-up band for the main event—Kid's Day.

Actually, I founded the day about 7 years ago after my son Sam pointed out that we celebrate Mother's Day AND Father's Day, BUT there was nothing to recognize…kids.

That's when I, in my most official voice I could muster, declared the first day of summer (June 21st) as…da-da-da-dant-da-daaaa…KIDS' DAY!!!!!

So ever since that day, we've let our kids know just how much we love having them as our children…and Father's Day has been relegated to a mile marker along the route to Kid's Day.

Now don't get me wrong, this holiday isn't on the same level as a birthday or Christmas, but we do set aside the day for our kids just like Mother's Day and Father's Day does for parents.

So, we make a few cards, buy a cheap gift for each of them that has to do with summer fun like a squirt gun, swim goggles, or a slip and slide (for all of them). Then we all play outside, go on a bike ride, get pizza, go for a picnic, or get ice cream from the ice cream truck. It varies from year to year.

Really, it doesn't have to cost much, except your time...and they're worth it.

Make your Kid's Day a good 'un.

Be real.

JUNE 22

Make it Hap'n Cap'n

A Note to your husband:

Hey Dad,

Just a little message from me, the Familyman, to you, a fellow familyman about the importance of family vacations. I probably don't have to tell you how vital they are to the sanity of your wife and family, but I may need to give you a little kick in the pants to make it happen.

After all, you're the captain of your ship, and I've met too many captains who for various reasons have neglected to steer their families into the vacation waters.

They always have plausible arguments like: we don't have the money, the kids are too young, we don't have time, this is my busy season, and we don't really need a vacation. These reasons sound somewhat convincing and oftentimes noble, but I'm not buying them.

I believe that every family needs and can take a vacation. Don't give me the victim mentality that says, "We're poor and can't take exotic vacations like everyone else." I'm not buying it!!

My advice is: Make it hap'n Cap'n! There are no victims in this game. The reason families don't go on vacation is because dads don't make them go. So here's my advice for making a vacation happen (when you don't have much expendable income):

1. Make a plan. Sit down and brainstorm. You might not be able to afford the Riviera but maybe you can afford a state park...or know someone who has a place you can use for free...who knows.

2. Let others know where you'd like to go (like Disney or Des Moines). You'd be surprised by how many people have connections and/or timeshares they don't use. It's not begging or pleading...it's just letting the body of Christ know what you're dreaming.

3. Check the internet on how to do what you're thinking. You'd be amazed at the cheap airline prices (think specials) one can find and the number of beaches within state parks.

4. Start saving. Just by saving out $10 a week, you'll end up with $520 to put towards a few days away somewhere.

5. Just do it. As my cousin Scott likes to say about the money he spends on vacation, "It'll grow back."

Finally, suck it up, take your place at the ship's wheel, and make it hap'n Cap'n!! Your wife and family need you to do it.

Be real.

JUNE 23

A Begrudging Dad

Hey Mom,

Hope you had a great weekend with your family. Besides a lot of rain and gray days, we had fun at my in-law's lake cottage. Although the bad weather kept everyone in, it did make for a lot of game playing. I'm not normally the game playing type...but I'm trying.

One highlight was that when the kids weren't inside, they stood outside in the drizzle fishing for the elusive giant carp...or bugle-mouth bass as they're affectionately known. The kids made poles out of sticks and 50-pound test line, attached a hook and some bread and waited until...BAM!!!!!

Finally, the sun showed its face and right before lunch my daughter asked, "Dad, will you take us tubing?" I knew it would come, and I knew that it would be coming at me because the day before, my brother-in-law bit the bullet and hit the lake in a boat loaded down with at least 150 kids.

I signed. "You don't have to if you don't want to," my daughter said to her bum of a dad.

"Well, I don't want to...but I will," I said dragging my comfortable carcass out of the comfortable chair.

So we loaded up the boat with kids, life jackets, tubes, and one begrudging-dad. I tried to act happy and goofy, but I know my daughter knew I was begrudging and told my wife so.

Oh, they all had fun, but I know I lessened the fun for my daughter because my heart wasn't in it. Sadly, I do that too often. I say, "Yes" but I let them all know that I'm begrudging, miserable, and that I don't like them for asking me to do 'it.' What a crummy dad.

Here's the deal, Mom; sometimes you do it too and your kids know it. They don't want you to say yes and then begrudge. They want you to say yes and enjoy. You know what? We can do that, but it doesn't always come naturally.

So, my fellow begrudging mom, when they ask you to do something... today, say yes and then enjoy it.

Be real.

JUNE 24

Math in the Kitchen

Hey Mom,

I just have to tell you that these are the exact words I was given for the topic this week: "Math in the Kitchen (YUM!)."

First of all let me just say, I'm a guy, and not to sound male-piggish, but this doesn't seem like a very guyish topic. And for the record, I never use the word 'YUM' in anything…EVER!!! So, I'm going to be silent on this topic and hope we're not discussing "Algebra in the Sewing Room" next week.

Of course the kitchen is a good place for math. The kitchen is where life takes place and involves real learning. The kitchen is all about measuring and cups, ounces, and…eggs. Just don't ruin the whole learning process by turning it into school. You don't need to have them write a paper, do a worksheet, or put on your lecturing hat. Just let them make cookies, have fun, and enjoy the process called learning.

And…send me a sample of your "lesson." I really like those no-bake cookies!!

Bon appétit.

JUNE 25

My Final Word on Algebra

Hey Mom,

I'm just going to say it. I've wanted to for a long time…but I knew I might unleash a firestorm of militant homeschool moms. But I don't care anymore. It's the way I feel and it's a free country. So brace yourself…here it is:

I think Algebra is DUMB!!!

There, I said it! Now, just to qualify my statement, I know there are some out there who use Algebra every day and who have been gifted by God in mathematics. That's the minority…the vast majority don't get Algebra and never use it (don't write me and tell me how we use it all the time to figure out…blah blah blah blah blah). Most of us don't use Algebraic equations to find out unknown distances, weights, or measurements…we just use good old common sense.

To me, the question begs to be asked, "Then why does EVERYONE think they have to teach Algebra to non-math destined kids?"

The correct answer: BECAUSE.*

I think that's a DUMB answer and we as homeschoolers can decide for ourselves whether we want to teach our children Algebra.

I took Algebra, Advanced Algebra, and even Advanced Calculus in college…and I couldn't solve a simple algebra problem today to save my life. That's because Algebra is DUMB (or maybe it's me that's dumb)!

That said, our kids have taken Algebra with the magical aid of Teaching Textbooks (what can I say? My wife is a math person). My kids love it…but I still think Algebra is dumb.

Be real.

**I know some states require Algebra.*

JUNE 26

How to Help the Struggling Reader

Hey Mom,

Once upon a time, long, long ago in the land-of-make-believe, there lived a dad. He was inexperienced, had young children, and was incredibly handsome.

One day, the incredibly handsome dad wrote an article about how simple it is to make every child a reader. In his mind, he thought he was offering help but upon looking back, the now older (although not much wiser) dad knows he may have furthered the lie that EVERYONE must be a reader, and for that he was sorry.

The truth is some kids become readers and some do not. I…er, the dad mentioned above, have some children who read voraciously. They read all the time, devouring books like chocolate chips cookies right out of the oven.

On the other hand, the dad has other children who, although they can and do read, don't read in the same manner as the book-gobblers. Instead of curling up with a good book, they draw, build, or experiment with science for pleasure.

The point is that not all children will become voracious readers. Yes, we sometimes limit the possibility by allowing them to fill their time with TV and computer games, but even if you remove all those distractions, some children and adults still aren't readers. And that's OK.

So have a wonderful day in the land-of-real, be patient with your struggling reader, and please forgive the stupid…although handsome dad.

Be real.

(Obviously NOT the dad in the above story)

Can I Teach Literature?

Hey Mom,

Can you teach literature? Does a one legged duck swim in a circle? Of course you can teach literature. Actually, I think literature can teach itself. All you need to do is read, read, and read to your child and get your child to the point where she can read herself…and then turn her loose.

If you let your kids read (& read out loud to them), they'll learn all kinds of things about life, God, and people. With the right books, they'll visit Narnia, listen to Pa play his fiddle, hear the snort of the black stallion, feel the fright of sighting the big white whale, and stand amazed when Jesus heals a man who was born blind.

About the only thing you can do wrong in literature is to teach it like the literature 'experts' say to teach it. If you reduce it to 'who is the protagonist', 'what is the meter', or 'name the themes throughout the story'…you'll ruin the whole literature experience. Plus, you'll kill the love of reading.

So just give them good books, let them read, get out of the way…and leave the protagonist to the antagonist.

Be real.

Getting Ready for College Writing

Hey Mom,

Cue the Brady Bunch 70's theme.

Here's a story about a man named y…

A long time ago I went to a public high school filled with professionals in the schooling department. I graduated near the top of my class and then went to a large university where I majored in Landscape Architecture. I'm not sure that I had an official writing class in all my time there, but I'm sure I had to write…although I did skip a lot of classes and might have missed something.

I graduated and went to Seminary where I had to write a bunch of papers. For most of them, I was ill-prepared and hadn't a clue about form or rules. In fact, I couldn't even type so I had to pay someone else to type my papers. I graduated, became a pastor…and boom—now I'm a writer.

Here's my point. I made it through high school, college, and seminary, and now I make my living by writing…and I really don't know how to WRITE.

You're right; I'm cynical about all the who-haw that says, "You need to be able to write if you're going to make it in college…they're not going to spoon feed you in college….blah blah blah blah blah."

Here's a newsflash for you: when your kids need to write, they'll write. It may not be perfect…and they may struggle through it, but they'll get it and do just fine. And you don't need to sweat it. Take it from me a writer who doesn't know how to write. Let those who like to write, write and those who don't… write when they have to. Who knows? It might be the non-writers who become tomorrow's writers.

Be real.

JUNE 29

In Times of Grief

Hey Mom,

I'm not going to say much, because in times of grief there is not much that can be said. But I think Charlie Brown unknowingly said something very profound. His lips got all squiggly and in agony, he said, "Good grief."

I think maybe he's right…maybe grief isn't all bad. In fact, maybe grief can be good, not that it feels good or we should run to find it (it finds us easily enough), but maybe the grieving times are when God's mercies are the sweetest. And those are the words and truths contained in the song, "Blessings" by Laura Story. I hope these words encourage you as they have me and so many others.

(Skipping intro)

Chorus:

'Cause what if Your blessings come through raindrops
What if Your healing comes through tears?
What if a thousand sleepless nights
Are what it takes to know You're near?
What if trials of this life are Your mercies in disguise?
We pray for wisdom, Your voice to hear
We cry in anger when we cannot feel You near
We doubt Your goodness, we doubt Your love
As if every promise from Your Word is not enough
And all the while, You hear each desperate plea
And long that we'd have faith to believe
When friends betray us
When darkness seems to win

We know that pain reminds this heart
That this is not, this is not our home
It's not our home
'Cause what if Your blessings come through raindrops
What if Your healing comes through tears?
And what if a thousand sleepless nights
Are what it takes to know You're near?
What if my greatest disappointments
Or the aching of this life
Is the revealing of a greater thirst this world can't satisfy?
And what if trials of this life
The rain, the storms, the hardest nights
Are Your mercies in disguise?
Are you grieving? Go listen to this song.

Be real.

JUNE 30

The White Flag

Hey Mom,

Let me just say that when you want to give up…you're not alone. Oh, I know you think you are. You can't imagine anyone feeling as down in the dumps as you do. You can't bring yourself to believe that others feel like tossing in the towel, too.

In fact, you're convinced that your perky homeschool friend, little miss what's her name, NEVER feels like you. The Greek word for that is BALONEY!!!!

EVERY home school mom feels like giving up now and then. It comes with the territory. That's what comes when you're doing something GOOD.

It's OK and normal to FEEL like giving up, but the important thing is to NOT GIVE UP.

That's what Paul was saying when he wrote, "Let us not become weary in doing good (and stop), for at the proper time we will reap a harvest if we do not give up…and throw in the towel." (Gal. 6:9).

So go ahead and rant and rave…maybe even threaten to put the kids in boarding school, BUT DON'T STOP.

Be real…painfully real.

Shallow but Thankful

Hey Mom,

I'm not sure, but I think my patriotism is a little shallow. When I think of Independence Day, I mostly think of the 4th of July filled with flags, fireworks, and food. The whole family gathers for the big weekend. Even in Northern Indiana, the weather is hot…4th of July hot, as grandpa pulls hot dogs and hamburgers from the grill and the kids shuck corn.

There's also the big fireworks display. I'm not talking about the BIG ones that the local Jaycees put on but the kind that come in a package from a parking lot fireworks' stand named Crazy Joe's.

The cousins 'aah and ooh' while the aunts scold their husbands for allowing kids to light dangerous fuses, and we all fall asleep to the sound of fireworks displays popping in the distance.

I'm half-ashamed at the shallowness of my patriotism. I hardly think about the incredible sacrifices made by so many men and women for the freedoms that I enjoy. I forget that the blood of hundreds of thousands of individuals paid for the flags displayed in every yard.

In a way, I guess that's okay. Those heroes died and sacrificed so that I might enjoy corn on the cob on a hot, Indiana day oblivious to the dangers they faced.

So this weekend…enjoy the sun, a cold slab of watermelon, your family, and the freedom to homeschool that we so richly enjoy in this great country, and may God continue to shed his grace on all of us.

Be real.

JULY 2

Freedom to Family

Hey Mom,

For all the problems we have in America, we still live in a great country. One of the perks of speaking at state homeschool conventions is that my family and I have been able to experience some of the best this USA has to offer.

We've walked historic battlefields, stood in the homes of former presidents, and looked out upon scenery that takes your breath away. My heart swells when I hear Kate Smith sing, "God Bless America…my home sweet home!!!"

God has truly blessed this country with freedoms that most of the world has never known. When you look at all that through the eyes of a child of God, you think…WOW! We're up to our foreheads in FREEDOM.

In fact, I love the Bible verse that says, “It was for freedom that you were set free.”

The sad thing is that most homeschoolers and Christians I meet seem bound and shackled like slaves who ignored the emancipation proclamation. Reminds me a little of the hamster my brother-in-law and his family decided to release.

They placed the open cage in the middle of the yard and walked away. After a couple of days, the hamster was still there. Even when they dumped it out of the cage, it returned.

I guess it liked cages, like most of us.

And yet…we’re FREE!!!!!!!!!

Kind of sad, huh?

So from one emancipated slave to another, get out of the CAGE!!! Forget what everyone else says you should be doing and start enjoying the freedom of being a child of the King. Live in freedom, eat in freedom, family in freedom, and homeschool in freedom.

And of course…be real.

JULY 5

Going Places

Hey Mom,

I love going places, and I know my kids do as well. One of the perks of being the Familyman is that I get to spend a big chunk of the spring and summer traveling around the country with the whole Wilson gang in our Familyman Mobile, our big old RV.

My kids have been just about everywhere in this great country of ours, but in all our travels I’ve NEVER used the word ‘geography.’ Somehow that word ‘schoolifies’ a good thing, and it certainly doesn’t increase the impact of the experience.

In fact, I’ve never made my kids write about where they’ve been or what they saw. I don’t ask them to give oral reports or verbalize what they felt. We just do things together as a family and then talk about what we saw in the same way you might talk about a baseball game you’re kids just played in…it’s just fun.

Now to be honest, some of them still couldn’t find Arizona on the map or tell you whether Minnesota was north or south, but who cares? The important thing is that they got to experience a slice of America WITH their family… and that is life changing.

So go…somewhere.

Be real.

Art for the Art-Deficient Mom

Hey Mom,

Truth: not all homeschool moms are created equal. Some like math, some don't – some are organized, some aren't – some love art projects and crafts, some despise them. My wife is in the latter group and often feels like a failure because she doesn't do fun, creative art projects with her children.

Fortunately, she has me to remind her of all her other great qualities (which are many) and remind her of the truth. The way I see it is if God had wanted OUR children to do cool art projects all the time, He would have made HER to like art.

Let me apologize on behalf of homeschool leaders everywhere for having given you false information and guilting you into thinking that good homeschooling moms should do art. It's not true. Your kids will be just fine if you skip that subject altogether.

Now having said that let me add that we have an art kid who spends most of his days drawing. He was made that way, so my wife has fed that passion, not by doing art projects with him but by getting him the tools he needs to develop that gift and by encouraging him in it. She's bought him art books, drawing pads, and computer software.

That's what homeschooling is all about: finding the gifts within your children and helping them pursue them. It's not about teaching what WE like anyway…but about what they like and are created to be.

So don't sweat art if art isn't your thing; they'll figure it out on their own if it's meant to be their thing. And, most importantly, don't feel guilty.

Be real.

JULY 7

Homeschooling Isn't the Problem

Hey Mom,

My wife had a conversation last night that troubles me. It wasn't that the person or conversation was necessarily troubling, it was the idea that homeschooling has some inheritably troublesome qualities.

The thinking goes like this, All these people got caught up in legalism, and they homeschooled…therefore the problem must be homeschooling.

I hear that same argument on websites like homeschoolers anonymous and other ex-homeschooling websites. We were abused, and we were homeschooled…therefore homeschooling is bad.

I don't doubt for one moment the abuse or the hurts that so many of US parents have put our children through, but it is NOT a homeschooling issue. Yes, some homeschoolers are susceptible to following every schmoe who comes down the pike selling stupid parenting advice…BUT it is NOT a homeschool issue.

People are already saying, "Stay away from homeschooling…it leads to bad things." But they are wrong, and if you follow their logic you will miss out on God's best for you.

Here's the truth: God invented homeschooling. It was His plan. He told the people more than once, "You teach your children…that they should teach their children…so that one day they would teach their children (Psalm 78).

Go ahead and be skeptical about the people who say, "God wants you to court, betrothe, wear dresses only, or have your babies at home." That's not in the Bible, but don't throw out homeschooling.

Homeschooling is just parenting. It's teaching your children in your home about all the things they're going to need one day in their home. It's a good plan…because God originated it.

So to all those who are linking fallen leaders, broken children, and weird philosophies to homeschooling, STOP IT. To you moms, who might be tempted to believe them, don't.

Enjoy having your children home. Smile as you learn and grow together. Don't believe everyone who tells you what you should be doing with your children. And love your husband most! That's homeschooling.

Be real.

JULY 8

Tips for Teaching Times Tables

Hey Mom,

You already know that I'm not a math guy. Normally, I play devil's advocate and tell you your child doesn't need most of it anyway. BUT when the topic is Times Tables and Everyday Math, I've got to play hardball.

Truth is: even as a non-math guy, I use 'times-ing' (also known as multiplication) all the time. And everyday math? I use it most every day! So your kids and mine need to know how to do these things (don't get me started on wasting time on quadratic equations).

There is no silver bullet, however. You just have to slog through…every day…flashcards…month after month…year after year, until they've got them. Some get them quickly; some take almost forever. But you've got to keep slogging. Don't give up or get anxious or frustrated. Just slog. And, my wife said to suggest TimezAttack*, a fun, computer game that you can download for FREE. Your boys (especially) will no longer fight you about having to practice with this cool and effective game.

Be real.

**www.educational-freeware.com/freeware/timez-attack.aspx*

***Another good option is XtraMath*

JULY 9

The Struggling Child

Hey Mom,

I know that if you have a struggling child then you've researched, asked questions, sought the advice of experts, and…beat yourself up everyday wondering what you can do to change that child.

But remember: no matter what your child is or isn't, they still need you to love and enjoy them. Sometimes 'schooling' gets in the way of that. It's easy to forget that God made your child exactly the way He wanted him to be…and He'll complete what He started.

You just need to plug away, not compare your kids or your situation to others, and enjoy the moment.

Be real.

JULY 10

Comfort-free Parenting

Hey Mom,

My fingers are stiff as I type this because last night, after two weeks of promising, we finally…camped in our backyard. It was everything I thought it would be…miserable.

I'm not sure I slept two hours the whole night. The evening was beautiful, warm and fall-ish. I even blew up the air mattress thinking that would eliminate the hard ground poking my old body. After singing around the campfire, I convinced myself that this was going to be the perfect night for sleeping out. "Not too hot or too cold," I told my four youngest children.

We bunked down for the night, and an arctic blast blew down from the North Pole and every animal that could howl, bark, or hoot converged into earshot of our backyard. It was miserable, and my eyes sting from lack of sleep.

I thought I would go insane from listening to all the hickory nuts and walnuts fall from the trees. It sounded like golf balls and baseballs falling from the sky with loud thuds near our tent. I kept wondering if the tent would be able to keep them from bashing us. Combine that sound with an evil sounding owl and a pack of dogs with insomnia, and it was one of the loudest nights I've ever experienced. Did I mention the trains and midnight drag racers? It was miserable. Oh wait, I think I already said that.

Right now the kids are watching PBS to keep quiet. I'm huddled over my computer with my hoodie pulled over my head to conserve heat thinking about last night. The truth is I may have thought it was miserable, but they will never forget…the night they camped out with their dad.

And while we were singing around the blazing fire, I could tell my little children felt stirred by the warmth. They kept hugging, holding, and kissing me. At one point I could tell my son Cal felt overwhelmed by the moment, and he said so sweetly, "You're the world's best dad."

Last night…the cold…the noise…the lack of sleep? It was wonderful. So it is in the dad-world.

My fellow parent, don't let your comfort get in the way of what matters.

Be real.

JULY 11

History Doesn't Have to be Boring

Hey Mom,

If you want to talk to someone who knows history, then Diana Waring is the person you need to see. She knows all kind of history…stuff. My kids love her audio history CDs and I think her History Music CDs are awesome. OK, enough of all this sentimental pleasantries, now on to the topic at hand.

Actually, I probably shouldn't even address the topic of making History exciting…because that what Diana does. I will say at the very least, don't ever make history boring. Don't settle for just a bunch of date memorization or boring 'fact learnin.'

I've learned that from dragging my kids all over the country to historical sites of all shapes and sizes. I've noticed how each family member is drawn to different aspects of history. Some like the battles, some the people or the relationships. Some of my kids like touching, others like seeing, and still others like hearing. And then there are some who don't like the history part at all, but they like the science parts of history, the getting dirty parts of history, the rocks and bugs part of history.

As parents we just need to know how our kids like their history and serve it up to order. AND don't be bothered that your children don't seem to appreciate the aspects that you or others enjoy.

Be real.

JULY 12

You Deserve a Break Today

Hey Mom,

Do you need to take a break from time to time? Who are we kidding? Moms don't need breaks...especially homeschool moms. They were created to live on a few hours of sleep a day, start early, and go late. They homeschool 365 days a year come rain, shine, or gloom of night. They are tireless...super moms!!!

Yeah, right. Of course you need a break sometimes, which brings me to my 'I hope you're planning on taking a summer vacation' message. You know why you need to take a summer break? BECAUSE MOMS NEED A BREAK SOMETIMES.

Actually, your books, tablets, curriculum, and school mind-set should have been packed away a month ago...and you should have let the homeschool monkeys out because they need a break, too.

~ A note to your husband: Dad, you need to make this happen. Truth is your wife does feel like she needs to be some kind of super, no-break-takin' kind of mom. You need to be her knight in shining armor and help her do what she needs to do. Try saying something along these lines. "Honey, you do an awesome job...but you deserve a break today...and I want you to take the summer off, because we all need it."

Enjoy your break!

Be real.

Ms. Frizzle Would Agree

Hey Mom,

If there isn't a wall plaque that says, "Life is a Field Trip," then there should be. In our school-tainted minds, field trip is synonymous with packing a sack lunch, boarding a big vehicle, and going to a predetermined location armed with a permission slip signed by a legal guardian.

We all went on field trips during our school days. I went to pumpkin patches, museums, and the Wonder Bread Factory around the second grade. I didn't learn a whole bunch...I mostly goofed off with my friends. I see field trip groups sometimes when we visit places as a family. Large groups of kids on yellow buses swarm the place. Luckily, we've figured out that they leave shortly after lunch and try to time our visits to coincide with their departure.

Summer is the perfect time for field trips because all the schools are on recess and don't clog things up. But here's the deal: field trips don't have to be learning-driven; they can be FAMILY-driven. So anywhere the family goes... is a field TRIP!!!

Need a few ideas?

-A state or city park
-A nature center
-The lake, ocean, or creek
-Your yard
-A nearby ministry where you can volunteer
-Grandparents house for some chores
-A friend's farm
-A local business/factory (call ahead)
-The local dump
-A car wash
-A big playground
-A local museum
-A big city you don't live in
-The library

Of course the list is endless, the process is not always fun, and it never goes according to plan...but it's still worth it.

Be real.

* *Ms. Frizzle is the star of the old animated series, "Magic School Bus."*

JULY 14

Games That Teach

Hey Mom,

Man, what great timing. Here we are on the eve of the great Summer Olympic Games*, and we're talking about using GAMES to teach. Some of my fondest childhood memories are of sitting around an old portable television with a fuzzy screen watching the summer Olympics with my family.

So here's what I would do: I'd plan to get the TV out and have two weeks of Olympic learning. Your kids are going to learn so much about other countries, the various events, and what matters and what doesn't (pay special attention to those athletes who have trained for years and then don't event place).

Now don't go and ruin the whole experience by trying to turn it into school but you might get out a big map to find places like Nairobi and Chechnya. Other important teaching tools would be loads of popcorn, ice cream and maybe even pizza for the opening or closing ceremonies. Feeling especially ambitious? Have your own summer games with events like watermelon seed spitting, running races, long jump, and heavy rock throwing.

Your kids will never forget these next two weeks.

Be real.

** There may not be any Olympics this year...but tuck this nugget away until they come around again.*

JULY 15

Grammar Woes

Hey Mom,

You might be one of the multitudes of homeschooling moms who worry about grammar. There seem to be a lot of you, who pass the time just before conking out for the night worrying about the lack of grammar your children know. Will they be able to write a sentence...get a job...survive in the real world!!!

First of all, don't worry about grammar (God said not to). Second of all, stop doing grammar if it's stressing you or your kids out. If you've been around long enough, you know what I'm going to say. I'm just about convinced that the only purpose of grammar is to give textbook printers another book to print and schools, another class to offer.

I make my living writing and speaking…yet I don't know diddly about grammar. I can't diagram sentences and don't know the difference between a direct object and an indirect object. Now if your child is planning on become an English teacher or an editor, it might come in handy, but to just trudge through the grammar treadmill because someone said, "Kids need to know grammar" is silly.

My opinion is if you know how to talk well…or…good (I'm never sure which word to use), you'll learn to write well. Hey, and if you need some help on grammar, there are plenty of helps.

The beauty of homeschooling is that if you think grammar is important, then you can teach it, and if you don't, then you don't have to. So if you think I'm all wet, then go ahead and teach your children about dangling parti-thingamajigs. But if you keep asking yourself, "Why do my kids need to know this stuff… it seems useless to me?" then allow me to swing wide the cell door and point the way out.

Be real.

JULY 16

Who Teaches Calculus?

Hey Mom,

Right now I'm chained to my computer with a look of defiance on my face. I will not back down…they can run over me with a tank if they want to… bamboo shoots under the fingernails…drip water on my head, but I refuse to let the engines of school push us into the school year. So I will NOT talk about calculus…whatever kind of animal that is.

It's only July 16th for goodness sake. When I was a kid that meant another month of summer vacation. Now, some poor wretched kids have already been in school a couple of days.

Oh, yes, school-balrog* - YOU SHALL NOT PASS!!

But I will say make these last days of summer special. Do that one thing you've been promising to do all summer, or spend the day at the lake, beach, or mountains. Do not give up the last days of summer without a fight. Your kids are counting on you to wring the last bit of fun from it before the tanks of school rumble down the street.

Enjoy today…I mean it!!!

Be real.

**The balrog is a fictitious creature mentioned in the Lord of the Rings. If you don't know what I'm talking about, ask your children or read the books.*

JULY 17

Help! High School Grammar

Hey Mom,

Now don't be afraid. Just because we're thinking about school and grammar doesn't mean we have to jump right into the icy waters; it's better to eeeeease into it.

Of course when the topic at hand is 'High School Grammar' is feels like jumping into a Minnesota frigid lake in the dead of winter. Again, all I know about high school grammar is from the accumulated experience at Danville Community High School. And what I remember about high school grammar is…nothing…nada…el zippo.

I'm sure we did some stirring exercises on sentence diagramming and parts of speech…but I'm drawing a blank on what those actually were. As you know from reading these posts, I'm not the brightest crayon in the box when it comes to grammar.

So my advice when it comes to high school grammar is…do whatever YOU think is best. If YOU love grammar and think it's important to master in order to live a productive life…then teach grammar. If on the other hand, you're like me and think it's all a bunch of hooey and don't want to teach high school grammar, then don't. God made you smart enough to know what's best for your children.

Eeeeeease into it.

Be real.

JULY 18

I Know…but Do They Know

Hey Mom,

I KNOW you love your kids, you KNOW you love your kids, but sometimes your kids don't KNOW you love them. You want to hear something really shocking? Sometimes your kids THINK you love school more than them.

Why? Because sometimes school becomes your priority.

"I know you don't feel good, but we have to get some school in today."

"No we don't have time to play a game (fill in your favorite); we have to get some school done."

"How could you have missed so many questions?"

"Why can't you get this…it isn't that hard!"

"What are you, dumb?"

You've forgotten that school is a tool not the end goal…not the main thing.

Here's how to show your kids that you love them: don't let school take their place.

If they're crying, stop and comfort the child. Purpose to see your child as someone to enjoy during the day, not someone who is bound and determined to make school hard for you. Stop worrying about how much you get done and be thankful you get to spend another day with you children. Quit thinking more of what others think about you and your kids, and start doing what you know to be right.

Make school a distant seventh in the race for your affection and your children WILL KNOW THAT YOU LOVE THEM more than anything.

Be real.

JULY 19

Homeschooling on a Budget

Hey Mom,

I probably should have had my wife talk about homeschooling on a budget. She's the number cruncher…the one who likes to account for every penny that we spend. I, on the other hand, am the type that would spend it 'til it's gone. But when it's gone…I stop spending.

My perspective is that sometimes homeschooling appeals to the dark side of the homeschool parent. Common sense says, "If I don't have enough money for 'it,' then I can't buy 'it.'" However, I've met too many homeschoolers who don't listen to common sense. They sometimes think, Yes, I know I'm out of money…but I really need this new curriculum or tool. That's when bad things start to happen; we teach our children some powerfully destructive lessons… AND husbands begin to resent the price of homeschooling.

So here's what my homeschooling on a budget entails: If you don't have the money (whether actual or budgeted), then don't buy it. Do without it for a little while. You'll probably find out that you didn't need it to begin with. Truth is, if you really need 'it', then God WILL provide 'it'.

But if you've got it…spend it!!! Dave Ramsey would die…and then roll over in his grave.

Be real.

JULY 20

I'm NOT Lovin' Math

Hey Mom,

I'm just coming off a long weekend and my brain may not be firing correctly, but let me give this "Middle School Math - Help Them to Love it!" topic a shot. I'd say not every middle-schooler is going to love math...you can't make every middle-schooler love math...and it may be YOUR middle-schooler that doesn't love math. In fact, they may grow up to be adults who don't like math. I'm one of those.

I was actually thinking about this very topic this very weekend as we relaxed at my in-laws' lake cottage. Mostly it rained, which kept everyone inside, so all 16 cousins and their moms and dads played games. To make a long story short, I don't like games. I never really have. It's kind of a family joke that Todd doesn't like to play games (like Herbie, the dentist elf).

This weekend I made an extra effort to play them...but for some reason my brain just doesn't work like some of theirs do. Their brains are fast and mine... is slow. They tried not to show it...but they snickered at my slowness and even rolled an eye or two because I didn't see the right move or use the right words.

Later, the reason I don't find enjoyment in some of their games dawned on me (I did enjoy Euchre). It's because my brain isn't wired like all of theirs. They like fast things...competition...and I don't. That's not an excuse to pull out of all the fun, just because 'it's not my thing', but it did kind of make me feel better for not liking certain things. Now don't read into it too much...maybe I would have liked it more had I grown up playing games.

But the truth is still the same...I think. Yes, your children of all ages need to know certain math, but they may never love it, and that's OK. Just plug away, and when they complain, don't get frustrated, say mean things, or give up. Just slow down a little and keep plugging. And by the way, you're a good mom.

Be real.

JULY 21

Your Kid is Not Going to be President

Hey Mom,

I don't mean to pop your bubble, but as smart and capable as your child is, he/she is NOT going to be the President of the United States. And the truth is: you're putting unbearable pressures upon your children by telling them those predictions.

I didn't realize just how much until last week.

We were at my in-law's lake cottage again surrounded by dozens of cousins of all shapes, sizes, and ages. One of my nephews was on summer break from a well known Christian college. In fact, just the week prior I had met a family in another state whose son had dropped out of that same college. The parents were heartbroken and had lamented to me that he had so much potential.

"They said they fully expected him to be the President or a congressman someday," I told my nephew, and I was blown away by his response.

"Every student here (at his college) has been told they'll be president or congressmen someday," he said almost disgustedly. "Then, they get here and realize they aren't the only one who is that smart and that capable, etc and they're blown away. That's why depression is such a huge problem there." Later in the conversation he went on to say, "It's only a matter of time before we have our first suicide."

BOOM!!!!!!!! Mind explosion.

He's right. I'd never realized the pressure parents have put on their children…that I HAD put on my children…because I've said similar things. We're setting our children up for failure!!! We should be telling our kids that they can do anything they set their mind to and that they can do great things through Christ, but every time we heap another unrealistic, future success prediction on our children, we pile up their future guilt of letting us (and God and everyone else) down when they don't achieve or desire our prediction.

The truth is most of our children are not going to become congressmen or future presidents. Most will become dads and moms living godly lives, and that is GREAT!!!

After listening to my nephew, I decided that I'm not going to predict future greatness for my children anymore. They may not do something great & impressive in the world's eyes, but they ARE already great NOW. And it's not dependent on what they do or don't do later.

So Mom and Dad, tell your children how special God made them, how much you love them, and how wonderful they are right now, but make sure it's not dependent on what they do in the future.

Be real.

JULY 22

The Home Maker

**Disclaimer – This article is from a male's viewpoint and any mean letters you might want to send me…don't.*

Hey Mom,

From the world's perspective, 'home' is a four-letter word, code for 'woman's prison'. In fact, I think the secular world would like to do away with the home and have children raised by institutions so that no one has to stay home—especially not women. Actually, I heard a radio program about "wife-less marriages," unions where the husband and wife equally share the responsibility for the home. Women need to be free…just the same as men. Oh, yes, the world hates the home.

Want to know something more sobering? I'm not sure the Christian world likes it much better. Even with homeschooling, sometimes it seems as if we do everything in our power to get OUT of the home. We stay busy running here and there and view home more like an Indy-500 pit stop, a place to get in and out of, not a haven to rest in, serve in, and enjoy.

Not all that long ago, the phrase "a woman's place is in the kitchen" was considered an honor. No more. Now it's demeaning…shackling…limiting… chauvinistic. Girls, whose only ambition is to be a mom and wife, are looked down upon…not only by the world but sadly by the CHURCH as well. Sometimes "we" even pressure girls to select a career so we aren't embarrassed by their lack of ambition.

Why is that? Because the church, like the world, elevates careers over homemaking.

So, is there hope for teaching daughters to love and keep their homes? Yep, but only by loving and keeping your home. It is the power of example.

Be real.

JULY 23

Home Ec Is for Boys Too…Right?

Hey Mom,

Before we discuss the topic of whether Home Ec is for boys, would someone explain to me what Home Ec is? Back in the day before a bunch of experts decided moms and dads weren't smart enough to teach their own children, there was no such thing as Home Ec…instead it was called HOME and it was the place children learned and the focus of their instruction.

Back then, kids were trained so that one day they could run homes of their own. And I guess even back then, boys, although not the primary home 'makers', needed to know how to take care of themselves and their families.

And so it continues. That's why my boys, as well as my girls, have one day a week for which they're responsible for all the family dishes (all day), have to vacuum and pick up, and do their own laundry. We don't call it Home Ec…we call it HOME.

Now I still believe that girls and boys are different. They have different gifts and different responsibilities. My boys are expected to do things their sisters don't have to do and my girls are responsible for things my boys aren't required to do…BUT everyone needs to know how to care for the needs of their home…including dads.

Be real.

JULY 24

Budgeting for School

Hey Mom,

Today's topic has two distinct audiences: moms and dads. Let me address the moms first. Okay ladies, history has taught us that occasionally you women folk buy curriculum like you buy shoes. The 'shoes' look good on others, are the latest fashion, and are only a little snug, so…you buy them. Who cares that you have a pile of other 'shoes' sitting in your closet that have barely been worn and look perfectly fine to the casual male observer?

You're ready to move on to new fashions, new ideas, new concepts...new shoes. Now, from a husband's point of view, that sometimes looks like a big waste of money. After all, you have plenty of 'shoes' that you had to have before. In fact, it can cause contention in a marriage and homeschool because husbands don't want to spend more money on something that's going to get a short workout and then sit in a closet or be sold on Ebay for a fraction of the purchase price.

So my advice to you, mom, is to make what you have work, buy only what you need, check out some of those overly expensive books from the library, ask and take your husband's advice, sell some of those barely used 'shoes' and use that money to buy new shoes. And all the while, view your shoes through your husband's eyes.

~ A note to your husband: Dad when you're spending money on school stuff, don't think

'shoes', think tools. Every man knows that the right tools make the job easy. The only drawback with good tools is that you pay for them. Now I'm cheap. I don't like spending money...even on tools. But here's the deal. When I use cheap tools, the job is a lot tougher.

Now transfer that to homeschooling. You, as the dad, need to make sure your wife has the tools she needs…tools that make her job easier and get good results. And suck it up, because it's going to cost…a bunch. So deal with it.

Be real.

JULY 25

Cutting the Clutter

Hey Mom,

Having me talk about decluttering a house is like having…my mom discuss the virtues of facial tattoos. It goes against my slob nature. But because I just hate leaving my space blank, here are a few tips I shared in the spring issue of The Old Schoolhouse Magazine.

The Familyman's Guide to Home Organization;

1. If you haven't worn it since high school, throw it out.

2. If an undergarment has more than 6 holes in it, throw it out…unless it's your husband's, which is good for up to 20 holes.

3. If you pick it up and don't know what it is, toss it.

4. Do not purchase or accept a game or craft with the word 'pieces' on it.

5. To help in the organization process, consider giving up your children for adoption.

6. Flypaper strategically hung around the house works like hangers for those hard-to-store items.

7. The space under the bed is meant to conceal things. In fact, if you place one concrete block under the foot of each leg on a king-sized bed it increases that space by 60 cubic feet, virtually eliminating all bedroom clutter.

8. By frosting the door of a shower stall, it can double as a food pantry.

9. Forget those 25 10-gallon plastic containers, which will end up empty in about six days anyway...instead get one big 250-gallon plastic container.

10. By placing TWO concrete blocks under the leg of each foot on a king-sized bed you can store most of the contents of your garage including a riding lawnmower and industrial strength snow blower.

Be real.

JULY 24

Homeschooling While Potty Training

Hey Mom,

Sometimes I wish I could just have my wife sit down with you and talk. She knows so much more about homeschooling and life than I do (I still know more about RVs!!!).

One of the things she often tells other homeschooling moms is not to look at homeschooling as something we ADD TO our lives but as just a natural PART OF our lives.

Is that not brilliant??!!!! She's right on the money. That makes the potty training dilemma…not so much of a dilemma. Instead of asking, "How can I homeschool my kids while potty training?" the statement becomes, "Homeschooling and potty training can go hand in hand because they're both just part of my life." It's not an interruption, but just part of school as much as it is a part of life.

Can you get as much school done when you're potty training? Maybe not… but that's OK. Maybe potty training is part of the lesson for awhile. Daughters watch and learn how to be a mom and siblings help a younger brother or sister learn a new skill and cheer them along the way. Those are valuable lessons.

That truth, by the way, applies to all those things we look at as 'interruptions'…sickness, character issues, house tasks, toddlers, elderly parents, teenagers…everything. It's all just part of life. And everyone knows that life is the best teacher and the best classroom to learn in.

Be real.

PS – I also know more about old TV trivia from the 60's and 70's than my wife.

JULY 27

My Child is Gifted…Now What?

Hey Mom,

Did you know that my children are gifted? Did you know that your children are gifted? THEY ARE ALLLLLL GIFTED!!!!! I don't just say that tritely; I believe that with all my heart, but sometimes I still forget it. And so do you.

We don't seem to forget the ones that are gifted in the way the world defines gifted. They're the ones that make us look really good in the world's eyes.

Sometimes we forget that the ones who the world would 'tag' as non-gifted are still GIFTED, created as masterpieces and given to us to nurture and enjoy.

This, my fellow parent, is my charge to you—now that you've realized you have gifted children…enjoy them. Let them learn at their pace, neither slowing them down or speeding them up.

What a gift to give your gifted child.

Be real.

JULY 28

Getting Ready for College

Hey Mom,

Greetings from vomit-central. I'm typing away on an iPad from my bedroom where my kids, Cal and Maggie, have been quarantined and are eating popsicles and watching videos. I'm on duty because my wife doesn't handle bodily fluids well...if she's forced to; she is prone to adding to them.

Up until last night, we have been stomach flu-free. All that changed so quickly, and now, here we are hoping we've stemmed the tide before we have an all out epidemic.

Regarding getting your kids ready for college, I think the first question to ask yourself is, "Does God want my child to go to college?" The answer might be different for different children. If you believe that is God's plan for your child, then go check out college prep expert Lee Binz. She'll be able to help you.

The really important thing isn't whether your child goes to college or not; the important thing is to enjoy your child and let him enjoy you and being home…for now.

Truth is college isn't that hard to get into. I even asked my college professor brother what his university would do with an adult who came to his school without a high school diploma and asked to go to his school. "If they really wanted to go to our college," he said, "we'd let him in."

There you have it. If they really want to go to college, they'll get in. So, relax.

Be real.

Never Give Up

Hey Mom,

It doesn't concern me that every homeschool mom on the planet wants to give up and toss in the towel from time to time (that's perfectly normal). What concerns me is that some WILL…or that YOU might.

Not long ago my sister (who homeschools) was talking to my wife about being discouraged in homeschooling and the fact that so many of her homeschooling friends have quit.

"Oh, I believe in it," she said. "I just don't think I can do it well enough."

It saddens me that my little sister feels that way…and that she's been fed a bunch of lies and that she believes them.

It saddens me too, that you might be thinking the same thing. I can't say anything that will take away the feeling that you want to give up…BUT I will say, "Don't act on that feeling, and DO what you believe is true…no matter what."

This is the truth:

Home is the best place for your children!

You are the best teacher for your children!

Your child is a masterpiece created by God just the way he/she is.

You can prepare them well enough for whatever their future holds!

Never give up!!!!!!

Be real.

Bugs, Bugs, Bugs!

Hey Mom,

Bugs…now that's something I can sink my teeth into…not literally, but topically. I mean, my boys have this thing for bugs. The bigger, stinkier, slimier…the better. Here in Indiana we've got our fair share of normal bugs, like walking sticks, praying mantis, daddy longlegs, and other insects that fly, wiggle, and crawl.

While we were in New Mexico we suffered a little bit of bug-envy and wanted so badly to see or catch a Vinegarroon or better yet, a Child of the Earth.

Now what kind of creepy bug must belong to a demonic name like Child of the Earth?!!

We never saw either…but there's always next time.

Here's the thing about homeschoolers though: sometimes we ruin natural learning in favor of the unnatural kind where little is learned. I'm a firm believer in that the best kind of learning (bugs especially) is the kind where parents stay out of it (unless asked by the child).

So, resist the urge to have your kids learn the body parts, write about them, or research anything (unless they want to). Just stand back and let them discover the world of slugs and bugs on their own. That kind of learning is unforgettable.

Be real…and be on the lookout for a Child of the Earth.

JULY 31

Outgrown Trike

Hey Mom,

It was a beautiful day today, but it feels like summer is beginning to wind down. It's amazing how quickly a summer passes…a year passes…a lifetime passes. As I was cleaning up all the yard trash (roller blades, bikes, toys, and my tools) this evening, I was struck by the thought that this might be the last year we use the blue bike trailer.

We bought it years ago when one of our oldest kids was just a toddler. Then I thought about all the life jackets that we've almost outgrown, the power wheel that sits unused and broken, and the red little tricycle that has seen its last rider.

Life passes whether you're having fun or not. Read this letter I got from a dad who knows that truth firsthand:

Hey Todd,

I shared your thoughts with a friend and had to forward you what he wrote back.

"If this Dad (talking about me) had to go through a divorce and suddenly not be able to see his kids much......he would enjoy every minute of anything they wanted to do."

I guess that's what I want to do…enjoy every minute of anything they want to do…with me. I know it's not possible to enjoy every minute…but I'd like to enjoy MOST of them because they're going by fast.

So, Mom, go and enjoy some of those minutes today and this weekend… you're running out of them.

Be real.

AUGUST 1

Lesson Planning and the Will of Todd

Hey Mom,

You want me to give advice on lesson planning? You might as well ask me to share my favorite recipes or all my advice on manicures. I just don't do lesson plans. If I prepared a lesson plan, it would include subjects like:

-Power Napping

-Spitting for Distance

-An Introduction to Body Noises

You know; all the important stuff. Thankfully, my wife does the lesson planning at our house.

However, with all teasing aside, I actually do have some advice when you're planning for the upcoming year.

First of all, make time for the most important stuff like baking cookies, reading aloud good books on the couch with the kids, playing board games, taking a nap, and hiding love notes in your husband's underwear drawer.

Second of all, refuse to let the "not-as-important stuff" keep you from doing the most important stuff. Sometimes lesson plans do that. Often, the lesson plan becomes everything. You write it out, get frustrated when you get off-track, make everyone miserable trying to finish it, and eventually feel defeated by failing to complete it.

So plan time for the important stuff, don't sweat the other stuff, and make your lesson plan a flexible guide, not a god.

Be real.

PS – If you need some other guidance on power napping or spitting, let me know.

AUGUST 2

A Penny Saved Makes for a Happy Husband

Hey Mom,

To preface what I'm about to say, let me state right up front that if I were talking to your husband, I'd tell him to spend the necessary money to get you the best homeschooling tools available. All men know that good tools make a job easier and that shoddy tools make a job harder.

But I'm talking to you and not your husband, and wives tend to be the spending side of their homeschool. My advice is not really a budgeting method as much as an overall philosophy-ish thing. From a husband's vantage point, homeschooling equals a money-sucking black hole leading to poverty and despair. Okay, so maybe that's a little over-dramatic, but I often hear moms say, "Oh, I shouldn't spend this much", or "My husband will kill me for buying this, but oh well, I'm going to buy it anyway."

I'm telling you, Mom, that's a good way to place your husband on the defensive or even antagonistic toward homeschooling.

So if you want Papa to be happy, talk about what you'd like to purchase with him…and then spend a little less. Your man will think you're awesome and more than likely, he'll even suggest you spend a little more.

That's all the financial advice that this financially-challenged man has to offer.

Be real.

AUGUST 3

Get Organized

Hey Mom,

I could probably get some kind of government money for being organizationally challenged. However, I did clean my office and desk off about two weeks ago…and it wasn't that bad. Actually, I feel a little better just by working in a clean environment.

Maybe you would feel better about school too by working in a clean environment. Instead of school today, you should spend a little while getting organized. I said instead of school because I think organizing, tagged onto doing school or regular stuff, can seem overwhelming. After all, who has time to get organized?

BUT if you could forgo school in order to organize, now that sounds do-able. I wouldn't tackle your whole life of clutter and disorganization…just take a whack at that one area that's been especially bugging you. It might be the school room, your book shelves, your bedroom closet, or the kids' dressers.

Pick one and cross it off the list. Make sure you involve the kids as well… because that's an important lesson, as important as regular 'school'.

I'm not sure, but I think you're going to feel better. Will it stay organized from that point on? Dream ON!! But it will be nicer for awhile.

Be real.

AUGUST 4

Your Struggling Reader

Hey Mom,

I think the whole idea of the 'struggling reader' is a bad concept and worded inappropriately. The phrase conjures up thoughts of a reading race with 'successful' readers crossing the finish line with smiles and exuberance and then one, lone, reading racer stumbling and gasping for breath half a lap behind.

Of course the bleachers erupt with applause for the 'finish line crossers.' The sole exception is the mother of the 'struggler.' She hides her head in shame, urging, coaching, threatening, and blaming herself for his lack of 'progress.'

That is a wrong picture and one that needs to change before we do any more damage to our children. The truth is: that kind of reading standard is not an accurate standard and sets some children up for failure and hardship.

The truth is: your 'struggling' reader is not struggling at all. He or she is just learning it or not learning it at the pace God designed him to learn it. Instead of pushing and threatening him, try plugging away and smiling with him. Just keep working at it each day a little at a time. Set aside your standards and SMILE as he butchers the simple (as in simple to you) words.

That said; I have to go work with that same reader today. I know your frustration…and it's all based on a LIE. Don't believe it. Your reader is doing just fine and will get it when he's supposed to get it.

Have a great day homeschooling your children.

Be real.

AUGUST 5

Define Literature

Hey Mom,

I just looked up the word 'literature', and did you know the word 'literally' means "things made from letters"? That's pretty broad and could include anything…made with letters. (Duh)

Here's the deal with me and literature: It just seems like a dumb thing to teach when a better way is to just read it. I know certain, brainiac people care about the meter, protagonist, and antagonist…but I don't. It seems to me like it's just a bunch of whooie for those who have nothing better to do.

I just want my kids to read. Some of my kids like to read classics, others like history, and one likes bugs and science. I don't care if they can attach labels to their sentence parts…in fact, sometimes all those labels can ruin the story, along with the love of reading. Plus…who CARES?!?!

So, my very simple thoughts on this over-complicated subject are: find the books your children enjoy reading and then…just let them read!

*Note – We also have a few children who don't find enjoyment in reading, and that's okay too. We still make them read (or read out loud to them) but are not distraught if they don't 'love' doing so.

Be real.

AUGUST 6

Listen to HIM

Hey Mom,

What is the DEAL??!!! Normally, I'd be enjoying summer right now, without a homeschool care in the world, but Wal-mart has already begun its school supply push…and we're even way beyond that now. Most of the public schools around us have already started (one started in July). That's sad to me, but sadder still, is that many homeschoolers have followed their lead and have also started.

I'm pretty sure that most homeschoolers didn't pray and think it through; they just felt the pressure, THE LIE, and caved in. That's the way it is with much of what we teach our children. The experts say we have to do sentence diagramming…so we do sentence diagramming, even though we think it might be a waste of time.

But that's the tip of the lie-perpetuating iceberg. We read that every child needs advanced algebra and geometry and then push our non-math children through it wondering what value it has for a non-math person. Authors say that every child needs to know Latin roots to succeed, play a stringed instrument, write novels, love history, read for hours, or be a scholarly theologian. But, is that really the truth?

Here's the nugget for the day: God made you smart enough to know what's best for YOU and your children. If you think something is a waste of time, then don't do it!! If you don't want to diagram sentences, do unit studies, study music, or start school in August…THEN DON'T!!!!!

God made you smart enough to figure out what's best for your family. Listen to HIM not THEM, and stop feeling guilty about it.

Be real.

AUGUST 7

Geography on the Go!

Hey Mom,

This is a topic I can sink my teeth into. In fact, we're getting ready for some On-the-Road-Again-Geography (Think Willie Nelson). In just a couple of weeks, I'll fire up the Familyman Mobile and we'll hit the open road to experience the best this country has to offer.

The great thing about this 'geography course' is that it is open to anyone. All you have to do is load up the car and head out. Why, in just a few hours of travel, you see changes in the climate, terrain, and plant life. I love it!!! I love going north, south, east and west (but especially south).

It's just amazing how different one country can be, and the wonderful thing about this geography lesson is that you don't have to grade it or even teach it… you get to experience it.

But that's the rub as I see it. Homeschoolers tend to ruin that kind of experiential learning by having the kids write a report about it or answer questions about it. Not us; we just want our kids to experience it without having to label it as official school.

Now, I know you might be reading this and thinking to yourself, but we don't have the money to take a long road trip. That may be true for a long road trip, but it's amazing to me how much you can see in just a few hours from home. It costs a little, but it's worth every nickel spent.

OK, sing with me…"On the road again, I can't wait to get on the road again…"

Be real.

AUGUST 8

Thinking Ahead

Hey Mom,

I know it's a little early to be thinking about homeschool conventions, but I want to put it into your hopper for next spring. There's just something encouraging about gathering with a boatload of homeschoolers that feels...good.

The great thing about homeschool conventions is that there are homeschool products to look over, speakers to hear, and other moms and dads to meet. Plus if you plan it right, you might even get a night or two in a hotel...WITHOUT YOUR KIDS.

I've spoken at homeschool conventions in just about every state and province. I've talked with homeschooling moms from Florida to Maine, from Nova Scotia to Hawaii. It doesn't matter where you homeschool; we're all in the same boat and face the same struggles and concerns. That's why conventions are so encouraging.

So let me urge you to take advantage of your nearest homeschool convention. You need it. Even if you think you don't...you do. Even if you've been homeschooling for decades and think you've got it all under control...you NEED IT!

I talked to a mom this weekend that hadn't been to one in years. Through her tears of happiness, she thanked me for what I shared and then said how grateful she was that she had chosen to come because she needed it...and so do you.

In fact, if you end up in a convention where I'll be...stop by and say hey.

Be real.

AUGUST 9

Make Your Kitchen a Science Lab

Hey Mom,

When I saw the topic at hand, "Make Your Kitchen a Science Lab," I thought cynically, why do I have to make my kitchen a science lab anyway? But after I thought about it, I realized that it's not so much about making it a science lab as it is about taking the time to let my kids explore in the kitchen. It's about my wife allowing my kids to help with what she's making and including them in everyday life that takes place in the kitchen. Yes, things will take longer, but real learning takes place in a natural, everyday type of way. So, yeah, I guess the kitchen does become a science lab naturally when you let your kids add the food coloring or the baking soda, or when they get to melt the butter or make the cookies.

The key isn't to turn your kitchen into a science lab; it's to enjoy your children while you're working in it. Don't shoo them out of your way. Let them be involved. That's the best kind of learning, when it's right alongside of us. They want to help; let them. So, use today to bake some warm cookies with your kids…and without even realizing it, your kitchen will have become a science lab.

Be real.

AUGUST 10

Bigger Than School

Hey Mom,

It's amazing how quickly things change. Just yesterday, I was thinking about today's topic, and I was going to encourage you to let your kids have a non-parent controlled lemonade stand. Then, I got a phone call.

I was just about to board a bus at the Chicago Midway Airport that would take me to the red lot to get my car when my wife called to tell me that a friend died suddenly.

"Oh, man," was all I could get out. I felt like a frying pan hit me in the face. I had just talked to our friend a couple of weeks ago in Florida. As always, she was so alive and vibrant. In fact, she makes me feel tired just listening to her. And now she's…gone.

Some friends of ours texted my wife and said they had spent the weekend with her, talking about her future plans with her recently retired husband. Future plans…if only she had known. But nobody ever really knows.

It's sobering but not because I feel sorry for her. She is experiencing everything that she, and we, have hoped for since placing our trust in the ONE who conquered death…but I still feel sober. I guess it's just another painful reminder that you never know. You never know when you say to your children, "Not today; maybe tomorrow..." that you might not get a tomorrow.

I leave you with that truth. If you're planning to do something with your family…then do it today, because you (or they) may be in heaven tomorrow.

Be real and go love your children and spouse.

Ministry Opportunities

Hey Mom,

Interestingly enough, a few weeks back I had a conversation with a home-schooling couple who seemed troubled by the isolation that some homeschool families have chosen.

"They seem to care little about the rest of the body of Christ…or even the lost around them," the husband said. "It just seems there is so much ministry to do as a family," his wife added.

Guilty…and she's right. In fact, my family can become kind of isolated, not because we try to…it just seems like we don't have a lot of extra time outside our own ministry, eight children and immediate family.

I could feel guilty about it (and maybe I should a little), but I know the truth is that I have a lot of ministry to do within my family. The Bible even teaches that one of the qualifications of my future ministry is how I do in my present family ministry.

That said; I still need to be looking for opportunities to minister to others WITH my family. And as you know, there are plenty of opportunities from the older couple that lives nearby, the single mom at church who could use a little help, to the family that needs an example and some friendship.

Back to the guilt-free part – if you feel like you're up to your eyeballs in little kids and family, rest easy…you ARE doing ministry and there are plenty of opportunities within your own home's walls. No guilt!!!!

Be real.

AUGUST 12

Hands-On Learning and Field Trips

Hey Mom,

I don't mean to alarm you, but you're running out of summer. This weekend all across America families are grilling hamburgers and having picnics as they try to squeeze the last drops out of summer.

This would be a great weekend to tackle a long put-off field trip to that nearby lighthouse, petting zoo, national park, lake, or animated movie that you have been thinking about taking in. Tell your husband that you'd really like to __________ this weekend…and that it will be a lot of fun.

The important thing is to get the kids there and then let them run around and do and learn the things that interest them. I know my kids get different things from the exact same fieldtrip destination. We went to George Washington Carver's birthplace and some of my kids enjoyed the historical significance, others liked the snake and turtle we saw along the walking path, and still others loved running and being outside.

Had I insisted that they do what I wanted them to do and learn, I would have frustrated some of them (if not all of them) and the 'learning factor' would have been lower. The beauty of fieldtrip learning though, is that learning takes place on individual levels…and it's FUN!!!! That is the best kind of learning.

So soak up the last of the summer sun, eat some corn on the cob, and go on a family field trip!

Be real.

AUGUST 13

The Curse of the Tire Swing

Hey Mom,

This year has been a weird travel season for us. We seem to pass by our home each week. So we travel out…stop at home and then travel back out. Actually, it's a bunch tougher on all of us and is much easier to stay out once we hit the road.

But I will say one thing; our yard looks a lot better since we're home to cut it each week. In the past it had that 'abandoned, haunted house look.' Just yesterday as I was cutting grass, spraying weeds, and picking up, I was stopped dead in my tracks by a haunting specter…the tire swing.

That steel-belted radial with white walls hanging by a rope, like a corpse dangling from a rope, stared at me unblinkingly. Sixteen years ago I got it from a local garage, cleaned it up, and hung it from a 200-year-old oak tree next to our house.

My oldest children have memories of being pushed as high as I could push and experienced firsthand my death defying 'scrambler.' But as we added more children, I found I spent less time out at the tire swing and answered the call "Push me, Daddy" with, "Have one of your brothers do it."

Then there was yesterday. The swing looked at me and in an evil voice whispered, "In a few years they'll all be grown and won't ask you to push them anymore…and then I'll hang here year after year through snow, rain, and sunshine reminding you that you were too busy to make time for themmmm…" The voice trailed off but I knew it would speak again.

So, I now proclaim to all who hear my voice that whenever my children ask to be pushed on the tire swing…I WILL PUSH. Hold me to it.

Mom, you may not have an evil tire swing hanging outside your house, but I would just about guess you have a tea set, a basketball hoop, a swimming pool, a swing set, or a trampoline that will sit outside or on shelves through the decades of decay reminding you that you should have spent more time paying attention to what matters.

Be real.

AUGUST 14

Nature Journaling and Geocaching

Hey Mom,

To tell the truth, I'm not much of a nature journalist. Back in the day, I had my kids journal about nature, thinking it would cement the things I taught them into their little noggins. I didn't feel like it really helped them learn anything more than just being out in nature did, so I'm not a huge fan of nature journaling. I'm not against it necessarily, and if you're someone who really likes it, then I say, "More power to you."

But if you dread the thought of journaling and it feels like another guilt-inducing device to you then I say, "Drop it like an old stinky sock and never think twice about it."

Now, I don't know much about geocaching…in fact, I've never even caught a geo, but I like the idea of it. I've talked to several parents who love it and describe the thrill of the hunt as they and their children go up and down roads looking for some hidden treasure guided only by their GPS device.

The thing I like about it is not that it teaches kids about navigation or how to use maps, but that it is a fun thing to do as a family. I'm all about activities that bring families together. Actually, you could add to the list of geocaching. You could go to the beach together, bike together, picnic together, eat pizza together, and anything else you can think of doing…together.

That's what summer is all about, Charlie Brown.

Be real.

AUGUST 15

I'm Bored

Hey Mom,

It's hot and sunny here in Northern Indiana...praise the Lord for air-conditioning.

Actually, I was talking today with my wife at lunch when she said to me, "I don't know what to do with the kids; they seem bored out of their skulls."

I was almost ready for the comment, because I was thinking the same thing as I saw them roam around the house. I know I should have said something understanding like, "You're right; maybe we can brainstorm about things they could do..." but I didn't. Instead, I jumped right up on the table and said, "That's okay; just let them figure it out."

I've thought about this quite a bit and stand amazed at the idea that moms feel they should provide constructive things for their kids to do so they won't be bored. I'm telling you mom, that's a losing battle and one that never ends.

"Thanks, Mom for the great idea about the Play-doh, but now I'm done... and I'm bored."

My theory is that you let your kids get so bored that they finally do something until they're not bored. I know I did as a kid. I slinked around the house until I decided I needed to build a tree house, play with GI Joes, or was assigned a chore from my dad (never underestimate the power of summer chores).

My advice on the boredom dilemma is to let your children be bored and figure it out for themselves...or give them chores. Now go and enjoy doing whatever it is you enjoy doing.

Be real.

AUGUST 16

"Let's Play a Game!"

Hey Mom,

Let's play a game?! Are you kidding me? Don't my kids know how busy I am? We just pulled into the driveway after being gone ALLLL weekend at a family camp in hilly PA.

I have tons to do, including writing this brilliant, little article that will minister to untold...dozens. I have emails to write, speaking arrangements to work on, products to produce, and gobs of other IMPORTANT stuff to do!!

Games take time…my time. Playing a game means stopping what I'm doing, setting it up, listening to my kids' incessant giggling as they make up their own rules, refereeing their bickering, and dealing with the nagging feeling that I should be getting something done instead.

It doesn't help when I see my wife, who is way better than I am, sitting on the floor in the midst of her busy day playing a game with our youngest. I just can feel the guilt being heaped on my busy head.

I've got to get this all done or nobody will!!!

Can I hear an AMEN?! You're busy too, right? Don't have time for games either, right?? After all, if we stopped in the middle of our busy day to play a game with our children nothing would get done………..except what really matters, right? Sigh.

I hate it when I'm right.

I'll make a deal with you. As soon as you finish reading this sentence let's both stop doing all the 'important' stuff we're doing and play a game with all the really IMPORTANT people in our house who would love a little mom and dad time. Deal?

Be real.

AUGUST 17

Life's Better at the Beach

Hey Mom,

I love the beach. I love the sand, the smell, the vastness, and all that you find on the beach. Some of my best memories are walking up and down a long stretch of beach looking for shells, treasures, and sea life. I love watching my kids battle the surf, dig in the sand, and giggle with delight as they race around in circles, overwhelmed by the size and openness. There's just so much to learn and experience at the beach. It's like a schoolroom in itself.

The only problem is that I live in Indiana…and that's about as far from the ocean as you can get. Oh, there are some big lakes around us (even one Great lake), but it just doesn't feel the same as the ocean.

So here is my thought about learning about sea creatures: go to the beach. You might live real close but it's been a while since you've let your kids explore…so go to the beach. Maybe you live in a place like land-locked Indiana. My advice? Go to the beach anyway. Get a map out and see how close you are to the ocean.

I'm just a short day's (12 hours) drive to a big chunk of the East Coast. I bet you can reach some salt water in about the same amount of time. That's not too bad…not for one of the greatest learning experiences God has to offer. Do a little Map Questing, a little planning, and do it.

Which brings me to a sore point…what is the deal with schools starting back up at the beginning or middle of August? Don't get sucked into that EVIL line of thinking. Stick to your summer guns and enjoy summer. You homeschool so you decide what you want to do. Do not let some academic, summer-hating, goofball trick you into giving up your summer!!! Go to the beach.

Be real.

PS - In Michigan, the public schools don't start until after Labor Day. Michigan, I salute you!!

AUGUST 18

The Perfect Curriculum

Hey Mom,

Here's the Familyman's Guide to Picking the Perfect Curriculum for Your Homeschool (drum roll, please): pick what you like and what works for your family.

If your kids like unit studies, but you don't…then don't use unit studies. If your kids like to read living books, and you do too…read living books. If you hate the math program you picked, then pick something else. If your best friend says, "You've got to use THIS curriculum because it is so wonderful and life changing," but it makes you tired just reading through the teacher's manual…then don't use it.

You know you and you're family better than any pencil-pushing-curriculum-expert or anyone else for that matter. So do what YOU like and what works for YOUR family.

One last thing: homeschooling is a process. We all started out using one thing and then changed as life changed. My wife loved one program with our older children, but got tired of it by the time she got to the younger children, so she changed. That's normal and okay.

Oh, one more last thing: each child is different. You already knew that, but sometimes you need someone like me to remind you. The curriculum that worked so well with three of your children just may not work with your fourth child…so don't use it with him.

So ask God for wisdom, use your noodle, and pick what makes everyone happy (or almost everyone).

Be real.

AUGUST 19

Go for Guidelines

Hey Mom,

This should be short…since my idea of a schedule is to bookend the day with waking up and going to bed. But my wife has different plans, and she loves to go into the new school year with a finely detailed schedule, breaking her school day into small, bite-size, time chunks.

Here's the deal: I know that by lunch time on the first day, I will find my wife sitting on our green chair staring off into the distance. I'll ask, "How was the first day of school?" but I know what she'll say before she answers.

"I can't do it…my schedule doesn't work."

That's how schedules work. You write one out, throw it out, write another… tweak and tweak until you finally get a good one. One that works….of course the school year will almost be over by the time you get to that point.

But that's the way real life works, and that's okay.

So don't be surprised and threaten to give up just because your first schedule doesn't work. Get back in there, figure out another schedule…and then tweak, tweak, tweak!!! Take comfort that you're not alone.

Be real.

AUGUST 20

Ready, Set, Go!

Hey Mom,

Here are my back-to-school thoughts for The New School Year Kickoff:

1. Remember what matters – Relationships always comes first. If you're kids are crying…take it as a sign from God that the relationship is out of whack. If you have to get less 'school' done in order to keep the relationship 'good'…do so.

2. Do what you believe – If you don't believe it's important to teach your children sentence diagramming, political science, or critical-whatever stuff, then don't do it. If you think it's important to teach your children how to balance a checkbook, walk with God, or blow bubbles in their pudding, then teach them those things. Do what you believe no matter what you might 'FEEL' from outside sources.

3. Find a friend who homeschools for the same reasons you do and stick to them like glue.

4. Be real – with that friend you found; be real…honest, transparent AND allow them to do so with you without judgment.

5. Get your husband involved. How? Whenever he involves himself in any way, LET HIM. Don't correct, criticize, or ask for more. Just let him do it the way he wants and then thank him.

6. Get my books, Lies Homeschooling Moms Believe and How to be a Great Wife Even though You Homeschool. They were written to be used individually AND with a GROUP (discussion questions). We sell them dirt cheap for group orders. Get your homeschool group to do it soon.

Be real…I already said that.

AUGUST 21

Abacus Abe

Hey Mom,

Once upon a time, I was at a homeschool convention and walking the aisles just to stretch my legs. Since I go to at least a dozen conventions per year, I try to be polite and smile at the vendors since I've seen and done it all. Well, on this particular day, I eyed some free candy and was about to swoop in when I was accosted by the lady in charge.

"I saw your candy," I quickly said. "Would it be alright if I had a piece?"

She wasn't about to miss an opportunity to sell her product…a math product. "Sure you can, but you have to let me demonstrate a simple concept."

I wasn't about to say, "No thanks," so I said, "Sure," instead.

She shared her simple math concept and proceeded to make me feel like the math-moron that I am. I couldn't learn her simple process…but I got my candy.

That's the thing with math; we each learn it differently. Some can memorize formulas, others understand the concepts, some thrive in the abstract, and some, like my son, Abe, learned with an abacus.

Yeah, you heard me right. My son who is a very concrete, sequential kind of learner was struggling with math on paper when my brilliant wife had the idea to try the old, dusty abacus. She spent a few minutes reading how to use it and WOW…it all clicked for him. He could answer any quadruple digit math problem with borrowing or carrying almost instantly with the abacus.

My mom-friend, that's the beauty of homeschooling. It's not a one size-fits-all program. Find what works for your child and go with it. AND if you have a math-moron kid, like me…don't be too hard on him.

Be real.

PS – My math-loving wife wanted me to plug the Teaching Textbook math curriculum as well. With many kids to teach and after trying almost every program on the market during our last 14 years of homeschooling, she has landed on TT. It's a great program, all of our kids have liked it, it frees up mom, & the people behind it are wonderful!

AUGUST 22

What About Socialization?

Hey Mom,

After almost a month of traveling, speaking, and enjoying some sun and warmth, we pulled into northern, Indiana yesterday afternoon. It got a little nerve-wracking on the way home with a 5-hour break-down delay…but God was gracious, and we got'er fixed and arrived home safe and grateful.

While on the road, we met so many homeschooling parents…who feel just like you do. They want to raise children who love God and are prepared for the future. They feel worried, unsure, and wonder if they're ruining them instead.

Would you listen to me and relax? I've seen their kids, which are like yours, and you're all doing a great job.

And as far as socialization…let's put that little question to bed…forever!!! It just doesn't hold water anymore. We've been homeschooling for decades, and the truth is homeschool kids are 'plenty socialized.' I speak to homeschool families as well as non-homeschooled families all over the country, and the homeschool kids are 'WAY' better at engaging and 'socializing' (in a healthy way) than their counterparts. Your in-laws, neighbors, and friends think the same (although they may not say it). Even an honest school teacher will agree. Home is the best place for kids, and it's the perfect place to learn (and practice) social skills.

Have a great week enjoying your children…and be real.

AUGUST 23

Balancing Character and Academics

Hey Mom,

We're in the midst of the big dig-out here in northern Indiana (No, we don't have snow in August…I wrote this in the winter time). To my children's delight we finally got some BIG snow. We played out in it yesterday, but today the temperatures have plummeted and it's bitterly cold. Too cold for playing out although we did spend some time trying to get our big van out of the driveway. It may be a while before we can use the other vehicles.

Of course I declared today a snow-day as did all the schools in the state... allowing us to put off the real world for at least another day.

It's sad to me how ingrained 'the lies' have been ingrained into our thinking that we actually, think that 'school days' only occur when 'school' is in session. How stupid is that? The truth is school really does happen 365 days a year. That's not just something I say to be "quaint."

It's also been beaten into our heads to the point that we have trouble believing otherwise that academics are every bit as important as character and godly living. It's just not true. We try really hard to balance the two areas... but almost always lean toward the academic side.

We would never say that but here's how it happens: School needs to get done...you feel behind...you're kids seem dumb...so you push, get frustrated, yell, threaten...all for the sake of 'learning.' You thought you were just doing academics, but the truth is, you are always teaching character...and here's what you taught them:

School is more important than everything.

Kids are a pain to have and make everything hard.

I (the mom) can't smile unless you please me by being smart...and you're not smart, that's why we have to work so hard on this.

Forget about all that stuff I read out of the Bible about loving and being kind to one another...just learn, learn, learn!!!!

Guess what they learn about character when you play in the snow with your children? You tell me, which one matters?

It's time for a snow day...even if it's still summer! □

Be real.

AUGUST 24

Go Ahead and QUIT!!!

Hey Mom,

Before you sell the books on eBay and stick your kids out at the bus stop, let me tell you a story. Actually, it's not one story but several stories combined that I've heard from lots of parents. It goes something like this:

"I homeschooled our kids for several years, but it was so hard. The kids seemed like they weren't getting it, and I didn't enjoy homeschooling anymore. I looked around at everyone else's children who were in school and they looked like they were learning so much and having the time of their lives. So...I put them in school." Then they pause and purse their lips together and add, "I thought we had problems before, but they were nothing compared to the issues we're facing now….it was like throwing gas on a fire."

So, go ahead and quit…but before you do, you might re-read the above paragraph. Those aren't my words. They are the words of moms and dads who did quit, who gave up because it was so hard.

"Let us not lose heart in doing good, for in due time WE WILL reap if we do not grow weary…(and stop). Galatians 6:9

Be real.

AUGUST 25

I Speak for the Kids

Hey Mom,

I don't know what your personal conviction regarding Dr. Seuss's The Lorax is, but I like the little guy. Yes, it may be an environmental propaganda story, but you gotta like a guy who can pick himself up by the seat of his pants. Of course, his famous line and mantra is, "I speak for the trees."

Well, today I'm feeling a little Loraxish. Not that I have anything to say on behalf of trees, but I feel like I need to speak for 'the kids' because of my trip last weekend.

I was speaking at a homeschool conference in Escondido, CA. It was a great time, and I met lots of folks, including more than a couple of mothers who were real close to tossing in the towel.

Mom after mom looked at me with tears and told me how hard homeschooling is and how they doubt their efforts. I of course told them that they can do it and sent them on their way a little more encouraged.

On the last day of the event I was at my booth surrounded by a small sea of people looking and buying books when a 10-year-old boy (whom I recognized from earlier in the day) came behind my table and walked up to me like he wanted to tell me a secret.

He brushed up against me, faced away from the crowd, and said with whispered emotion, "Please tell my mom to keep homeschooling me," and then he walked away.

I never saw him or his mother again, but let me tell you, "I'm the Dadax and I speak for the KIDS."

Mom, you may feel like tossing in the towel and selling your curriculum along with your children, but don't stop homeschooling. Your children may not say it, but they want you to keep trying. They want to be safe at home. They may even say, "I don't want to be homeschooled anymore," but what they are really saying is, "Keep homeschooling me (only do it differently than you do now)."

If you have to take a little break today to get perspective, do it. Just don't stop homeschooling.

I speak for YOUR kids!

Be real.

AUGUST 26

Stretch Your Homeschool Dollar

Hey Mom,

I definitely should have my wife write on this topic. I'm not a money/budgeting kind of guy. My wife, on the other hand, loves number crunching and budgeting, and if she was a squirrel, she could gather a hoard of nuts from the Sahara Desert (in other words she knows how to make a dollar stretch).

She's really busy right now, so let me just imagine the kind of advice she would give:

1. Make eBay your best friend. Most likely, you'll pay a fraction of the retail cost by looking for used curriculum and supplies instead of new. Used curriculum sales are a good option too. Give yourself some extra school money by selling the unused curriculum that has been cluttering your shelves. My wife is working through a small stack of books that she's selling on eBay right now.

2. Be content and use what you have. There are indeed times to change curriculum, but most of us hop from curriculum to curriculum in hopes of finding the 'silver bullet.' Chances are the curriculum you want won't be any better than what you have, so stick with what you presently use or see if you can borrow what you need from a friend.

3. Work with your husband. If your husband thinks you're breaking the bank to homeschool, he may not be real excited about doing it. In fact, he may want you to quit because of it. So talk with him. Decide together what you should spend and then don't go over it. We've seen so many homeschooling moms stand at our convention booth and say, "I've already spent all that I was supposed to…but I really want these books." I'm telling you Mom, that's a good way to put a burr in your husband's homeschool saddle. So once you've spent your budgeted homeschool money…don't spend any more. Need more money? See advice #1.

I think that's all she'd say.

The only thing I would add is…

Be real.

Cursive Shmursive

Hey Mom,

Just got back from a homeschool convention in South Carolina and on the way home, we stopped for dinner at Culver's for their incredible butter burgers and frozen custard. As we sat around the table, I mentioned the topic of Cursive Writing and ignited a small firestorm of discussion.

One of my teens was 'for' teaching cursive writing because..."It's just good to be able to do", and one was against it because..."No one uses cursive anymore except to sign their name." I have to admit that I think it's a waste of precious time, because a homeschooler's time is precious...and I NEVER write in cursive.

Today, people type on computers or print to fill out the Publisher's Clearing House giveaway. The thing is...cursive isn't required and is hardly used.

But out of that passionate conversation, ONE voice spoke truth (and it wasn't mine). My wife wisely said, "I'd say, if you have a child who wants to learn to write in cursive, teach him/her. Otherwise, it's not that big of a deal."

Wow, I've got a smart wife. She's right, you know? In this case, it really is about the child and not about the skill. The fact is you have a limited time of teaching. You can't teach everything. Cursive is a fading and non-essential skill. BUT if you have a child who wants to learn it (we've had a few)...you should teach him how to. If he's sloppy at it and can't seem to get it...let it go.

That's from my smart wife!!!!

Be real.

A Bunch of Kids

Hey Mom,

Sniff, sniff...smell that? It's the smell of autumn!! The nights are cooler, the flowers have faded, and things just feel more snuggly.

Your assignment? Enjoy autumn with your children and call it homeschooling. We've forgotten some of the joys of homeschooling, such as the fun of spending a nice day outside together...looking, sniffing, and feeling one of the most wonderful times of the year.

It amazes me how complicated we've made homeschooling. The topic at hand about homeschooling different aged children at the same time hints at that. It's almost like we're discussing how to breathe or use a spoon. These things come naturally because they're part of God's design.

I believe God's design for training our children was altered a long time ago when some group of unemployed, smart people (who needed jobs) convinced parents that they were more capable of teaching their children than they were. After time the 'experts' weren't satisfied with one-room school houses because more people needed jobs so they broke the children up into various age groups and classes. So that's been the standard ever since, BUT that's not the best way to learn.

Family is the best way and place to learn, no matter how many ages are learning at once. In homes, there are interruptions, urgent demands, and constant distractions like fall days, chocolate chips cookies in the oven, and spontaneous games of Candy Land. That is God's design and the best way to learn and LIVE.

You get to do it every day and are so blessed to be able to teach your children at home, all of them at once.

Go have some fun and do school.

Be real.

AUGUST 29

Moms is Moms

Hey Mom,

This is going to be quick because I'm loading up for a convention in Greenville, SC and just got back a couple days ago from speaking in Long Island. Here's my take away after talking to a lot of New Yorker moms: Moms is moms.

I don't care if their speech sounds Cajun (New Orleans), Norwegian (MN), Hillbilly (TN, NC), Genteel (GA), Cowboy (TX, OK, AZ), Asian, Mexican, Crocodile Dundeeish, or Taxicab driverish (NYC)....Moms is moms.

We all face the same struggles, hardships, and defeats. We have hard-to-handle toddlers, mouthy teenagers, bills to pay, jobs to do, homes to maintain, cars to fix, and wives to love. We are an army of often-bungling moms who don't have the luxury of giving up but keep doing what moms and dads do... because we're moms!!!!

You're part of the team.

Be real.

My Child Said WHAT?!

Hey Mom,

A couple weeks ago we were sitting around the table eating and laughing when one of my older children said a word that stunned my wife and me. It just hung in the air like a vulgar cloud. We glanced at each other and by the innocent look on our child's face, we knew he had no idea what the word meant.

Later my wife and I talked about it, wondering if we should bring the word to his attention so he wouldn't say it again in public. That's the thing about some of the words our children sometimes say (or most assuredly WILL say); they just don't have the same grid as a 40-year-old does. They hear words... that are just words. Sometimes I think we freak out and explain too much and get angry when we just need to sit still and remain quiet.

So there are times when we should remain calm and assess, and there are times when we need to say something. It's okay to say, "They may talk that way, but we don't talk that way EVER!" Sometimes you'll even have to dole out some chastisement to deal with habitual offenders.

Here's the deal about some of those bad words...they might have LEARNED THEM FROM US!!! Sometimes, we let them slip in moments of frustration or during homeschooling. It doesn't mean we shouldn't correct our children, but if we want them to grow up NOT saying those words then we better stop saying them ourselves.

You can say, "Do as I say, not as I do," but they WILL DO what you do, regardless of what you say.

So to boil it all down...don't freak out, deal with the real issues, examine your own words, and...

Be real.

AUGUST 31

They Just Don't Get It

Hey Mom,

As long as there are homeschoolers, there will be non-supportive family members. If you're fortunate enough to have supportive family members, you need to thank them. Thank them for believing in you and in homeschooling.

Thank them for keeping quiet when they could be critical. Thank them for the encouragement in what you believe.

Now if you're like most of us, who have a few non-supportive family members in the closet, then let me say, "You're not alone." We've all had (or have) relatives who say critical, hurtful, discouraging comments. To give them the benefit of the doubt, I really believe they don't mean all that much by it. They are just 'status quo' people. They like normal, they lived normal, and they don't know what to do with non-normal...so they say dumb things.

I think the temptation is to get defensive, quote successful homeschool statistics, or get argumentative. I think that's the wrong approach. Instead, let your children do the talking...not literally, but let their homeschooled behavior/character speak for your efforts.

Homeschooling and being at home has positive effects on your children. Your non-supportive family members will see it and they will come around. I've seen it in my family. We had some who were skeptical...and then they watched our kids grow up and you know what? They say nice things to us now...because they see the difference.

So again, to recap:

1. Don't be surprised...you're not alone.
2. Don't get defensive.
3. Let your children do the talking.

Oh yeah, and although you might think you need to have it all together... don't pretend to. Above all...

Be real.

SEPTEMBER 1

Autumn in Indiana

Hey Mom,

I love this time of year. I love the changing leaves, the smell of campfires, and the crisp cool air. It makes me think of orange construction paper, apple cider, and frosted sugar cookies.

With all the sights, sounds, and smells, it's no wonder that there are so many fall activities that you can enjoy as a family. One of our favorites is the annual pilgrimage to one of the local festivals in my neck of the woods, whether it's the humongous Johnny Appleseed Festival in Ft. Wayne, IN, the equally humongous Nappanee Apple Festival, or the very impressive Mississinewa 1812 festival in Marion, IN.

My kids love walking the grounds observing blacksmiths hammer, rope makers spin, and musicians pound on dulcimers, while civil war canons boom in the distance. And there's the smell of kettle corn, chicken and dumplings, and wood smoke as we eat our peanut butter and jelly sandwiches that we packed because we're too cheap to eat all that expensive food.

But what my children like most is handling the sharp, hunting knives, throwing tomahawks, and trying on Little House on the Prairie bonnets. It gives them a taste of life a hundred and fifty years ago.

About the only negative thing about those festivals are the port-o-lets/port-o-johns/port-o-potties. I'd rather explode than use one, but my kids don't mind. In fact, I've even seen them peer into the open stool lid and holler, "Look at all that stuff down there!"

Gross. Praise the Lord for sanitary wipes.

Anyway, if you're looking for a great fall, family activity, then surf the web and find one that is happening near you and go, but please don't try to schoolify it. Don't make your kids write a paper, take notes, or prepare a report on what they see and learn. Just let them enjoy it...and your time as a family.

Be real.

SEPTEMBER 2

'Fall' in Love With Homeschooling

Hey Mom,

I'm sorry, but this is such a woman topic...I mean what guy would ever talk about falling in love with homeschooling like it's his wife...or football season?

In fact, I'm pretty sure that the vast majority of homeschooling moms never fell in love with homeschooling to begin with. And why should they? The way homeschooling has been portrayed, even by most homeschooling experts, is that it's supposed to be like traditional school, only it's at home. Who would love that? I know I never did. About the only people who could say that they LOVE homeschooling like that are those few people whose gift is teaching... and would probably be school teachers if they weren't homeschooling moms.

The vast majority of moms I meet look tired and discouraged and would love to find a more enjoyable way to homeschool.

I think there is a better way, one that every parent can fall in love with again. It's called parenting. That's what homeschooling really should be, just a mom and dad who love, train, and teach their children...at home. They don't necessarily need a lesson plan, a curriculum guide, or an expert telling them what they should do.

Parents just need to be reminded to slow down and enjoy their children and the privilege of being allowed to train them for adulthood. That doesn't sound so bad, does it?

The same way I would counsel a person who is struggling to love his/her mate, I would also counsel a homeschooler who is struggling to love her homeschool. Cut away all the externals and concentrate on the relationship and let the externals take care of themselves.

On a beautiful fall day it might mean raking up a big pile of leaves just to jump in, not to study them. It might mean taking a hayride for fun...not as a field trip. It might mean going to pick apples, having a campfire, or cutting out pumpkins from orange construction paper because it's fun...not because you can count it as school.

Be real.

SEPTEMBER 3

LOL

Hey Mom,

At this moment, I don't feel very humorous. We just pulled in the driveway from a long road trip to Baton Rouge, LA, and we're all cranky and leaning toward the mean side. But here's the deal about humor: it sometimes takes the passage of time before normal everyday occurrences and struggles seem humorous.

It's the same way with homeschooling. Homeschooling may not seem funny now, but in a few years or decades, you'll remember it differently. In fact, I guarantee the things you will be sitting around the Christmas tree laughing about it in 30 years will be the struggles you're going through right now.

You'll giggle about how you never thought that ONE kid would ever read, how you thought you'd go insane trying to get them all to sit still, or how you worried about scarring your children for life. And you know what? You're going to miss those wonderful, hard, humorous days.

So maybe we both need a little reminder that the trials and tribulations of this homeschooling life...are what will bring us the most joy in the future. So enjoy them right now...and laugh.

Be real.

SEPTEMBER 4

You Can't so Don't

Hey Mom,

I've said it before and let me say it again: you CAN'T do it all AND you can't fit it ALL in. I'm not sure what it is about homeschooling moms and that fact, but most moms seem to fight it.

They, or I should say, you, work so hard to try and fit it all in. You see an interesting book and think I really should read this to the kids. You read or hear some curriculum expert say you need to cover 'this' topic and think I can add it in between math and lunch.

Mom, you can't do it all or fit it all in, so deal with it. You can't read every good book, cover every single subject, and learn every cool instrument. You CAN help your kids enjoy learning (by not trying to cram in too much), however, which helps them desire to learn.

Just do what you can, fit in the most important stuff, like playing games with your children, and leave the other stuff by the wayside along with the guilt.

Have a great day with your children ...

And be real.

SEPTEMBER 5

Start at the Very Beginning

Hey Mom,

For just a moment let's pretend this isn't summer and it's OK to think about school: When you think about spelling I go to the wise sage...Julie Andrews. I mean she hit the ball out of the park when she sang to those eager Von Trapp children, "Let's start at the very beginning...a very good place to start. When you read, you begin with A - B - C. When you...uh, spell you begin with C - A - T."

She and the kids went on to sing a wonderfully memorable song...but I'll just go on to say to start simple and don't expect too much. After all as the good doctor Todd has said on more than one occasion, "Good spellers were created that way...and not so good spellers? Well, they were created that way as well.

Go ahead and plug through those spelling lists of age-appropriate words. If they're not reading or speaking the words, they shouldn't have to spell them. Along with that, don't rush your spellers. You won't get better spellers by having your three-year-old learn to spell the word d-o-g.

OK we've spent way too much time thinking about school it's time to get back out there and do summer!!!

Be real.

Here's a fun song by a group with a lousy name. Check out the Crazy ABC's song by Bare Naked Ladies (I hate their name...but the song is worth a listen if you want to laugh and think).

SEPTEMBER 6

Only One

Hey Mom,

Can I just say up front to all of you moms homeschooling an only child... stop apologizing for having ONE child? You don't need to do that, and it bothers me that we in the homeschooling world have made you or anyone else feel the need to apologize for the number of children you have.

Moms come up to me all the time and apologize for having one child... or two...or NINE!!! There is nothing spiritual about the number of children in your quiver.

That said I also know there is a lot of pressure on only-child-homeschoolers. The pressure at first comes from others' questions, such as: "Shouldn't you have him/her with other children? He needs interaction with kids his age...it's not good to be at home all day long by himself..."

What's worse is that those outside voices become inside voices and you begin to replay those comments in spite of the conviction that you believe you should homeschool your child.

Listen to me, Mom. If you believe you should homeschool your only child, THEN homeschool your child. I really believe that only children benefit from being homeschooled. After all, we want our children to know how to interact with and get contentment with their future family. The best place to learn all that is in YOUR HOME!!!

Experts tell us to get them out of the home and into the world. But your child needs to see how he fits into the family and that a family is a family no matter how many children there are and what better place to learn that...than at HOME.

And even if you feel like you need to keep up a good appearance, fight the urge and...

Be real!

An Ordinary Homeschool

Hey Mom,

Ordinary. I love that word. It feels unpretentious, humble, and earthy. It's a great descriptive word for every homeschool family…because we're all ordinary…or the same.

We all have high expectations, often accompanied by feelings of failure. We say things we wish we hadn't and fail to say the things we know we should…to the people we love the most.

We get overwhelmed by the messes, the stinky attitudes, the perceived expectations of others, the loneliness, and the job of keeping it all together. We worry about our children's futures and if we will have done enough to prepare them.

But amidst all the ordinary, something extraordinary happens in all of our homeschools. Relationship. We get to be with our children even when we'd rather be doing something else. Our children get to see us at our best and at our worst. They get firsthand experience at home about how a family should function and what it should look like. They feel the safety of being home and the joy of not being labeled.

Every day we get to be together. The limited hours of our life will be spent together…learning, laughing, crying, and being ordinary.

That's an extraordinary life! You are so blessed.

Be real.

Picking Again?!

Hey Mom,

Still have curriculum decisions to make…maybe for the second time? Oh, you've come to the right guy. That's me, Mr. Go-To Curriculum Guy. It's not that I know two licks about the difference between one curriculum and another, but I do know one truth that will solve all your curriculum problems.

Are you ready for this? Here's all my curriculum-choosing wisdom boiled down into one nugget of undistilled brilliance: God made you wise enough to figure it out.

That's it! Truth is you know your children way better than some curriculum guru does. Oh, he'll throw you his pitch about how if you use his stellar curriculum your children will top the charts on...every scale. Go ahead and listen...but you know better.

You and your spouse are wise enough to figure it all out. If you don't want to do it 'their' way...THEN DON'T. If you don't like the curriculum that everyone else LOVES, then don't use it. I don't care what anyone says you should use. If you like something else or don't like curriculum at all...then do it your way.

Because...GOD MADE YOU, THE PARENT, SMART ENOUGH TO FIGURE IT OUT.

Be real.

SEPTEMBER 9

Beware the Fog

Hey Mom,

As I type this, the windows in our home are open. It was cool this morning—just the kind you'd expect in September around here. It's actually kind of quiet in our house right now, which is odd. It feels very 'schoolish', although we're pretty fresh into the school year.

I hate the back-to-school feeling. It always hit me as a kid around this time of year and it hits me now that I'm all grown up (I'm 50, by the way). I think as homeschoolers we feel the weight of a new school year even more than normal people. It creeps in like a thick fog, blotting out the sun of summer and the TRUTH of why we do what we do.

I know other homeschoolers feel it. They start asking in hushed voices around the middle of July, "So when do you start back up?" But, there is always the perky homeschooler who is so excited to begin. She has all her curriculum lined up, her lesson plans detailed out in 3-minute increments, and giggles at the thought of all they're going to learn in the coming year.

But then there's that fog. It spreads and covers every homeschooler like a shadow of doubt that gnaws at your bones. In it comes haunting whispers saying your children would be better off if someone else were teaching them... you're ruining them...they're missing out on so much...life would be better if you didn't have to homeschool...everyone else's kids seem to be doing okay...

But here's the truth and the reason I'm writing this column: that fog is a lie. If you believe a lie long enough, it sure sounds like the truth. My fear is that you'll act on that lie, Mom, and miss out on the joy and benefit of homeschooling your children. That's why you started right? You thought it would be fun...good, and now you hate the thought of it and wonder how you're going to make it through another year.

Mom, you're in the fog of lies that homeschooling moms believe. Take comfort in the fact that you're not alone. In fact, I believe that EVERY SINGLE homeschooling mom believes these lies (dads don't – if they believe any lie it's the lie that they're better than they really are).

Here's a fog shattering truth.

God gave your children exactly the mother they needed for the coming school year.

That's you!!!! And it's true. God looked at your children and knew they needed you with all your strengths, flaws, and failures. Hey, if you want to find someone smarter to teach your children, they're a dime a dozen, but if you want to find someone better to teach your children…there is no one. You're the best.

I know, some of you are nodding and thinking, "Yeah, but you don't know me; I barely made it through school myself. I'm lazy and skip more days than we should. How can that be good for my children?"

I know this – You, with those qualities, are perfect for your children. Still others are saying, "Yeah, but I'm the type who takes all the fun out of life. If I don't have my kids in tears by 9:30am, I don't feel like I've done my job right. How can that be good for my children?"

I know this – You, with those qualities, are perfect for your children. Quit beating yourself up over it. When your children say, "Mom, you're no fun!" you respond, "And that's exactly the kind of mother GOD KNEW you NEEDED!!!!"

It's true. So quit comparing yourself to other moms and how they do school or life (you may have to stay away from Facebook). You do it the way God made you to do it and enjoy those children of yours. Because that's all that matters.

Mom, it's going to be a good school year.

Be real.

SEPTEMBER 10

Learning on the Go

Hey Mom,

As is our custom, we'll be hitting the road for a fall loop next month. Not only will we be speaking at homeschool groups and churches along the way, but we'll end our time with some much needed R&R down in sunny Florida.

We love homeschooling on the road and 'on the go', but I'm going to be upfront with you. If you think you're just going to transfer your normal HOMEschool to ROADschool, then you're in for a world of frustration. We've found that it's a lot harder to do all the normal school stuff while you're truckin' down the highway.

But if you put your pre-conceived ideas of what school should look like aside…then you'll have opened up a whole new world of learning.

That's the great thing about school 'on the go'; you get to see, smell, feel, and experience things that others only read about. Growing up in a public school, I'm sure I read about the Civil War, but by the time I reached high school, my only retained knowledge of it was that it involved some guys in blue and gray and Abraham Lincoln won it at Gettysburg.

But my kids have walked the Civil War battlefields, seen their weapons, walked the stairs in Lincoln's home, played in the grassy area where he gave his address, sat in Ford's Theater, and stood before the place where Lincoln was buried. That's school at its finest.

I won't pretend that all my kids are Civil War experts (although I have a couple who are), but they all seem to pick up their own bent along the way. Some like the events, other like the relationships, and still others like the bugs in the grass.

The best homeschooling takes place in the real world. It might happen in your yard, down the street, or in a town called Gettysburg.

Be real.

SEPTEMBER 11

I Stink at Balance.

Hey Mom,

"I stink - you stink - we all stink at BALANCE!"

It's true; we're all prone to being unbalanced. Since that is the case, the important thing is to make sure you're unbalanced in the right direction…or the one that will cause the least amount of problems.

For busy husbands and dads, I would say that if they're going to be unbalanced to make sure they're unbalanced towards family. If they have to drop a ball in the great juggling act…they should drop it in the work/career department. Like you, I've met plenty of men who have been unbalanced towards work and have regretted it. I have never met a dad who was unbalanced toward family and regretted it.

So…for homeschooling moms I'd say to make sure you're unbalanced towards the relationship with your children. If you have to fall short, fall short in what you teach them NOT in how much you enjoy them. It's easy for a child to make up in the information category, but it's almost IMPOSSIBLE for them to make up in the relationship department.

For some of you, that will be reassuring; for others of you, let that be a warning.

So go ahead and be unbalanced, just make sure you're unbalanced in the best direction.

Be real.

PS – Actually, what I just wrote isn't being unbalanced...it's the way God intended life to be lived.

SEPTEMBER 12

Never Listen to the Mom with the Pointy Tail

Hey Mom,

Hope all is well in the mom department at your house. I just got back from a great men's retreat at Hidden Acres Christian Center in Iowa. There's nothing better than being with 350 dads who all face the same stuff.

Right now, I feel like a cartoon guy who has a dad-dressed-in-an-angel-getup on one shoulder and a dad-dressed-in-horns-and-a-pointy-tail on the other. One is encouraging me to take my kids sledding today, and the other is offering some mighty good excuses why I'm too busy to even consider it.

"Your kids are growing up...and you won't be able to go sledding one day."

"Do you realize how many projects you have on your desk? They won't get done themselves, you know."

"It's only one afternoon."

"It's ALL afternoon!"

"Your kids need the time with you."

"They don't care about time with you."

"What matters most?"

"You have to provide for your family...don't you...don't you? Pay attention when I'm talking to you.........I'm talking here...DDD!!!!

Mom, got a good and bad mom on your shoulders today? Don't listen to the practical mom...the bad mom. She has some pretty good arguments about why you shouldn't do what your kids would love to do with you. If you listen to her, you'll have chosen foolishly.

Listen to the good-mom...who often speaks for God, Himself.

Don't hear the good-mom anymore? Then let me speak for him.

"Hey Mom, don't waste your time on Facebook, that project, or hobby. Your kids will be gone before you know it. Besides, you'll still have time to get it done. It won't take that long. You've been promising for a long time…do it!!

Be real.

SEPTEMBER 13

Change of Seasons

Hey Mom,

I don't know about you, but I'm NOT ready for the seasons to change. Normally, I like the crisp mornings, the vibrant colors, and the smells of fall, but I'm not ready this year. Where did summer go??!! Maybe it's life on the road that shortens the season, but I think the more likely culprit is age. It just seems to me that the older I get, the faster the seasons change.

Errma Bombeck is right about time going faster, comparing it to the faster the toilet paper roll spins the closer you get to the end.

I don't like changing life-seasons either. What happened to my little boy who was our guinea pig into homeschooling who has been out for two years now? I used to be the newly married guy, now I'm that old guy who has been married twenty-five years. The seasons are changing too fast…and I DON'T LIKE IT!!!

I like the way things are NOW…I don't want them to change.

But, things are going to change whether I like it or not, so I BETTER LIKE IT.

You better too. So go enjoy some hot chocolate, make a fall craft, and hug your growing child like you mean it...and before you run out of seasons.

Be real.

SEPTEMBER 14

Spellin'

Hey Mom,

Before I talk about speling, let me just tell you that I'm about to hit the roed with the hole family on a speakin' loop in just a cupple weeks. You can sea my skedule on are websight.* If we happn to be in yur nayborhood, stop in and sey, "Hay."

Now back to the speling thing. You know my wife has tried all kinds of different helps…from words lists to secquetial spelling. But my theory is that those curriculms only highlight good and bad spelers. Trueth is, I have good spelers and bad spellers at my house and after working through spellin programs, the good spellers are 'gooder' and the bad spellers are only slightly les bad.

Aktually, I'm one of the bad spelers. I can memorize the words, write the words, rewrite the words, learn cute little tricks…and I still can't spell them. My wife and dauwter can see a word once and remember it for the rest of their lives. I can check and recheck my work and still can't see mispleled words… AND I'M A WRITER!!!! (praize the Lord for proof-readers).

So…go easy on your non-spellers. Give them the lists, teach them the tricks, and then love them when they still can't spel worth a dime.

And of coarse…be reel.

**www.familymanweb.com/speaking/speaking-schedule/*

SEPTEMBER 15

A Decent Paragraph

Hey Mom,

Once again, I'm in a topic that puts me in way over my head*. I don't know how to help a child write a decent paragraph…I can barely write one myself… and I'm a writer. My thinking is, instead of trying to get your child to write a decent paragraph…work on allowing yourself to accept 'decent'.

Because you're a homeschooling mom and have trouble assessing what qualifies as a decent paragraph, I'll do it for you. So here's what makes for a decent paragraph:

1. It should have some words in it…and some of them should be spelled correctly.

2. I would have them write like they speak, minimizing grammatical rules.

3. Then I would read it and say, "Looks good to me…you did a great job." I wouldn't correct it or modify it. The more you correct, the less they'll want to write.

4. For those kids who like to write, let them write. For those kids who don't like to write…I wouldn't make them write too much. Let them spend the most time on the subjects they do best.

5. If you just can't help yourself and think you need to get your child to write better, then check out Andrew Pudewa's writing program (Institute for Excellence in Writing). My wife uses it and loves it. He's a good egg.

Be real.

**Kind of makes you wonder why they look at me as a homeschool expert, doesn't it?*

SEPTEMBER 16

What About Sports?

Hey Mom,

FYI - I am a red-blooded American male...who doesn't care for sports. Growing up I played them all, I just wasn't very competitive and couldn't wrap myself around the idea that people took it seriously. Seemed like a game to me, but to others, it was far more.

Maybe it's one of the reasons my kids don't do sports. Not that I'm against them or think less of others who like them. It's just that it doesn't seem all that important to me if my kids play them. Besides, they get plenty of playing on their own and every Tuesday night a group of my kids play pretty completive volleyball with about 40 other young adults. It's awesome.

That said; I sure don't mind NOT having to cart kids to games and practices during the week or weekends. The two years that we played Upward Basketball about did me in...and it was only eight weeks long!!!

Some non-sports families feel the pressure from family members, "You need to have your kids play sports...that's how they learn to work together as a team...it's fun...great memories...you're going to ruin them if you don't let them..."

My answer? Whatever. You do what works best for your family and your children. If you like sports and want them to be involved...do them. And if you don't...don't. Not every kid has to be involved in everything.

My kids get to travel all over the country, but that doesn't mean your kids should or are less than mine. You might have horses...but that doesn't mean I need to get them. Others might grow gardens, play instruments, build boats, or breed whales...but that doesn't mean everyone should.

That said, go play kickball, basketball, or nuke'em* as a family tonight.

Be real.

*Nuke'em is a great game for the whole family to play. You play it with a volleyball or badmitton net. Put half the players on each side of the net. Then instead of hitting the ball like volleyball, you thow the ball to the other side. If they catch it, they get to throw it back. If they drop it, the person who dropped it is out. You can get your team members back in by catching the ball with one hand. The first team to lose all its players is out. My kids love it.

Be real.

SEPTEMBER 17

Creative Math Facts

Hey Mom,

I have as many math and science skills as I have organizational skills. I can add, do some subtraction, and know how to construct a dominant/recessive gene chart of the fruit fly (that has come in handy). Soooo…it seems to be asking a lot from me to write about creative ways to teach math and science.

By its very nature, math is drudgery for many people. You make math fact cards, slosh through the basics, fake your way through the higher math equations, and then spend most of your life adding, subtracting, multiplying, and dividing.

Let's move on to science. That's a different beast. The world around us is all about science. Any child given the freedom from spending their days in a schoolroom can learn plenty. Here's a sample. A typical day at our house the kids might see our cat eat a squirrel, mold growing on leftovers in the fridge, bugs climbing on the screens, a toad or snake in the grass, rain filling the puddles and creek near our house, crawdads hiding under rocks, dust collecting on the TV screen, and fruit flies swarming our kitchen. That's science. In fact, my kids have a science tutor—GOD!

Throw in an Apology Textbook* for future trivia game information and you've got science nailed.

There you go. Expert advice from a non-expert…and you got it all for FREE!!

Be real.

**www.apologia.com*

SEPTEMBER 18

I Love 'em

Hey Mom,

I love homeschool conventions. I know some who have been there, done that and think they don't need them. In fact, I met a homeschooler who had homeschooled for over 15 years and never knew there were any conventions.

My advice is if you homeschool, you should go to your state's annual homeschool convention.

There's just so much to see and hear, and other homeschoolers you'll meet who need encouragement or can encourage you in your homeschooling journey.

That said; I know that homeschooling conventions can be overwhelming. So here is my advice for navigating and enjoying your homeschool convention: God made you smart enough to homeschool your children.

Go ahead and listen to the workshops, the vendors' spiels, and friend's advice, but if it sounds too hard, too overwhelming, or too…UGH…then don't do it and don't feel guilty about not doing it. God made you smart enough to figure it all out.

You pick out the stuff you like and leave the stuff you don't like behind.

Take deep breaths occasionally and introduce yourself to the person who looks just as confused as you feel. Who knows what might become of a 'chance' meeting? Also, mention it to your husband now so he can begin to warm up to the idea.

Be real…and maybe I'll see you at a local homeschool convention near you.

SEPTEMBER 19

PE

Hey Mom,

Let's just get right to the point. PE is 'schoolified' playing. It is a break from sitting in a classroom and gives students an opportunity to play and stretch their legs. Now I know some would say, "Oh, contraire…Physical Education is more than play." To which I would counter, "Baloney."

How is playing dodge ball, whiffle ball, or kickball more than playing? Homeschoolers specialize in playing. After all, book work should only take a homeschooling family a fraction of the time it takes the institutional school, and there should be lots of playing and free time.

Please don't call it PE. Somehow that feels like we're playing their game, BUT if by state law you have to have PE, count it all. Every time they run, skip or walk…count it!! This summer you should have gotten a whole year's worth of PE…and then some.

Be real.

Cherish Today

Hey Mom,

I was speaking in hot and humid Houston, TX last weekend. I almost melted, but I'm back in cool and crisp northern, IN enjoying a little M&P (mayhem and pandemonium) with my brother and sisters and their families.

We were in the midst of life yesterday morning when Debbie, my wife, called on her way home from an orthodontist appointment with my son Ike (15). As soon as I answered my phone I knew something was wrong. There was emotion in her voice and I thought, "How can an orthodontist appointment go bad?"

Then I heard her tear-filled words, "We were in a wreck…but we're OK." She filled me in on the details (a car slammed into the back of their car as she was stopped for a police car that had pulled a car over in front of her) and I made the hour trip to pick them up. On the way home she described the event and I felt so grateful to God for having spared my wife and son. It could have been bad.

It felt (and still does) sobering to realize how quickly things can change. In fact, the thought strikes me that catastrophic events always start as a normal day.

You have breakfast, read the paper, run off to work…and then next thing you know there is an accident, a shooting, or a call from the doctor. There's no warning…no little indicator light to announce, "Buckle your seatbelts because things are about to change…forever."

I wonder how we would adjust our lives if there was such a light or warning. We'd end the argument we were in right now, we'd hug and tell those around us how much we love them, we'd linger at home instead of rushing out…we'd…do things differently.

Dad, I don't know how the rest of your day or week is going to turn out. Maybe you'll get a call today. Can I encourage you to love that family of yours today…or even RIGHT NOW like the red warning light is about to go off. If you've got some apologizing to do, DO IT! IF you've got some words that need to be said, SAY them now through a text or call. Don't assume that you've got time or that things can't change between breakfast toast and bedtime, because they always do.

DO IT!

Be real.

SEPTEMBER 21

Can I Teach Everything?

Hey Mom,

When the question is asked, "Can I teach EVERYTHING," I quickly respond, "Yes, you can teach EVERYTHING...and No, you can't teach EVERYTHING."

The truth is if your kid needs to be taught it...you can teach it. You may not be an expert in every area, but you can direct them in the right direction. There are online and DVD helps as well. So in a very practical and real way, you CAN teach everything in your homeschool.

The just as true truth is that you CAN'T teach everything. You only have a certain amount of hours in each day and you just can't get to everything. I know some moms who get excited about teaching first-aid to their children and then worry about how to fit it in to the rest of their very full schedule. It never dawns on them that they have the authority and opportunity to teach first-aid INSTEAD of something else.

The same goes for any other subject. If you want to teach welding, then your child might not be able to do geography. If you want to teach sports, then they might not be able to do music. If you want to do music, then they may not be able to do art. If you want to do welding, sports, music, and art...then they may not be able to do science, spelling, and history. Because you CAN'T teach EVERYTHING.

Did I make myself clear? I didn't think so.

Be real.

SEPTEMBER 22

The Comparing Game

Hey Mom,

There's something exciting about the start of a new school year. The smell of freshly sharpened yellow pencils, along with new art boxes, new schedules, new classes, and unknown books to discover await everyone. Anticipation hangs in the air and the halls of learning replace months of footloose and fancy-free summer living. You can almost taste the excitement as you jump out of the starting blocks.

Your heart pounds and you feel the pure rush of adrenaline as you experience the race into the new school year…but THEN you glance to the side and compare yourself to other moms. You see one mom whose kids are playing instruments and you think to yourself, "MY children should be playing the violin." So, you buy or rent a truckload of stringed instruments and announce your new plan to your children.

For the first three days it is fun, but THEN you glance over and see another mom whose children are learning to paint with watercolors and you think to yourself, "That's what we should be doing." So, you visit your local art supply store and load up on all kinds of supplies and announce your new art agenda to your children.

And it is fun for the first day and a half, although it's hard to find time to paint in the midst of homeschooling, life, and violin lessons. THEN, you glance over at yet another homeschooling mom who posts on her Facebook page that her children (all under the age of twelve) have helped start a home business and saved enough money to buy a house…debt free.

"That's what we should be doing," you think to yourself. So, you FORCE your husband into starting a family business so your children can earn a living and learn something along the way. And it's a lot of fun…NEVER!!

By now, you're exhausted, the kids are cranky, and your husband isn't talking to you, but you still look around and see all the neat things everyone else is doing and think to yourself, "That's what we should be doing."

Stop it! Stop playing the comparing game. It is a game where there are no winners. In fact, everyone loses. I know my wife plays it from time to time. In fact, I remember one time, when I was speaking at the New York State homeschool convention, and she was browsing the vendor hall during some down time.

At one point, I heard live blue grass music being played from somewhere within the hall. Winding my way through the people I finally found the source of the music—a family with at least ten children playing blue grass music. Man, they were awesome, dressed in their little matching Hee Haw outfits. I'm telling you, there was even a tiny little kid on a mandolin going to town.

That's when I prayed a prayer that struck me as funny and one that I've remembered all these years. I can remember standing in the crowd and praying, "Dear, God, please don't let my wife SEE THIS."

I just knew that if she did, she would feel like we were some sort of loser family because we didn't play any instruments or have a family band. I am not going to haul a big string bass around the county in my RV, I thought to myself.

Ever since then I've told the story a bunch of times to moms who feel the same way. I'd just about bet that you probably feel the same. You are constantly comparing yourself, your children, and worse yet, your husband, to other homeschooling families that you know or know of. AND IT'S KILLING YOU!!!!

Here's the thing: just be you and let those other families be them. If they like to play instruments, fine. If they like to paint 'perty' pictures, fine. If they run home businesses, take RV trips around the country, write novels, or compete in synchronized kick boxing, FINE.

Every family (including yours and mine) has its own giftedness from God. The trick is to do what you do and stop comparing your weaknesses against someone else's strengths. My wife is tempted to do that.

My wife, Debbie, doesn't like crafts. She doesn't like the preparation, the mess, or the open-endedness. Her idea of an art project is to say to the kids, "Here's some paper and crayons…draw something." So when she goes over to a friend's house who loves crafts and sees a full scale model of Jerusalem made out of paper mache on the kitchen table, she comes home feeling like a failure.

Here's the deal: my wife has gobs of strengths. She's organized, disciplined, talented beyond measure, and breathtakingly beautiful. BUT she's got weaknesses. Lots of them. Truth is no one is created with all strengths. That's what the Bible is talking about when it says that the body is made up of many members, all with different abilities. Some members are toes, others are ears, or fingers, BUT no one is the ENTIRE body…including you.

You have weaknesses galore. The important thing is not to compare your weaknesses against someone else's strengths. If you do, you'll lose the comparison, and you'll spend all your days trying to be something you were not made to be.

You need to face the fact, that you (your kids or husband) may not ever play a musical instrument, paint a picture, own a home-based business, travel the world in a sailboat, own your own little farm, spin yarn from yak hair, or have a ministry in churches.

Your children may not be able to carry a tune in a bucket, design their own clothes, or write stories that others will read, but they do have gifts and talents. Your job as a parent is to fan and enjoy those gifts. That's the beauty of homeschooling. So stop comparing your weaknesses against other's strengths. Actually, you probably should stop comparing period because all comparing leads to either pride or misery. Both are destinations you should avoid.

Hey, would you mind if I gave you one more little nugget of advice from Todd, the Familyman, not from God? Facebook is the mega arena of the comparing game. The posts are filled with pictures of gourmet meals, angelic children, romantic marriages, and smoothly run homeschools. Only problem…it's a LIE.

Those well-meaning folks have only shown the triumphs and successes, not the down and dirty. I know more than one mom who has had to pull herself away from the comparing arena so as not to…compare. Each time she visited Facebook, she walked away feeling discouraged and eyeing her own family like the enemy of her success and happiness. Enough said.

So, to wrap it up, enjoy the coming school year. Do what you do best and forget the rest. Go ahead and try something new out, but if it doesn't fit your family's gifts and talents…toss it and don't feel guilty. And when you visit your friend's home and they are practicing their instruments, painting murals, or solving the problem of world hunger, smile, be amazed, but DO NOT COMPARE!!!

Your family is amazing. Just ask God.

Be real.

PS - Whew, that was a long one.

SEPTEMBER 23

Two Kinds

Hey Mom,

There are two kinds of people in this world: those who like to teach and those who don't. The first group loves lesson plans and curriculum, schedules and class room activity. The second group dreads textbooks and routine classroom activities.

But with that said, it doesn't mean that everyone can't homeschool and find joy in doing so. The truth is homeschooling was called 'parenting' way before it was called homeschooling. And parenting should bring joy…even when it's hard and monotonous.

So to those of you who don't like the school teaching of homeschooling, I say find a way to do it that fits you and your children. Focus in on what matters most (like enjoying your children), ditch the stuff that steals your homeschool joy, and just plug away at the essentials (even if you hate doing them), and don't feel bad for not LOVING the school part of homeschooling.

And of course…

Be real.

SEPTEMBER 24

It'll Get You

Hey Mom,

When discussing the whole techno-dilemma, I think there are few people who would argue the idea that it is indeed a monster.

You probably feel it yourself, as most parents do, but there is a disconnect when it comes to taking action based on what you feel to be the truth. And while the tech monster can and will gobble up your children, it also gobbles up parents. In fact, you might be in the techno-beast mouth right now.

The defining question that needs to be answered is this: are you a better parent (or spouse) because of the technology? Or, are you a better or worse mom (or wife) because of your smart phone, Facebook, or blogs that you follow?

If you answer "Better," then the monster isn't a monster but a friend, BUT if you say "Worse," then you're being consumed by the monster.

The sad thing is that I've met a lot of moms and dads who say, "Oh, I know it's a problem (or addiction), but I'm not giving up my iPhone or Facebook."

There it is: it's easy to talk about the monster, but not many are willing to do what it takes to slay it. I know it's not easy…but it's time to do battle with the monster that I call the techno-beast. In fact, I have a few resources to help you.

1. Taming the Techno-Beast parent booklet
2. Taming the Techno-Beast Student Workbook
3. The laugh-out-loud Taming the Techno-Beast seminar CD.

Be honest and be real.

SEPTEMBER 25

SAT

Hey Mom,

Honest … the first thing I thought of when I saw the letters ACT, SAT were rhyming words FAT, BAT, & CAT. That's the way my mind works. In fact, when I took the SAT my junior year of high school, I didn't even know people studied for the thing. I just thought it was more of a 'survey' of how much you knew.

I went to college and then seminary and never gave it two thoughts again. Of course now, in homeschooling circles, those three letter words seem to get a lot of air-time, as if a bad score might doom you to a life of servitude and ditch digging.

Nothing could be further from the truth. Actually, my first two children have not taken either test. The first has already completed his bachelor's degree (through College Plus*) and the second is nearing the end of a technical animation school (Animation Mentor**). I'm not opposed to our children taking the SAT, MAT, ACT, BAT tests. But I'm not going to have them take them just because others take them and suggest that my children should as well.

I was talking to my college professor brother and posed the question, "So what would your state college tell a twenty-five-year-old guy who never graduated high school and never took any of those tests but says, 'I want to go to college'? Without hesitation he answered, "We'd let him in." That's what colleges want. They want someone who wants to go to college, not someone who just goes because it's the next thing to do after high school.

All that to say, RELAX. Don't let people scare you to the point where you frustrate your children and stop enjoying them. Not everyone needs those tests and if your child does, you'll figure it out.

By the way, Bill Gates got a near perfect score on the SAT (1590) and Bill Cosby got a 500. Both are geniuses. So are your children.

Be real.

**www.CollegePlus.org*

***www.AnimationMentor.com*

SEPTEMBER 26

You've Been Warned

Hey Mom,

Not to alarm you but…WE'RE RUNNING OUT OF TIME!!!!!!! Mom, this family thing is going to be over before you can snap your fingers. I was smacked in the face by this fact the weekend when we celebrated my oldest son Ben's (18) high school graduation.

My daughter Katherine made a big poster board display with photos of Ben from birth to the present. At one point, I walked over to the display and was looking at the photos of my oldest son when suddenly my vision began to blur with tears and a tennis ball made its way up my throat.

It's all going to be over soon, I thought. It won't be long before my house and RV will be empty and this chapter of life will be over. The same is true for you too, Mom. So don't miss it. If you've been contemplating a Family Adventure…take it. If you've been talking about buying something for your family, watching every episode of a special family movie, a change of careers for your husband so you can spend more time as a family, or camping out in your family room, do it, because it's going to be over soon.

Don't say I didn't warn you.

Be real.

End of the Table

Hey Mom,

I had that feeling again—the one where you feel a deep sense of accomplishment. It's not an arrogant, burst of pride; it's more like a warm, solid feeling of this is good.

I got it last evening while we were celebrating my oldest son's completion of his bachelor's of arts degree. Like all things worth celebrating, it took place at a Mexican restaurant. It was all ten of us, plus my son's fiancé, Rissa. Somehow I got pushed to the end of the long table giving me a good vantage point to watch everyone interact. That's when I got the feeling.

I was eating chips and watching all eight of my children talk, laugh, and interact when that warm flame of contentment and satisfaction covered me. I was enjoying some of the fruit that dads and moms down through the ages and across the globe have experienced, and it felt good.

I know the feeling won't last very long, but I know it will visit me again from time to time. It won't come because I have a big bank account, accumulate a lot of toys, or attain some important position or ministry. But from time to time, as my children and their children gather together and I sit and watch it from the end of the table or my comfortable rocking chair, I know I'll get that warm feeling.

Maybe it's the same feeling that God had when He looked at his newly created 'children' and said, "It is very good."

Haven't felt that feeling in awhile? Try sitting at the end of the table.

Be real.

SEPTEMBER 28

For the Last Time...

Hey Mom,

I'm getting tired of the question, Can you homeschool high school? Of course you can. Don't believe the LIES that say it's different than teaching the younger grades. Others will scare you and fill you with doubts, but you can do it. God has given you the means to teach your high schoolers at home.

Now, you might need some helps like DVD programs, online aids, or some special video instructions, but your kids will be better off if you teach them at home during high school. Plus high school is the time where they can explore their own interests. Homeschooling allows that, institutional school hinders that.

My children have learned animation programs, how to weld, and have written books because they were homeschooled during high school.

I could go on and on about all the EXTRA things they'll learn IF you were to put them in school during the high school years, but I don't think I need to do that. Besides don't you remember YOUR high school teachers? In fact, my brothers and I were sitting around our family's lake cottage just this past week talking about how TERRIBLE our high school teachers were. You can easily do better than that.

So let's just leave that question behind about teaching high school at home and promise to never re-visit it again. You are not only capable of doing it; you were designed to do it...so do it.

Be real.

SEPTEMBER 29

Habla Mongoliono?

Hey Mom,

The question, "Should I teach my child a foreign language?" is often asked by homeschool moms. Many experts would answer, "Definitely," and have the statistics to strengthen their case.

I, on the other hand, am not an expert. I don't do statistics, in-depth research projects, or construct elaborate polls. I'm just a dad who encourages parents in what matters most. So, if a homeschooling mom or dad comes up to me and asks, "Should I teach my child a foreign language?" I respond back with the question, "Do you WANT your child to learn a foreign language?"

If the answer is yes, then I say, "Then you should do it."

If they answer no, then I say, "Then you shouldn't do it."

Some might accuse me of waffling, but to tell you the truth, it doesn't matter what I think. The important thing to remember is that God made you smart enough to teach your children. If you want to teach them a foreign language, then do it. If you don't like languages, and your children don't have a gift for learning languages (you know if they do or not), then don't do it. Don't let others guilt you into doing it and stop feeling like you're somehow letting your kids down. If they are meant to learn a foreign language, then they will learn one.

Have a great day doing and teaching what you think is best.

Be real.

SEPTEMBER 30

Support Groups

Hey Mom,

I was about to start this article with this statement: "You need a homeschool support group." Then I thought, who am I to tell YOU what you need. You know what you need better than I do.

Actually, I was just talking to my wise wife last weekend about this exact subject. She explained to me that there are different seasons in every homeschooling mom's life. It ebbs and flows to where she needs different things, different years. Some years she needs a support group for fellowship, some years her kids need more activities, and other years she just feels too busy to add another thing. And that's OK."

Man, she's smart. She's right too. So here's my advice. If you need a support group, find one. And if you don't, don't let people 'guilt' you into joining one.

A note to your husband: Dad, your wife may not need a support group, but she does need support. In fact, she needs your support. She needs you to take ownership of your homeschool, believe in it, and then cheer her on. Don't know how to do that? Figure it out! And, buy my book Help! I'm Married to a Homeschool Mom and I'll help you.

Be real.

Making it Happen

Hey Mom,

I love the idea of homeschool co-ops (definition: a group of homeschooling moms who gather together with purpose and for support). Of course, the purpose behind the homeschool co-op varies with each group.

Some meet to share teaching responsibilities, some meet for field trips or activities, and others gather for social reasons or just to encourage each other. The important thing to remember is to pick a group that meets YOUR needs (no, you're not being selfish). For example: if you need encouragement that can only come from another homeschool mom, then don't go to an 'academic focused' co-op. If you do, I guarantee you'll leave each meeting feeling more discouraged than when you arrived.

Don't have a support group? Then start one. Don't be scared; it doesn't have to be any more than inviting your homeschool mom friends for an hour or two to sit in a circle and talk and/or pray. See if a couple husbands or older teens would play some games with the kids while you meet or meet at night and leave the kids at home.

If you don't know what to talk about, ask the ladies these simple questions: Why do you homeschool? What is the hardest part of homeschooling right now? Fill In the blank: "I sometimes feel like tossing in the towel because ________________."

That should get any group of moms talking and sharing. The trouble will be stopping them when the time is up.

If you feel the need for encouragement or don't feel like there are any good co-ops in your area, I'm betting there are other moms who feel that way as well. So start a group. You don't have to name it, have refreshments, or have a program. Just find a place to meet and … meet.

By the way, did you know that if you live within 5 hours of northern Indiana, you can have me speak to your homeschooling group during the school year? I love speaking at support groups and co-ops and because you live close to me, it's super easy. Just go to my website and click on the "Speaking" tab on the tool bar to get the ball rolling. You can see my speaking schedule there as well.

Be real!

What Grade?

Hey Mom,

There are many things that homeschooling parents fear, but one of the greatest fears is the dreaded question by NON-homeschoolers: "So what grade is Josh in?"

As soon as the question is asked, the air passage becomes constricted. You're about to answer when, nightmare of nightmares, the child whose name was mentioned speaks first. "I don't know. Mom, what grade am I in?" Or better yet, the said child answers like he has never heard the phrase before, "What do you mean?"

When that happens, the parent laughs nervously and goes for the quick recovery. "Oh Josh, you're such a teaser. You know what grade you're in." Not waiting for the child to answer, the now embarrassed parent answers for him, "Fifth … yeah that's it … probably."

I remember when one of my kids answered this question while I was right beside him. "I'm in sixth grade," he said to the guy who asked him. I looked at him like he was a liar. There is no way you are in sixth grade, I thought. Later, I found out from my wife that he WAS in sixth grade.

Here's the deal: grade levels don't mean diddly, but for embarrassment purposes, pick a grade …any grade and tell your child at the beginning of the school year, "You're in the _______ grade." Have your kids role-play a few minutes by taking turns asking each other what grade they are presently in.

That way, when someone asks, your child has an answer, and you don't have to go through the embarrassment of looking like your children have been raised by wolves.

Be real but pick a grade.

OCTOBER 3

Use Your Hands

Hey Mom,

Everyone knows hands-on learning is the best way to learn. High schools and colleges advertise and promote it…and your children do it every day of the year.

Just this morning, my two youngest boys Cal (8) and Jed (6) were outside early. In fact, when I came down for breakfast, Cal walked in through the front door dressed in shorts and wearing big heavy winter gloves. Instantly, my mind went on alert at the sight and I said, "What are you doing?"

"Dad, there are a ton of ants outside…come and see."

There were a ton of ants swarming on our sidewalk, eating whatever ants eat, and my kids were learning! But I didn't spoil the moment by pointing out thoraxes and ant patterns, I just said,

"Cool!" and left them to observe.

Mom, go and do the same. Let your kids do life. Refuse to point out thoraxes, and then if you want…count it as a day of your school year, because the real honest truth is: they will learn more by hands-on learning and exploration than they will staring into the pages of a book.

You can put that in the bank.

Be real … and pick up some ant spray.

OCTOBER 4

A Leftover Kind of Mom

Hey Mom,

The nerve of some people. My wife actually accused me today of, and I quote, "Giving everyone else your best and then giving our family nothing afterwards."

Doesn't she know I'M THE FAMILYMAN??! I work myself to the bone encouraging other moms and dads to give their ALL to their families. Without my message they'd waste their lives, pouring their energies into their careers and other people at the neglect of their families. Can I get an AMEN?!

What? What do you mean she has a point? The nerve of some people.

The thing that really galls me is…she's right. I do use most of my smiles, words of encouragement, and debonair, witty charm on complete strangers and give the worn out, leftover-me to the people I love the most. In fact, even as I write this, a wave of shame and regret washes over me.

When will I ever learn?

I have some mending to do tonight…and first on the list is my wife. Then, I need to be aware of what I dish out to my family and give them 'at least' what I give to others.

How about you, my fellow parent, short-order cook? Do you give the people at church, homeschool co-op, or ministry your right-off-the-grill best, leaving only leftovers for your family? Maybe it's time that you begin to serve your family some heaping helpings of Mom-first…and leave the leftovers for the fridge.

Be real.

OCTOBER 5

No More Pedestals

Hey Mom,

Awhile back, the homeschool world was rocked by the unfolding drama of a leader's fall. I'm not exaggerating when I write that I still feel the shock of it. I guess I'm not so shocked by the failings of the man but by how easily so many people were duped.

To clarify, I'm not even talking about those who were directly involved in the leader's ministry. I'm talking more specifically of all the people (usually homeschool moms) who looked in from the surface and thought to themselves, Wow, if only we could be like them.

Then one October day…KABOOM!!!

Here's the take away: what you see is not always reality. That means your elevation of friends, neighbors, homeschool buddies, and ministry leaders are not usually accurate or reasonable.

You must stop comparing lives and believing LIES. You must quit wanting to be like 'them' because the truth is 'them' aren't even like 'them.' What you see is not always what you get. This big homeschool scandal is a reminder of that. So stop idolizing people, following blindly, and pushing your family to be like 'them.'

Be who you are and like your family the way they are. And just in case you ever start to think too highly of me and my family…let me just set the record straight that we've got issues (just like you do)!!!

It's going to be a good day.

Be real.

They Keep Pounding

Hey Mom,

You know the thing about lies homeschooling moms believe is that they're so unrelenting. Like waves against the shore, they continue to pound day after day, month after month, year after year. They have the capability of undermining roads, homes, and cities with disastrous effects.

Oh, you can build walls, levees and dikes…but the waves are still there… POUNDING, looking for that one small crack or weakness to exploit.

My wife and I have dedicated the last ten years of our life reminding others of the TRUTH and yet…the lies pound away at us (especially her). Even the other day while I was in Boise, ID, my bride called and said she needed a little pep talk. She was falling for the lies.

It wasn't the lie that she was failing in homeschooling necessarily…just failing as a parent in general. I think the feeling was intensified because she was going to be around other family members, family members whose children didn't seem to struggle with 'issues' like some of ours.

"I mean they don't have children that have done this…" she said. "They won't understand…maybe we've failed in this area…their kids seem so understanding and easy…"

We talked and then I reminded her of what she already knew: that we can't control every aspect of all our kids' lives. They have to make choices and some will be different from ours (although we made some of the exact same choices back then that we're so bothered by now). We're not going to play the game of pretending everything is all neat and tidy, and we won't spend our days apologizing for their differences. We'll just talk about it, deal with it, and love our children no matter what.

I'm telling you, if you let those waves of 'assumed criticism' get to you, they will wash every ounce of joy from your life. So let the waves pound, but do not…I repeat, do NOT… believe those lies.

Keep praying, do the best you can, love your children, and don't apologize for them or their actions.

Be real.

OCTOBER 7

Home Disciples

Hey Mom,

I don't know about you, but I cringe every time I hear the word discipleship. I don't know what it is…it just feels so unattainable, especially as it pertains to family. I know what people mean by it. They just mean that it's important to train our children to be followers of Jesus. But when I see or hear the word all I can envision is working through a booklet, getting up really early, and tossing in the towel after a few days.

I'm thinking instead of calling it discipleship, we should just call it parenting. After all, that's what it really is…just plain old parenting. Discipleship sounds so…lofty, spiritual, and official. Parenting is so normal and you do it every day, 365 days of the year.

You don't have to go through a lesson guide, a discipleship program, or keep score. Just walk alongside your children every day and keep diligently pointing your children to God while you model trust, love, and service. Example is true discipleship…I mean parenting.

As one smart person once said, example isn't the main thing…it's the ONLY thing. He or she was right. Our children learn how to follow Jesus by watching and walking alongside us, as WE follow Jesus. It's like Deuteronomy 6, moms and dads teaching their children when they wake up, lie down, and go to the grocery store. It's everyday…it's…it's HOMESCHOOLING. You don't have to worry about how to do it, because you're already doing it,

So happy disciplining!

Be real.

OCTOBER 8

Never Forget

Hey Mom,

Any homeschooling family has my respect, but a military homeschooling family gets a double portion. If you fit into that category, thank you for making the sacrifice so the rest of us homeschoolers can practice the freedom of homeschooling. I can only imagine the extreme stress of having a husband who is sometimes gone for long periods of time. So thank you.

Now, a note to all you non-military homeschooling families: make sure you don't forget those who make sacrifices for our country and for the freedoms we enjoy, especially in the next couple of months. It's easy to over look them in all our busyness.

This time of year is a great time to be extra sensitive to their needs. Start by bringing their family to the attention of your children during school today. Get their thoughts on how your family could encourage them during Thanksgiving or Christmas.

You might adopt their family and take them special homemade goodies, pool your money and pay for their Christmas tree (someone once did it for us), invite them over for Thanksgiving dinner, or offer to watch the kids while their mom runs errands.

I know it would be easier to not do anything, but she's counting on you. Besides that kind of generosity is a huge lesson to teach your children. You can be thoughtful AND count it as school. Win win.

Be real.

OCTOBER 9

Kids & TV

Hey Mom,

TV is bad…but I love it. I know this sounds contradictory, but I was raised on television. I was fed a steady diet of educational television, was greeted by it when I stepped off the school bus each day, spent Saturday mornings glued to it, and gathered around it with my family each night like colonial families gathered around the fire.

So when my wife and I got married, one of our first purchases was a TV. Even though we guarded our eyes and our home, TV was the one porthole of sludge into our family. Even though we didn't watch crummy programs, they were still only a channel or two away. Plus TV was a huge time waster and when our children came along, we found they liked watching Barney (& a host of others) better than doing…anything.

So thus began our TV journey. During the course of the last 25 years we've gotten rid of our TV, got a new one, watched videos only, purchased Netflix, and have contemplated getting TV guardian. I guess what I've learned is that it just isn't as simple as I once thought.

I know my wife would like to get rid of it at times (except for HGTV) but…it's just not that easy. I do know that TV can still be a porthole of worldly sludge if we allow it to be. We still have to guard what comes in and limit the time our kids spend watching it. It's a battle that never ceases. And one that we need to talk to our kids about so that they make that battle their own.

It isn't easy...but parenting never has been (even when TV hadn't yet been invented).

Be real...and keep fighting the battle.

OCTOBER 10

Family Devotions

Hey Mom,

I heard somewhere that if you want to be a spiritual giant, you need to have family devotions. All the great men of the faith did, at least that's what everyone says. Apparently, they got up a couple of hours before dawn, gathered the family around the table, read the Scriptures for two hours, prayed for three, and then sang great hymns of the faith, while the children listened quietly as mice.

Well, this is one spiritual 'guppy' whose family devotions look more like a blue light special at K-Mart. One kid is standing on his head on the couch, one is hidden under a blanket, one is 'quietly' strumming a pint-sized guitar like the lead guitarist in a heavy metal group, and another woke up grumpy at life while I babble away like a Baptist missionary preaching to a bunch of Papua New Guinea natives who have no idea what I'm saying!!

We try singing, but it's hard to sing, yell at kids, and worship God at the same time. Sometimes I have to stop in order to send one child to the bathroom for me to deal with later. Finally, I ask one of my kids to close us in prayer before someone gets hurt. Amen.

Ahhh...wasn't that relaxing and uplifting? NOT!

So, you know what I'm going to do?

Try again tomorrow.

That's all I can do. I know spending time together as a family for 'devotions' is best. It must be because it's so hard, and all the good things are hard.

How about you? You up for God's best? Here are Todd's Tips for Semi-Successful Family Devotions:

1. Keep it short – think baby steps.
2. Ease into it. Why not just pray as a family? Take prayer requests, have different people pray, and that's all.
3. Make it simple-There is no magic recipe for making family devotions a piece of cake. Just read a few verses out of the Bible, talk about them, and pray.
4. Throw away all your expectations of heaven on earth.

5. Lastly, and this is the most important rule - Let your husband lead, and be satisfied with whatever he does. When he finishes, thank him and don't ask him for more. If he skips the next day or month, let him. But the next time he leads, thank him and don't ask for any more.

Be real.

OCTOBER 11

Don't Do It

Hey Mom,

My advice on comparing is: don't do it...ever! Don't compare yourself with your friends, the people you read about in homeschooling magazines and blogs, homeschool celebrities, or 'real schools.'

You see, what ends up happening is that you compare your weaknesses against others' strengths, and you can't win that game. So don't do it. You have plenty of gifts and strengths of your own, but you can't have every gift or strength.

Some like crafts - some don't. Some are organized - some aren't. Some did undergraduate work at MIT - some barely made it through high school. Instead of lamenting the fact that you're not what some are, thank God for your strengths and capitalize on them.

Now, as for comparing your homeschool to a 'REAL' school, why would you compare yourself with something that doesn't work? In fact, you know what? Public schools compare themselves to us. They know that one-on-one teaching is more effective and that real-life learning is more successful. They sit around in committees and try to make their school environment more like home. They have students plant gardens, hike through the woods, learn to cook, build stuff, and learn to relate to others. That's what you do everyday... and it's working.

So stop comparing yourself to them or anyone else. Ask God what He wants your school...I mean home to look like and then do it.

Now if only I can get my wife to stop comparing.

Be real!

Mom and the Time Demanders

Hey Mom,

It's been a fast and furious couple of weeks on the road. The RV has run like a dream, the speaking events have gone well, and the sun is shining as I type. Actually, it's just coming up as we sit in our favorite campground in Florida for a little R & R (not sure what that stands for…ranting and raving?).

You would think vacation would be an easy thing for a dad. It's just playing, right? Nothing to it, right? HA!!!! Nothing could be further from the truth. I'm thinking vacation might be the best testing ground for moms and dads. You have to set aside your ideas of fun, ease, and self. And that's hard for me.

I have all these Hallmark pictures of family burned into my imagination. The families are all smiling, laughing…frolicking. My family doesn't seem to frolic much. We specialize more in debating and mess making. Right now a couple of my kids are carving pumpkins into… accident victims. Their guts are spilled all over the concrete pad and our whole site is covered in bikes, wet towels, and junk!!! No Hallmark commercial here.

Maybe that's why I see so many moms and dads on their cell phones or computers here (as I type away on mine). It's easier than real life sometimes, but I can't help but feel like they're missing out on REAL life with REAL people…no matter how messy and time-demanding they may be.

In fact, I need to wrap this up and get back to my little time-demanders. The sun is barely up and they're raring to "go and do." So…I need to go and do.

You may not be on vacation…but your messy, time-demanding family still wants you at the helm and involved. Don't pull out and hide in your "staying-busy world," your phone, or on Facebook.

Be real.

Those Hard Kids

Hey Mom,

I may not know diddly about 'special needs kids', but I do know there are certain non-negotiable needs that ALL children, including special needs kids, need from their moms and dads.

So, special kids need…

To be loved unconditionally
To be liked unconditionally (which is way different)
To be shown how to trust in and follow God
To be corrected when behaving inappropriately
To be prepared for adulthood
To be shown they are not the center of the universe
To be shown forgiveness
To be shown patience
To be cuddled
To be chastised
To be tickled
To be told, "No"
To be told no matter what, "I will always love you"
...notice that I didn't even mention algebra or sentence diagramming?!

Be real.

OCTOBER 14

Relax!!!

Hey Mom,

The other day my wife was talking to...let's just say "another home-schooler." The conversation revolved around college and the plans she had for her soon-to-graduate child.

My wife summed up the woman's attitude toward steering her child in the college direction as...well...OBSESSED. She was bound and determined to get this kid into a specific college one way or the other. She was relentlessly pushing her son towards a better SAT score, a sports scholarship, and any other way she could think of to make sure he got into the college of her...er, I mean his choice.

My kids noticed it too and thought she was a little NUTS.

I'm not against college. I'm not against higher learning and institutional universities. BUT I am against putting a round peg into a square hole. Not only does it hurt the peg but it's also a losing proposition.

This particular kid has abilities, talents, and gifts, and wants to pursue a certain type of ministry, but all his mother can see is a specific COLLEGE and a specific degree (in something more versatile than what he wants to do)!!! She's so bent on that destination that she's pushing him into it, will most likely cause him to rack up debt (unless he gets that sport scholarship), and then doom him to a life of doing something he doesn't even want to do.

If this mom sounds like you, can I urge you to...RELAX? It's not your job to get your kid into college, trade school, or the work place. Your job is to fan the flames of passion, give them the tools to accomplish what they are made for, and allow them to grow up by failing or floundering.

The big LIE that has been perpetuated by politicians, leaders, and homeschoolers is that everyone needs to go to college and have a marketable degree. That, my fellow parent, is a bunch of malarkey. Not every kid needs to go to college in the same way that not every kid needs to speak Russian.

What are we doing here...squeezing our children into boxes? Some kids are made to fit the box...but some are not. Mom, let your child be what God wants him/her to be. Quit thinking it will look bad on YOU and quit letting fear of their future drive you to the point of obsession. Think only of what God would have for your child and then stand back and cheer him on. Don't tell him why he shouldn't...but why he should.

I'm telling you, that is FREEDOM and the recipe for joy and success. But it starts with you relaxing and leaving the results up to God.

Be real.

OCTOBER 15

Ounces, Pounds, Cups, and Pints

Hey Mom,

In my opinion, kitchen math should definitely be considered higher math. Like the song New York New York says, "If you can make it there...you'll make it anywhere."

No kidding. Advanced calculus has nothing on tripling a batch of sugar cookies. Not only is the math way over my head...but to add insult to injury, you have to clean up the dishes afterwards.

I know plenty of moms who may see the value of math as it is involved in the kitchen but would NEVER count it as real math. In fact, I have home schooling moms come up to me all the time to tell me how their children do all these real life 'math' applications but they're afraid to count it as real school.

Homeschoolers of the world, you can count almost anything as school... because almost everything IS school. If you want your children to bake cookies, cook dinner, or make a smoothie in lieu of math...DO IT!!! And don't feel guilty.

But they still have to clean up the kitchen.

Be real.

OCTOBER 16

History Is Not Dead

Hey Mom,

Unfortunately, I've got to make this quick. I'm sitting on the front porch of a friend's house on the side of a mountain in Las Cruces, NM. Being on the road, we get to see such neat people and cool things.

Just yesterday, we walked among the Petroglyphs at the Petroglyph National Monument, tomorrow we're going to White Sands National Monument, and the day after that, we'll go to Carlsbad Caverns. That's the great thing about RVing, we get to see history and geography alive.

Now you may not be able to travel around in an RV, but there are things to see and do within a couple hours drive of your house. In fact, my son told me about a cool phone app made by the folks at the History Channel that will tell you what great historical sites there are…where you are.

The important thing is to quit talking about it and do it.

Be real.

PS - check out these great websites: www.roadsideamerica.com and www.historical-sites.find-near-me.info

OCTOBER 17

Teachable Moments

Hey Mom,

You deserve a break today, so take one. Now, just because you take a break from school doesn't mean that you get a break from teaching. In fact, the best learning takes place when you're not doing school. It comes in the form of everyday lessons learned from teachable moments.

Just so there is no misunderstanding, I am NOT talking about contrived teachable moments that look and smell like school in disguise. "Let's go out into the back yard and play…and while we're there we'll draw pictures of what we see and then discuss it." Yuck.

What I'm talking about raking piles of leaves, the messes that need to be cleaned up, and the moments when someone is crying, stung, or afraid of the thunder and lightning. It is in those moments that we get unplanned opportunities for teaching.

By the way, you're teaching all the time as your children watch how you love your spouse, your children, and your neighbors. Those are especially life-impacting lessons.

Don't miss these because you're too busy getting your stuff done, thinking about school, or keeping things clean. Enjoy a little break, your children, and all those wonderful teachable moments.

Be real (what a great lesson).

OCTOBER 18

The Year of Freedom!!

Hey Mom,

Smell that? It's the smell of change...and it's blowing fresh upon the homeschooling world.

I know many of you heard the news about a homeschool leader that rocked the homeschool world recently. I don't know all the details, but I know that one of the bi-products it could produce is freedom to lots of well-meaning homeschoolers. It's time we stop believing that certain people have the 'magic formula' for family or homeschool success.

For years, many of you reading this article have trudged along trying to do all that 'the experts' told you to do...or NOT TO DO. You tried doing more, doing without, doing...doing...doing, with varying results accompanied by a deep sense of failure and thoughts that you should do more...and be better.

After this terrible...mess, it's time to say, "No more." It's time to put away guilt and condemnation for good and experience the freedom and joy of parenting and homeschooling again. The truth is not every family, homeschool, and parenting style looks the same. There are some who like to write out their family vision and some who don't give a hoot about a family vision. There are some parents who watch TV and some who don't. There are some homeschoolers who like classical style and some who don't. There are some mothers who like to wear dresses only and some who like to wear skinny jeans.

I know I should stop...because you get the idea, but I can't. There are some parents who celebrate Christmas and some who don't. There are some families that have family devotions and some who just can't seem to make it happen. Some wives like to cook gourmet and some like to eat out. Some kids grow up with homemade oatmeal and others grow up with Frosted Flakes, and we need to stop judging people for not doing what we do and stop following people who feed us that line of thinking.

The only common denominator among us all is that we are God's children and that we all struggle in family and homeschooling. I'm telling you there is freedom in that truth.

It's time to set aside false expectations, appearances, and comparisons and make this year, the year of freedom. Be what God has called you to be and enjoy and appreciate your husband and children for who God created THEM to be without trying to change them.

And the next time you hear anyone telling you how to have the perfect homeschool, family, or marriage, RUN AWAY!!! That's the thing about us homeschool freaks, we're prone to following rule givers. My fear is that we will not have learned our lesson and are prime targets for the next 'expert' who comes along peddling his 'godly formula for family success.'

Take a whiff and have a great day!

Be real.

OCTOBER 19

Mama Said There Would Be Days Like These

Hey Mom,

Mom, there will be days when your homeschool blows up…your kids will see you at your worst and you'll feel like tossing in the towel. You'll think to yourself, this can't be good for my children…they'd be better off in REAL school.

Here's a survival secret: don't quit. Ask forgiveness and take some time to rebuild relationships, but don't abandon ship and give up on homeschooling. The truth is everyone has bad days (or weeks)…EVERYONE!!! Don't believe that lie that says you are the only one that does. The thing about doing something worthwhile is that worthwhile things are HARD.

But here's what God says about the hard times: "You will reap a reward IF you do not grow weary and stop" (Galatians 6:9). That's a promise…a promise to you.

I've seen too many homeschoolers hit the rough spots, give up, stick their kids in school…and then regret it. In fact, I've had them come up to me and say, "I thought I had problems before, but when I put my kids in school we ended up with way bigger problems."

Mom, you may be going through a hard patch right now (as in today). Keep swimming. Ask forgiveness, repair the relationship(s), and assess areas that are causing added stress, but never give up.

And know this: YOU ARE NOT ALONE.

Be real.

OCTOBER 20

You Don't Gotta

Hey Mom,

Whew! The trailer is loaded and we're about ready to embark on another tour of homeschool conferences and another family adventure. Actually, I feel a little like a chicken with my head cut off as I run from one last minute project to another...all the while crossing paths with my headless chicken wife who is doing the same.

Tomorrow it won't matter...because we'll be on the road and it will all be behind us. We've already had a couple of great conventions, and I look forward to a long string of others. I hope you're planning to attend your local homeschool convention.

There is nothing better than walking the aisles surrounded by scads of other homeschoolers. Somehow it's encouraging to know we're all in it together. My one bit of advice as you go into it is: don't feel like you have to do what they say you should do.

I mean those homeschool vendors will be on you like buzzards on a gut-wagon. You've got to use this...gotta do this...think through this...be able to master this...AND do it in LATIN!!!!

Here's the deal, you don't got to use that...do that...think through that... master that...or do it in Latin...if you don't want to or think it's best. Those experts have nothing on you when it comes to knowing or teaching your children. In fact, they come in a distant second to your personal expertise. So don't let them (or me) coerce you into doing what they think is best.

You do what you think is best and don't for one second feel guilty about it. I met too many homeschooling moms this past weekend who know what they believe is best...but felt hog-tied into doing something different just because of the pressure. So stand strong, mom!!!

Be real.

OCTOBER 21

You Think You've Got Problems

Hey Mom,

Sometimes when you're in the midst of the muck, you just need to step back and get a little perspective. This especially helps with homeschooling, because you believe the lie that you're ruining your children and that they would be better off if you "stuck them in school."

Now I know the truth, and I could tell you the truth, but I think the truth sounds louder when someone else speaks it without even knowing it. That truth speaker was my neighbor's daughter.

They've been our neighbors for the last 17 years but have been 'frail' the last several years. This winter was hard on them and a month ago the husband, who is suffering from dementia, fell and broke his hip. Since then, my wife has been pretty involved in their life and been on the phone many times with one of their adult daughters. In fact, it was one of those daughters who was the perspective giver.

She was the daughter our neighbor always compared to us. "She's got SEVEN children and she homeschools too," she would often say in her quick, Hispanic-accented dialect.

A while back, my wife was on the phone with that daughter and she said something like, "Yeah, I used to homeschool, but I didn't think I could handle it anymore so I put them all in school and pretty much ruined their lives." Those were her exact words, "RUINED their lives."

She didn't elaborate but from where she now stood, she saw that homeschooling was good for her children and "sticking them in school" was not only not good for them…but even RUINED their lives she felt. Wow, those are strong words and give the weary homeschooling mom (AKA – YOU) some perspective.

Be real.

OCTOBER 22

Online Learning

Hey Mom,

Here are the ground rules for today's article on On-line learning:

1. I am not going to talk about the many evils and dangers of the internet, Facebook, or the techno-beast*.

2. I am going to restrict my comments toward higher learning…specifically, post high-school.

Now that that's done, let me begin by saying, "Colleges and Universities BEWARE!!!! On-line learning is going to put many of you out of business."

We live in a time of great educational change. I have witnessed firsthand the on-line shift with two of my children. My oldest, Ben (21), has a BA through an accredited online university. He completed it in about two and half years at a fraction of the cost with no debt. Now I would never say that it is better than a traditional university...but it is EQUIVALENT.

Those who argue otherwise...are blowing smoke. I have a traditional degree (as well as a master's) and my son's degree is no less than mine. It involved hard work and diligence (mine didn't).

But that's not my only exposure. My second son, Sam (20) is just a few months away from completing an on-line, post-highschool program with Animation Mentor. Without going into all the details, it is taught by animators at major studios with the purpose of training animators for the industry.

It is an amazing program, and my son has excelled in it. But here's the deal: MOST of his classmates have already completed an art degree (some in computer animation). And according to the grading scale, he has surpassed most of them (he's homeschooled after all).

Here's my point: Online study is going to rule the higher education world. It's more efficient, more focused, and more practical for this world in which we live, BUT it is not for everyone. Your child might need to go a traditional route, or a non-school route, a trade route...a paper route.

The philosophy that works for homeschooling in elementary and highschool also works for higher learning. Don't believe me? Just wait a few years and you'll see it offered everywhere.

Be real.

**Feel like the techno-beast has taken over your home? Check out our Taming the Techno-Beast Combo (for parents and a student workbook). It's time to get control before it consumes your family.*

OCTOBER 23

The Power of Birthday Cake

Hey Mom,

Hope you're enjoying some nice fall weather in your neck of the woods (North Dakota moms...sorry).

We just celebrated my son Abe's birthday on Tuesday and it was a great day. You know, every kid should have a birthday. For us, it's the one day of the year when they are king...and the world revolves around them.

They get to pick their own favorite breakfast, eat what they want for lunch, eat candy throughout the day, do something special for dinner, open gifts, and stay up late watching a special video that they've been looking forward to while eating popcorn (with extra butter).

I know for Abe it was a great day, not so much because of all the stuff we did but that he was the center of our attention. It seems that certain kids tend to blend into the crowd; they're easy-going and don't demand your attention so they're easy to overlook. Abe is that kid.

Actually his birthday reminded me that I need to work harder at spending time just with him. For lunch, he chose to go to Golden Corral. So the two of us went, stuffed ourselves silly, and talked the entire time.

Throughout the day, his mom played games with him, and we made extra efforts to tell him how great he is and how glad we are to be his parents.

By the end of the day, I could tell he was overwhelmed by our love AND by his love for his mom and dad. He must have hugged us each a half-dozen times and said, "I love you soooo much," and he meant it. That's what birthdays do...and every kid should have one.

So Mom, got a kid's birthday coming up? Make it a good one. Even if you don't, spend a little extra time with that easy-to-overlook child of yours. Take him to breakfast or lunch, play a game with just him, or stay up watching a video together.

After all, he loves you soooo much.

Be real.

OCTOBER 24

Exit Stage Left

Hey Mom,

I'm not sure where, but somewhere I heard that actors are taught how to 'make an entrance.' The phrase got me thinking that maybe dads need to learn how to... 'make an EXIT.'

It all started a couple of weeks ago. I was speaking in Cleveland and was busily gathering my stuff in the morning to hit the road in time to stop by the Christmas Story House.

I said my quick goodbyes and then dashed to the car, slammed the door shut, slipped into reverse and started backing up. That's when I looked up and saw my son Abe standing outside the front door holding four fingers up for me to see (I – love – you – more).

At that instant, I forgot all about my destiny with A Christmas Story House and my speaking engagement...and only saw my son with his four fingers sticking up and a soft lump lodged in my throat. I jerked the car to a stop, rolled down the window and yelled out, "I LOVE YOU ABE!!!"

He smiled and went back inside feeling safe, satisfied, and loved. We had said goodbye the right way. Nothing was left unsaid...or undone. I thought about that on my drive east and even since then. I imagined being killed in a car wreck and never coming home…but having left things 'done.'

I can't always say that. Sometimes I run out without saying goodbye and my wife is upset with me, the kids are out of sorts, and I storm out, glad to be gone. Then I imagine…what if? What if something happened to them or to me and I neglected to say, "Goodbye and I love you?"

It happens all the time. Moms tiptoe out the door to go to the grocery, to a friend's house, or to Wal-mart…and never come home. Gaping holes are left behind that could have been avoided had MOM just said goodbye.

So, my fellow busy parent, can I encourage you to 'make a good exit?' Maybe you're about to head off to the store. Slow down, say your goodbyes and I love you's, and hold them tight and make sure everything is left…done.

Be real.

OCTOBER 25

Feeling Like a Baby Water Buffalo

Hey Mom,

I don't mean to complain, but sometimes I feel like a baby water buffalo surrounded by a pack of hyenas. Everyone gets a mouthful of skin and then starts tugging. The biggest usually wins, and the baby water buffalo always loses.

Now that may be a tad graphic, but as a homeschooling mom I bet you get my point.

Sitting in my office, I can hear one of the hyena's footsteps right outside the door. The door flies open and my son blurts out, "Hey Dad, when can you help me make my shelf?"

I return the 'blurt' with the first answer that comes to mind, hoping to loosen his grasp, "Later." He walks away…for now.

Earlier, they were biting and pulling, "Dad, can you play a game with me? Dad, can you wipe me? Dad, can you take me to Wal-mart? Dad,…."

"I have a job here, people!!!" I feel like shouting. "What do I look like…a baby water buffalo chew toy!!??" I don't say that though. Instead, I get snappy and put them off, hoping…hoping that they'll forget what they asked of me but knowing…they'll be back. They always come back.

My fellow chew toy, I know you feel pulled a dozen directions by family, homeschool, and other responsibilities, but not everything that pulls…matters. The important thing is to do what…does.

Get back in there. I gotta go build a shelf.

Be real.

Heart and Smarts

Hey Mom,

It's interesting to me that we often view character and academics like they're two Middle-Earth foes battling it out for dominance. I think we have that idea because someone, somewhere, told us that we should teach character as a subject, in the same way other academics are taught.

And so the problem arises, how do I have time for both? What if I do one at the neglect of the other? What if I make a mistake and doom my child to a life of stupidity or worse, moral shipwreck?

Here's the deal: character isn't taught in the same way as academics, but it is often taught while we teach academics. The truth is: character is taught all the time…and you're the teacher. Your children are watching and learning as you shop at Wal-mart, run errands, make a meal, clean the house, do your taxes, and interact with your husband. They see what brings you joy and how you handle hardship. They listen to your words, catch your attitude, imitate your actions, and observe what you value.

When you make academics your main emphasis, you ARE teaching them character. You are showing them that what really matters in life is NOT how they behave or the relationships that they have, but what they know.

Academics are needed, but they are not what matter most. How does that look in your homeschool? You open up the books and do your lessons, but you don't measure your children by their achievement. You take breaks happily when people need you, and you see homeschooling as a wonderful opportunity to spend time with your children 'teaching' character.

One of my wife's favorite quotes is: Children are great imitators. So give them something great to imitate.

Have a great day with your family!

Be real.

OCTOBER 27

Get Your Nose Out of the Phone

Hey Mom,

I don't really mean to be an anti-technology nag, but every once in a while I just can't help myself. In fact, I feel a little like Popeye when twisted into a pretzel by his arch-nemesis Bluto. Something snaps in the normally pleasant sailor and he announces, "That's all I can stand, I can't stands no more!" He swallows a can of spinach and then springs into action.

The Bluto in my life is a nameless lady that I saw in our local Subway a couple of weeks ago. I wouldn't have noticed her had it not been for her Dakota Fanning-looking daughter with stringy, bleach blonde hair who sat next to her swinging her feet happily.

As I watched the little girl sit, eat, and look around, I noticed that her mother sat there fixed on her iPhone typing away and reading messages. In fact, during the entire time, I'm not sure she said one word to her daughter. And then we left.

Last week, I was back at Subway with my bride and the pair was back... stringy blonde hair, iPhone in hand. This time I paid close attention to the girl and her mom and can verify that the mother did not say ONE word to her little daughter as she stared at her phone.

At one point, the girl even said something to her mother and she never responded. I had half a mind to say," That's all I can stand..." and walk over to the mom and kindly add, "Your daughter who is right beside you needs you way more than some Facebook post or 'friend' living in Timbuktu."

I didn't, but I wish I would have had the guts to. I'd be doing her a favor. I'd be doing them all a favor if I kindly remind those iPhone zombie parents that they're missing out on God's best...and stealing precious time from their children.

That's why I'm writing you today, Mom...to tell you to stay off your phone when your spouse or children are in your presence. Fight the urge to check, post, or respond. Wait until you're alone, go to the bathroom, or chuck the phone off a cliff. I know I should mind my own business...but I'm feeling very Popeye-ish.

Be real.

OCTOBER 28

Because You Love Them

Hey Mom,

I think I could be a truly happy dad...if...if only...my dog would drop dead. If you're a pet lover, I'm sorry to sound so harsh, but I just don't like our little Chihuahua, Chewy. I'll spare you the details, but he has issues. A few of my kids actually love the animal, but not me. In fact, they know I'm not... uh...fond of the little guy and run to his defense when I'm ready to 'vent'.

I know I should at least pretend to like him for their sake and was even bothered a little when a dad-friend of mine chided me for not loving the dog… for them.

"No, way," I said to myself…"not that dog!!!"

Then yesterday, my son Abe came up to me and asked, "Dad, how do you spell Chewy?"

A few minutes later he asked how to spell, barks at strangers.

"What are you writing, a for sale sign?" I jokingly asked.

He just smiled and asked a few more spelling questions. On the last word, I looked over his shoulder and saw him writing a paragraph in his best handwriting about our dog that I hate. I expected a jumble of words and was startled to see a warmly written memory of one boy's dog and how much he loved him. It listed his guard dog qualities and how much he liked sitting in the big bear chair in the sun. It was like he just wanted to be able to remember his dog when he was older.

That's when I thought, I need to love that stupid dog…because my son loves that dog.

So, Mom, let me say to you, "You need to love that stupid ______ because your child loves that _______.

Be real.

OCTOBER 29

No Giving or Taking

Hey Mom,

I remember the good old days when as a kid we use to go trick or treating in our suburban neighborhood in Indianapolis, IN. It was just so much fun. Back then I didn't know Satan had anything to do with it. We didn't know anyone who looked down on trick-or-treating. Everyone did it…and it was fun.

Now, Halloween seems to be a determining factor in one's salvation. Some folks do it and other folks shun the idea, refusing to acknowledge the day. The most spiritual of them all call it Reformation Day instead. For the record: we've done it all.

Here's the deal Mom; if you like to trick-or-treat on Halloween, go and have fun and stop feeling guilty about it. I know one year I took my kids out and my wife said, "Don't take them by so-and-so's house." We knew they didn't do Halloween and hid in their basement to avoid the 'evil ones'.

On the other hand if you don't like Halloween, go ahead and skip the day, do what your family normally does, and then let others do what they do… without heaping any guilt on them.

When someone asks you to go trick-or-treating with them just say, "That sounds like fun, but we don't do Halloween. Thanks for asking and I hope you get a ton of candy."

Here's a side note, to all you non-halloweeners. For years, my wife and I hosted a little oasis in our very busy Halloween town. We opened our garage, served coffee, hot chocolate and powdered doughnuts. It was a great outreach to our neighborhood. Just an idea.

Be real.

OCTOBER 30

I Needed That

Hey Mom,

The sun is shining…finally. For the last several days, we felt like Noah in his ark…his dripping, leaking ark. I'm telling you, we have been in a torrential downpour from Tulsa to Atlanta. I've got drips dripping from spots that never leaked before…more items for my fix-it list. And yesterday morning, I noticed that one of my tires was flat.

God was gracious…again…and thirty minutes later we had a new (reasonably priced) tire.

Is it just me, or does life seem hard sometimes? The days seem gray, the problems unending…and then it gets harder. That's how it was last Saturday in Tulsa. Almost from the moment I woke up, things went from bad to worse. Oh, nothing was leaking, but everyone in my RV seemed to be mad at me.

I can't remember all the details, but my wife was upset, my children were on edge, and I was freaking out because I had to speak in 30 minutes!!! In fact, one of my kids did something, and I chewed him up and spit him out crying. Then, ten seconds later I apologized from the pit of my heart and he forgave me…but I was a quivering blob of a crummy dad as I gathered my notes and walked to the room where I was suppose to speak.

That's when God sent me a reminder of how good I had it. As I picked up my notes, a half sheet of paper slipped to the side. I LOVE YOU was printed in big red marker. I knew my son Abe had written it because he's always writing me notes about how much he loves me. But somehow this particular note penetrated the gloom of my heart like a shot of sunlight.

"Todd," God seemed to say, "yes, it may be hard…but it is good and they love you…in spite of yourself."

Mom, parenting, marriage, or life might be hard right now, but let me remind you as I was reminded, "It is still GOOD."

Be real.

OCTOBER 31

Thanks Mr G

Hey Mom,

There's just so much to do when you'll be gone for three months. It seems that for every item I check off the list, I think of two more. Oooh, I just thought of another. On top of that, the kids don't seem to FEEL the weight of packing and leaving. In fact, Maggie has come up to me twice as I type this to ask me what color a princess's bow is in some movie (she's coloring).

You know, it's hard being a familyman...trying to do the important (like helping Maggie) and still do the things that need to get done (like replacing the drain plug on the RV's water heater). Maybe the hard thing is remembering which matters and which doesn't.

A couple days ago it was so clear.

You see, every Tuesday morning for the last twelve years, I've had breakfast with Mr. G. A week ago, he died. The funeral was Monday. The church was packed and there wasn't a dry eye in the place. He was loved and will be missed by so many.

As I sat up on the platform, I had the unique perspective of watching everyone's face as they listened to some of his daughters, grandchildren and friends share fond memories. At that moment it was crystal clear; I knew what was important. God, my wife, my family, and friends. RVs, lawnmowers, cars, and Familyman Ministries didn't even enter the equation.

If only I could remember that daily...if only YOU could remember that. If only you could remember that doing that thing with your son is more important than the math lesson you need to cover, and that spending time helping your husband on his thing is more important than the project that is consuming your thoughts...if only...

Whether we remember it or not...it's still the truth.

Be real.

NOVEMBER 1

The Election

Hey Mom,

Election time is where the homeschool rubber meets the road. Do we really believe God sets up kings and presidents and that "He's got the whole world in

His hands"? Or, do we show our children by our gloom and doom predictions that all we've taught them about God is a bunch of hooey (to use the Greek word)? To hear some Christians talk, you'd think that God steps down from His throne every November election day.

We can teach them all we want about God through reading the Scriptures and memorizing Bible verses...BUT they LEARN the most from the way we live when 'school' is not in session.

We don't watch TV, but on Election Day we plan to plug in the TV and watch the presidential coverage. I'm sure we'll cheer on our favorite...but afterwards, no matter who walks away as winner, we will pray for our new president and thank God for setting him in place.

Here's one more thing to think about...the absolute truth is that what takes place in YOUR house is way more important than what happens in the White House.

Be real...and trust God.

NOVEMBER 2

The Blah Days to Come

Hey Mom,

The best time for family fun is during the winter. Even as I write this, the Wilson family is celebrating our very first snowfall. Now don't be impressed. All we do is pick up some inexpensive wintry gifts, have dinner at Long John Silver's (don't ask), and enjoy hot chocolate and a warm fire as we savor one of the best things that God has given us— family.

We started off the morning by reading Isaiah 1:18 about being washed as white as snow. As on every first snowfall, I remind them about the theology of snow and how God 'might' have created it just to give us something to compare our 'purity' to.

Here's the deal about family fun time; my children may not remember my theological teachings, but they'll never forget how important they are to me. I can just imagine that when they have children or grandchildren of their own (when I'm no longer here) that they'll look out the window and see snow falling like feathers from the sky. They'll walk outside, feel the bite of cold on their skin, see the falling snow and think not only about how their sins have been washed white as snow...but also how much their dad loved the first snow and how much he loved them.

I'm telling you Mom...your kids won't feel that way about your math lessons or much of your homeschooling, but they will feel it about family nights with videos and popcorn, board game nights and make your own sundaes, or spending the whole day reading a book, baking cookies, or decorating the house for Christmas.

So...let me encourage you to spend your day today doing what's most important...having some family fun.

Be real.

NOVEMBER 3

Find a Smiley Way!

Hey Mom,

We were enjoying some family R&R recently when my sister-in-law told me about a friend of hers who was thinking about not homeschooling.

Honestly I was shocked, not because I think you have to homeschool to be in the center of God's will, but because I knew this mom. If there was anyone who 'looked' the part of a homeschooler, it was her.

I knew her plate was full…I mean really full. Not only did her youngest child need 24/7 full-time care because of his condition, but their family was also facing other hardships on top of that. My sister-in-law said her friend felt like she was letting her kids down…like she wasn't doing a very good job. That's what led her to the conclusion that she might have to give up on homeschooling.

Now, I'm not going to talk to her, but I will give the same advice to you that I would give to her. If you believe in homeschooling but feel like you're failing or hate every minute of it, THEN find a different way to homeschool!!!!

Maybe, just maybe, trying to do 'school' in your home doesn't work. The truth is trying to do school in SCHOOL doesn't work. It's a failed method and system so quit trying to copy it.

Instead, do it the way YOU want/need to do it. If you just want to sit around and read to the kids then do it. If you want them to watch educational DVDs then do it. If you want to do workbook pages, then do it. If you want them to experience life with a family (even a sick child) then do it.

Homeschooling is God's idea, and He didn't make it that hard. Yes, it's daily and has unrelenting challenges, but it should still be enjoyable (except when it's not). So if you feel like giving up but still believe in homeschooling, THEN find a different way to do it. And quit worrying about what everyone else will think.

Be real.

Flash them THE FOUR

Hey Mom,

Got back from sunny…wwaaarrrmmm Tampa, FL this week with a slight sunburn and then was slapped in the face with freezing cold, Indiana snow. The snow piles are mountainous and the temperatures brutal.

Even with the wickedly cold temperatures, the kids have been tunneling through the plowed piles around our driveway. I go outside and their heads pop up like snow-covered prairie dogs.

Two evenings ago, I was on the second floor looking down on them from the warmth of the house watching them play. My son Ike (14) was laying in the snow…just thinking about…snow. I can remember the exact feeling of lying in the snow…in the cold…in the twilight, when all the sounds were muffled and the air crisp.

At some point he looked up and saw me through the window. I waved and smiled. He looked up and smiled, and then he felt a sudden warmness and held up four fingers with his gloved hand. I smiled again and held up four warm fingers.

To anyone looking on, it would have looked like a wave of the hand, but to Ike and I, we had communicated I love you more without uttering a word. And it felt good.

For the last several years, FOUR fingers has been a signal for I Love You More at our house. It use to be three fingers which meant I Love You…but somewhere along the way Ike turned it into a FOUR fingerer.

Now, every night we exchange 'Four Fingers'. In fact, some of them can't go to bed unless I've flashed "The Four."

Here's the deal, Mom; signals are important. They allow parents and their children to communicate how much they love each other without uttering a word. It comes in handy at airports, school plays, wedding days, big gatherings…and on snowy days when words don't work through a window.

If you don't have a signal…get one…and then use it tonight.

Be real.

iMom

Hey Mom,

I hope you're doing great; I'm feeling a little somber. It started last night as we were gathered in the family room to watch one of the original Anne of Green Gables movies. My oldest son Ben walked into the room and announced, "Steve Jobs just died."

I imagine it was a little like that evening in the 60's when they announced that Walt Disney had died. Ben is my techno-kid, so for the last 2-3 years he's kept us abreast on all the latest Apple inventions and upgrades, Apple stock, and the news that Apple passed Exxon as the most valuable company in the world.

Today, the tech-world is eulogizing him…recounting his story, his unique personality, and the gizmos he invented that have helped shape the modern world.

To tell you the truth, I can't stop thinking how all he worked for, sacrificed for, and cared about…didn't really matter in the end. Don't get me wrong. I think all the iGadgets are cool, but I would just about bet that he wasn't thinking about iGadgets during his last few moments.

In fact, his name will soon fade (my little kids didn't know Walt Disney was a real person), and someone else will control the iUniverse.

The truth is that some things matter and some things don't…iThings don't matter but iMoms and iWives DO.

So, Mom, go love your husband and children…and change the world!

Be iReal.

NOVEMBER 6

Early Stages and Beyond!

Hey Mom,

I don't know what it is about writing an article in a magazine or book that makes others think you're an expert, but I'll try my best not to disappoint. In your mind try to picture me sitting in my leather, wingback chair. I'm wearing a tweed jacket and a brown bow-tie. My glasses are perched on the end of my nose, with legs crossed, and I'm speaking in quiet, professional tones. Let's begin.

Every child goes through different stages of learning and life. The hectic, early years can be exhausting and overwhelming. But there are four definite things that parents, especially dads, need to do to provide them with as the building blocks of success.

First and foremost you need to love them unconditionally. That means no matter what...with no strings attached. You are patient when you'd like to scream. You forgive quickly, even when they don't ask for forgiveness and restore the relationship when it's been strained. You don't withhold yourself when they've made messes, disobeyed, or can't seem to get what you're trying to teach them. You love them...no matter what!

Secondly you need to listen with your eyes. Whenever your child is talking to you, you need to stop doing what you're doing, look them in the eyes, and work to make what's important to them...important to you. And when I say 'work' I mean work, because it is work to listen. I know Lego creations, dolls clothes, or playhouse arrangements may not seem important, but when you sincerely listen, you convey to the child who is talking that he or she IS more important than whatever you're doing at the moment.

Thirdly, you need to smile often. This may be a tough one because sometimes in the midst of homeschooling and life you don't feel like smiling. You have important stuff to do and children get in the way. Can I ask you a question? When was the last time you smiled at your young child? Smiles are powerful and when you smile it says, "I like you and I like being with you."

Fourthly, you need to show physical affection. Whether you grew up in a touchy-feely family or not, your child needs you to hold, hug, and touch them. Girls and boys have the same need and without physical affection bad things can happen. As a dad that might mean wrestling on the floor, putting them in a head lock from time to time, or pulling your little girl up on your lap.

Now as your children enter the teen years they move into different stages with felt needs as well. Now they need you to...love them unconditionally, listen with your eyes, smile often, and show physical affection.

This may not look exactly the same as when they were younger and may even be a little bit more difficult, but the need is greater than ever.

Then as your children move into adulthood they move into a final prolonged stage. Guess what they need from you? Bingo. They need you to love them unconditionally, listen with your eyes, smile often, and show physical affection.

Mom, sometimes we get so bombarded with differing opinions that we forget what really matters. I'm telling you, as I remove my bow-tie, each of your children need these four things from you. They need them as toddlers, teenagers, and beyond. If you do the things mentioned above, you will have prepared them for success and will have assured healthy, loving children who will in turn be able to love and train their children. Those four things provided at all stages of childhood can change the world.

Be real.

Don't Be a Bumper Sticker Mom

Hey Mom,

I love the open road. In fact, I think inside every man is a truck driver wanting out. I especially like sitting behind the wheel of our big Familyman Mobile on a cool summer evening (my kids know it's my favorite time to drive). There's just so much to see as you crisscross across this great country of ours.

Now I'm not just talking about wonderful destinations like Gettysburg, Valley Forge, or Gravity Hill. I like the actual highway sites…the old rusty Pacer that still runs the road, the vanity plate that proclaims GR8DAD, and all those wonderful bumper stickers that give you a glimpse into each car owner's life.

Actually, I just saw one while tooling through Chicago a couple of days ago that not only caught my eye, but also struck a nerve in the deep dad-recesses of my mind. The bumper sticker was just three words on a plain background, but it spoke volumes.

-Deer Hunter's Widow

At first I wasn't quite sure what it meant, but then I realized that a longer version would be, "My husband is gone so much during deer hunting season that it feels like I'm all alone in our marriage."

I'm sure the person bought it as a joke, but I felt myself getting mad as I stared at the tail end of that car. In fact, I had half a mind to follow the car to its home and chew out the guy for abandoning his family in favor of sitting out in the woods with a bunch of buddies and white-tailed deer.

As the car pulled away, I began thinking of similar bumper stickers that might have a market.

-Golfer's Widow
-Businessman's Widow
-Pastor's Widow
-Football Fan's Widow
-Internet User's Widow
-TV Watcher's Widow

I was on a role and intended to write an email to my dad friends regarding my thoughts when I thought of one more…

-Homeschooler's Widower

The disconcerting truth is that homeschooling can be such an all consuming activity that husbands get left alone to fend for themselves. Oh, the homeschooling mom may make time to feed, clean, and care for the basic needs of her husband…but she's not really there.

Her thoughts are always on school, lessons, achievements, and failures. They may share an occasional moment of intimacy but her mind is simultaneously thinking, "If I drop off Tiffany at piano at 3:30pm, I can probably get back home in time to finish up a science experiment with Josh and read Michael the last chapter of his book.

She may think she's doing a great job balancing all her duties…but her husband feels like a widower, last on the list of her priorities.

To bring this a little closer to home, ask yourself if YOUR husband could feel like a homeschool widower? Some of the symptoms are: half-joking remarks he makes about how you're always thinking about homeschooling or the kids, a lack of commitment to his family, or even resentment towards homeschooling itself.

Men feel and say these things because they feel like they have lost their spouses to homeschooling. Now I know you might be thinking he needs to get over it because homeschooling does take a lot of time (read – all your time). After all, you can't just throw an education together. It takes planning, time, and effort, and you just don't have enough time to meet all his needs. He just needs to grow up and deal with it.

If you're thinking something like that, let me remind you that God called you to love your husband (Titus 2:4) not your homeschool. I can run down through a mental list of several moms who loved their homeschool at the neglect of their marriages and when that happens, homeschooling doesn't quite seem so important anymore.

But here's the good news: It's easy to lift the lid from the homeschool coffin and climb back out of the grave. Your husband doesn't need all your time and energies…he just needs to feel like he's your #1 priority.

Here's what I suggest: Start today. Draw school to a close a little earlier, fix his favorite meal, have the kids help clean up before dad gets home, put on one of his favorite outfits, give him a steel-melting kiss when he walks in the door, and linger in his arms.

After dinner, forget about grading papers and planning lessons, and instead give your man some of your undivided attention. Ask about his day, snuggle up in his arms, watch a movie together, or dish him up a big bowl of ice cream.

I'm telling you, it doesn't take that much to move a husband out of the homeschooling widower category into the madly in love with his wife and family category. He just needs YOU to make him a priority, to care more about him than you do about your curriculum, your progress, the latest gadget available on the internet, and…school.

If you do that, then he won't need a Homeschool Widower bumper sticker… he'll get one that says, MY Wife Homeschools and She's My Hero.

Be real.

NOVEMBER 8

No Matter Who Lives in THAT House

Hey Mom,

I'm dragging a little today after my big birthday celebration. It's not that we painted the town (especially at my age)...it's just that every single member of my family, including me, is under-the-weather. It's nothing serious, just the common, congestion-hacking-droopy sails, kind of cold. Hopefully today's looking a little clearer, and we can pick up a little steam.

Anyway, hope you survived the election. Although it didn't turn out like I had hoped, the world goes on spinning. Really, no matter who occupies that house on Pennsylvania Avenue, I still have a job to do. I have to get up every morning and be 'da dad.

I can't bemoan which party is in control, what the economy is like, or what catastrophe looms on the horizon...I'm still 'da dad. I have a job to do: to love my wife and to love, train, and prepare my children. Whew...I think it would be easier to bemoan.

So, Mom, if you're all bent out of shape and gloomy, suck it up and get back in the game. Plan something fun for this weekend. Plan a date with your husband, rent a family movie, or get pizza and have a game night. Then, at the end of your time, thank God for still being in control...because HE is.

Be real.

NOVEMBER 9

Busy Wasting Your Time

Hey Mom,

Got back from speaking in Escondido, CA and am on my way right now to speak in Lansing, MI (talk about whiplash). The RV is primed and ready. I got the new water heater and water pump installed and have crossed off all my RV fix-it projects. New week we're off to Winston-Salem, NC...

Right now I'm super busy packing, fixing, and doing. My kids don't seem to recognize that and as I'm up to my eyeballs in busyness one will often shout to me, "Hey Dad, can you play basketball with us...can we play kick-ball... can we go on a bike ride?"

I usually answer, "I'm busy right now." I explain how this is important stuff and they walk away without complaint, but deep down, I know I'm exchanging stuff that matters for stuff that doesn't.

So hear me loud and clear, Mom (I'm talking to myself as well). The next time one of your kids says, "Hey Mom can we…will you…," drop the unimportant stuff you're doing (even if it's school) and say, "Yes!"

Is that hard to do? You bet. Does it come naturally? Never. But do it anyway.

Be real.

NOVEMBER 10

A 100-Year Vision

Hey Mom,

Sometimes in the midst of homeschooling, we forget that we're impacting the future. We get so bogged down in math facts, reading lists, and curriculum that we forget that what we do matters not only for our children but also for our great grandchildren. In fact, that's what the passage in Psalm 78 implies:

"But tell to the generation to come the praises of the Lord,
…That they should teach them to their children,
That the generation to come might know, even the children yet to be born,
That they may arise and tell them to their children,
That they should put their confidence in God and not forget the works of God, but keep His commandments…"

Talk about impacting the future…and the children of children yet to be born. It reminds me of the old preacher who was asked by a young father, "When should I start training my children?" He thought about it for a moment and then answered, "100 years before they're born."

Mom, listen up right now. What you do with your children in your home TODAY affects people, communities, and governments 100 years from now.

Hard to believe when you're up to your eyeballs in poopy diapers and bad attitudes, but it is truth. So get back in there and change the world!!!

Be real.

The Dark Side

Hey Mom,

I'm afraid that in the quest to "do family right" many homeschoolers have forgotten what IS right and the results are horrifying.

The sudden exposure of a recent homeschool leader scandal revealed an ugly trend that has developed over the last several years. Parents have devotedly followed 'leaders' who set unrealistic standards, impossible goals, and offered simplistic solutions to complex situations. As a result, they parented and homeschooled out of fear and control.

I see a significant group within our circles who are tossing homeschooling out with the garbage.

The more I probed, the more people I found talking horribly about homeschooling.

Sadly, the biggest trash-talkers were NOT non-homeschoolers who have always misunderstood us, but our own children who were homeschooled for much of their growing up years.

These bitter homeschooled kids are using what happened as a reason to TOSS IT ALL OUT!!!!

May it never be!!! Many of us ARE guilty as charged of blindly following leaders who seemed to have all the answers. We did put undo pressures on our children. We did live in fear of doing 'it' wrong. We did put 'school' ABOVE the relationship with our children. We did falsely believe that rules would keep our children's hearts. We bought into the bold face lies that reduce godly living to eating certain foods, doing certain activities, and abstaining from others. Even if our motives were good, our practices were wrong!

Many of us need to apologize to our children and chart a new path...BUT hear me loud and clear. I believe with all my heart that homeschooling is part of the solution NOT the problem, and it is still the best way to impact the future.

Love your children and be real.

NOVEMBER 12

Showing Not Just Knowing

Hey Mom,

I KNOW you love your kids, you KNOW you love your kids, but sometimes your kids don't KNOW you love them. Do you want to hear something really shocking? Sometimes your kids THINK you love school more than them.

Why? Because sometimes school becomes your priority.

"I know you don't feel well, but we have to get some school in today."

"No, we don't have time to play (fill in your favorite game); we have to get some school done."

"How could you have missed so many questions?"

"Why can't you get this…it isn't that hard!"

"What are you, dumb?"

You've forgotten that school is a tool, not the end, not the goal…not the main thing.

I'll tell you how to show your kids that you love them…don't let school take their place.

If they're crying, stop and comfort them. Make it your purpose to see your child as someone to enjoy during the day, not someone who is bound and determined to make school hard for you. Stop worrying about how much you get done and be thankful you get to spend another day with your children. Quit thinking more of what others think about you and your kids, and start doing what you know to be right.

Make school a distant seventh in the race for your affection and your children WILL KNOW THAT YOU LOVE THEM more than anything.

Be real.

NOVEMBER 13

FaceTube

Hey Mom,

I just wasted a few minutes of my life reading an article that broke the news to me that I live in the 38th happiest state in the country, and that North Dakota is number one having moved up 30 spots in the last year according to a recent Gallop pole. The article came highly recommended by some nameless

Facebook user amidst all the other highly recommended articles in an ocean of highly recommended articles on Facebook.

I don't know about you, but I think it's time that someone stands up and says, "This is stupid." I mean how many amazing articles can a person ingest in one sitting? There's Ten Amazing Photos about Your Toes That You Have to See to Believe, a titillating article on the Twelve Foods in Your Fridge that Will Kill You by Days End, and a gripping true story of How a Woman in New Jersey Ate Her Piano.

The maddening thing about Facebook is that there is ALWAYS another must-read article to peruse, another breath taking series of photos to see, more life changing mumbo-jumbo that you must implement before it's too late…so much so that it's sucking our real lives away.

What did we do with all our extra time before Facebook? We spent it with people!!! We looked at them, moved among them, and interacted on a physical and emotional level. Now we sit in front of monitors clambering for the next article or post. You know I'm not overstating it…because you can barely wait to run back and 'like' something.

Someone should calculate how many hours and lifetimes have been diverted from interacting with real family members and wasted on reading about an 87-year-old yoga teacher or the top 15 sink holes in America. It's got to be staggering!!* And yet, we swarm around our screens like flies on a dung pile.

When will we stop? When will we say Facebook is a bad thing and that it is killing families, causing moms to ignore their children, husbands to ignore their wives, and teenagers to avoid real life? I haven't even touched on the fact that it has fueled a multitude of affairs and heaped up despair and depression on many of its users.

We hate it and love it…vow to turn it off but can't stop posting, viewing, and liking.

Maybe I'm just an old dad who remembers a time before Facebook and has a hard time going with the flow. Or maybe…it's time to say good-bye to Facebook for the good of our marriages, our families, and the world.

Be real.

**According to my calculations based on the info provided by Statista…874 million active user a month each spending an average of 22.52 minutes per day = 37,447 years wasted per month!!! Or 468 lifetimes flittered away on Facebook per month.*

There's a Happy Day a Brewing

Hey Mom,

I don't know about where you live, but today looks to be a good day. A little nippy…but good.

It's just amazing how one little 'issue' can skew how you view everything else. That's the way it is with the lies homeschooling moms believe: they distort the way you view your children, your marriage, and yourself.

Why just a couple of weeks ago we spent the day with a great family. Our kids played well with theirs and the adult conversation was easy. I think it was the next morning when I woke and rolled over to my wife that I could tell a little dark cloud seemed to be hovering over her head.

"What's bothering you?" I asked, hoping it had nothing to do with me.

She stared at the ceiling and said flatly, "She (the person's house we just left) does such a great job with her kids. They all seem kind to each other and obedient. She is just so intentional in her mothering." She went on with her observation, and I knew she felt discouraged by her own mothering. I tried to tell her otherwise, but that's the thing with lies…they often speak louder than husbands.

Well, that was that. Life carried on and I didn't think much more about it until recently. Out of the blue the other great mom emailed my wife and basically said, "How do you do such a great job with your kids? They all seem kind to each other and obedient…"

In fact, as my wife was sharing the email with me it sounded like a word for word recording of what my wife had said a just a few weeks before. That great mom believed the same LIE that my wife believed. And they believed it about each other!!!

Thing is, YOU believe the LIE about your best friend, my wife, the great mom, the moms in your church, and just about every other homeschooling mom you know. Guess what? They ALL believe it about you, too.

Don't shake your head at me. YES they DO!! That's the power of the LIE. The truth is: you're not perfect, you're never going to be perfect…you're going to have gaps and failures. But everyone else does as well…EVERYONE.

I'm telling you, this kind of perspective is like having your ear unplugged. It not only makes everything 'look' better, it's also the truth. Once you realize that, you see everything as it was meant to be seen: your children, your husband, and yourself.

It looks to be a good day.

Be real.

NOVEMBER 15

A Quick Trip From 'Is' to 'Was'

Hey Mom,

Why is it so hard being a parent? I want to do the right stuff, have the right attitude, and treat my family with love because I know what's most important... but it's just so hard.

I seem to blow it more often than I succeed. I say mean things to the people I love the most, and I get a chip on my shoulder towards family members that I love more than...anything.

Just the other day I was driving down the road thinking about...stuff, when the thought struck me like a bug on the windshield that one day my kids will go from saying, "My dad is..." to "My dad WAS..." It will be here before I know it.

I almost said out loud, "I don't want to go from IS to WAS!" That thought highlights my feeling lousy as a dad. Why don't I live in those thoughts every day? Why don't I remember that the thing bugging me at the moment is NOTHING compared with being with my son or daughter at that moment? Why is it so hard?

As I type this, I can hear God's voice answer, "Because that's the way it is, Todd. Quit your wallowing in self-pity and failure. Dad-up, and get back in there and love your family!"

Sigh. He's right. We moms and dads can't always live in those truths of what matters most, but we can get back in there and love our families.

So Mom, no matter how you've been mom-ing lately, let me urge you to... get back in there, and love your sons, daughters, and husband. You might even need to skip 'school' today to do it.

Be real.

NOVEMBER 16

Like Mother Like Son

Hey Mom,

Remember that old 70's anti-smoking commercial that coined the phrase, "Like Father, Like Son?" Well, I felt a tinge of that today with my son, Jed, and it felt good...and scary.

It started out just like any other day. I was getting dressed and about to grab the first shirt on top when I remembered my wife telling my mom that I always wear what's on top, which ends up being the same thing over and over so I decided to dig deep and wear something different.

I dug out a blue-striped, rugby shirt out and pulled it over my head. Later, I bumped into Jed, and he looked up at me in surprise and beamed a big smile.

"We match!" he said pointing to my shirt. "I've got one like that."

He disappeared and then reappeared a few minutes later, proud as all get out, wearing a shirt almost identical to mine. We took a picture together and my little boy hugged his rugby-clad papa. I could almost hear that soothing narrator's voice say, "Like father, like son." It felt good knowing my son wanted to be like me...and then it felt scary knowing my son wanted to be like me.

It's a two-edged sword...and I wield them both. If that doesn't terrify you, nothing will. But that's what makes what we do so powerful. That's why we can't afford to coast, slack off, or quit. There's too much riding on it...er...us. Jed needs me to show him how to be a dad, a husband, and a man. Actually, all eight of my children do.

Guess what? So do yours..."Like mother, like..." You know.

Be real.

PS - Rodney Atkins wrote a great song about this very thing called Watching You. Buckle on your country music seat belt.

NOVEMBER 17

Preparing to Answer Questions from Family at the Holidays

Hey Mom,

The way I see it, you only have a few options when dealing with the unavoidable homeschool questions that well-meaning Aunt Bertha asks every Thanksgiving AND Christmas.

1 – Pretend that you don't hear her and hope she goes away.

2 – Act like you're choking on a turkey bone and hope that in all the commotion she forgets what she just asked.

3 – Take the bold approach, stand your ground, and say in a commanding voice, "Yeah, we're still homeschooling, you old busy-body...what's it to ya?

4 – Smile pleasantly and make comments about the food..."My goodness, Jane's noodles are tender this year...Did you ever taste such tender noodles?"

5 – Before she can ask about homeschooling, beat her to the punch line. "So is your daughter still sending her children to that pagan institute which is Hell-bent on their destruction?!"

Or better yet, just answer her questions, confidently knowing that you're doing what God would have you do. Don't feel like it's your job to convince her (or them) of all the benefits. Just answer the questions and let your children be the PROOF. They'll see the difference.

~ A note to your husband: Dad, it's your job to be a knight-in-shining-armor and protect your sweet damsel from dragonish relatives. Stand up, take the brunt of the questions, and let your wife hide behind you.

Be real.

NOVEMBER 18

Be Ye Thankful

Hey Mom,

For what it's worth, I think the only way to cultivate an attitude of thanksgiving is to say 'Thank you.' Start by thanking God as a family for all he has done. Then thank your daughter for baking cookies, your son for taking out the trash without complaint, your husband for going to work each day, or your wife for doing the laundry again.

You might be saying to yourself, "But I shouldn't have to thank someone for doing what they should be doing anyway." You're probably right, but if you don't thank them…they won't learn to be thankful.

To be honest, my children say thank you about everything. If we stop in at someone's house, they say as soon as we leave, "Thanks for taking us…" If we go to McD's for 50 cent cones, as soon as we're in the van they say, "Thanks for getting us…" If I take them to Dollar General for a bottle of glue, as soon as they are in the van they say, "Thanks for taking me to get…" Sometimes when they thank me I want to say, "You don't have to thank me for taking you to church!!" But I don't…because I know they are being grateful and God is pleased.

You know what? They don't say thank you because we've shown them the "be thankful" verses in the Bible or because we had them study "thankfulology." They do it because we give thanks to God as a family all the time, and we try to thank them for their contributions.

So…cultivate a thankful attitude by saying, Thank you.

Thanks for listening.

Be real.

Thanksgiving

Hey Mom,

Wow! Is it possible that Thanksgiving is almost here? That means Christmas is in…auggg! Maybe it's better if we just take one holiday at a time. You know, if you think about it, Thanksgiving is really only thanksgiving if you GIVE someone thanks.

If you just think it and never say thank you, it's really thankskeeping. That's the great thing about the holiday. It gives us an official reason to thank God and the people who need thanking.

This year I've got a plan. Actually, I stole the idea from my sister-in-law, but I've always believed that the best parenting ideas are the ones you steal.

It's really pretty simple. All you need is a jar or container, a few slips of paper, and a pencil or pen. Then place the container along with the paper and pen in a conspicuous place like the kitchen or dining room table.

Next, gather the family and instruct them that for the next week they are to write down what they're thankful for and place it in the container. Then, on or near Thanksgiving Day, take a few minutes and gather your family together and read the slips of paper out loud. Then pray and thank God for many of the things written down.

That's it.

Matter of fact, I think I'll announce it tonight at dinnertime.

By the way, I'm thankful for you and all that you do as homeschooling moms and dads. Keep up the good work and…

Be real.

NOVEMBER 20

Clarence

Hey Mom,

I want to wish you a Happy Thanksgiving with your family. After all, you have so much to be thankful for this year, and you have a great wife and family. Do you know how many guys would kill to have it as good as you do?

Jimmy Stewart forgot that and it took an angel named Clarence to remind him of his wonderful life. You got gypped; instead of an angel in an overcoat... you got me.

So let me remind you that although others may have nicer cars, bigger houses, humongous incomes, and take luxury vacations...you have a wonderful life. In fact, there would be an awfully big hole and a lot of hurt if you weren't there.

That's true, for thanksgiving day and the coming month. Thanksgiving just screams family. Can I encourage you to immerse yourself in THEM? Play games, go shopping, cut down a Christmas tree, string outdoor lights, go out for pizza, go ice skating...anything, but just do it with them. Don't get so busy that you miss out on what really matters.

Be real.

NOVEMBER 21

A Premier Mom

Hey Mom,

As I write this, we're less than a week away from the premier of the Hobbit 3.

We'll be there opening night, not showing back up at home until close to 4 am. The kids are pumped, but it sounds exhausting to me. If you were to show up at our theater, you'd see me in my best, homemade, Gandolph costume. I'm only doing it because my son Abe wants to dress up and needs a little moral support.

Actually, you won't be seeing me in my costume, because I'm not going to post the pictures. You know there are just moments that DON'T need to be posted, published, or put on display. They are special family moments that are sacred and should be stored in scrapbooks and in memories, not on Facebook.

In fact, can I encourage you to cherish those special times and ponder them in your heart? Don't cheapen them by posting for others to 'like.' Believe it or not, Mom, our kids are beginning to wonder if we are 'doing these family things' just so we can post them so others can 'like' them.

So, want a never to be forgotten memory? Go to the premier of a special movie, stay up late and watch a string of Christmas movies, have a special meal, or play a silly game, but don't post it for others to see...ponder it in your heart. I know your kids will.

Be real.

Up and Gone

Hey Mom,

The sun is shining, and for those of us in northern Indiana...that's a treat. No shortage of rain and gray skies here. I'm ready for some sunshine!!!

I'm struck...again, by how quickly these mom and dad-years are passing.

Last night, my wife and I had the rare treat of watching a video in our room...alone (almost as rare as sunshine in Indiana). We watched Parental Guidance starring Billy Crystal and Bette Midler. It was a great mom and dad movie and left us all warm and fuzzyish.

The thing about warm and fuzzy movies is that they also leave behind a bitter aftertaste of 'my children are growing up too fast'. It didn't help that four of my children were away at the time, making it pretty easy to imagine them out of the nest and myself...old.

I guess I'll leave this on your plate for the week: your kids are going to be gone soon so squeeze all you can out of the time you have left. Smile more, listen intently, and don't sweat the small stuff...especially school.

Be real.

Thankful for Other Homeschoolers

Hey Mom,

There are those unexpected moments in life that alter courses, directions, and philosophies. Bob was the homeschooler who "did that" for me. It must have been about nine years ago, when my wife and I attended the Indiana State Homeschool Convention.

Like most everyone else in attendance, my wife and I scanned the list of workshops trying to figure out how to best use our time there.

I'm not sure of Bob's workshop title, but it had something to do with how to have the best homeschool ever. So my wife and I attended, expecting to discover the miracle curriculum that would guarantee success.

I can still remember the small room where the workshop was held. People came in, sat down, and waited. I guess we had been there a few minutes when a white-headed man with a clean, starchy mustache walked in with an armload of books.

While most presenters used PowerPoint presentations and sat glued to their notes, Bob stood in the front of the room, leaned back against the table, and talked to us like we were sitting in his living room.

Now, I don't remember all of what he said, but I'll always remember his opening statement. "First thing you ought to do," he said softly, "is go out and buy a big, comfy couch." He then went on to share stories about kids, living books, education, and unforgettable life experiences.

He changed my homeschool philosophy and life. In fact, I do what I do now because of Bob Farewell.

When I asked my wife who most influenced her, she mentioned Bob's wife, Tina as one of the people who gently steered her down the path of "life learning" instead of trying to reproduce the classroom at home.

Over the years, we've traveled some of the same paths and have spent some time getting to know the Farewell's. In fact, I think they have so much to offer homeschooling families so stop by their website*, sign up for their email newsletters, and tell them Todd sent you.

For them, I am truly thankful…as I am for you. I count it an honor and a privilege to be part of your life.

Be real.

**www.bobandtinafarewell.com*

NOVEMBER 24

Saying Thanks to Our Families

Hey Mom,

Saying thanks to our families is a great idea! I wish I had thought of it first. What a great time to give an official 'thank you' to the people we love the most and often take for granted.

So here's what I think I'll do:

1) Thank God for each of the members of my family.

2) Verbally tell each of my children and wife why I'm thankful for them (the more specific, the better).

3) Write a note on a quarter-sized sheet of paper thanking each family member for being in MY family. Then I'll place the note on his/her pillow to find on Thanksgiving night.

Actually, I'm going to quit writing this article and start writing those notes (I'm guessing it will take a grand total of 10 minutes). I'm not going to tell you what to do...but I'd recommend you do the same.

Happy Thanksgiving...and be real!

NOVEMBER 25

Thankful for You

Hey Mom,

OK I'm officially freaking out here. I don't know if you've noticed or not…but it's THANKSGIVING!!!!!!!! I'm not ready for Thanksgiving. I'm lagging behind, but my kids are in full swing and have been pestering me for a week about decorating the house for Christmas.

Time goes by too quickly. This whole holiday thing will be over by the time you read this email…just a dim shadow in the great rearview mirror of life.

But that's the great thing about Thanksgiving; it forces us to slow down just long enough to catch our breath, reflect, and give thanks to God for all that He has blessed us with and brought us through in the past year.

And like Bob Cratchit once said, "I am truly a blessed and happy man."

Part of the pondering has led me to be thankful for all of you and our ongoing friendship. It's good to know that there are people out there who face the same trials that I do. It's comforting to know that you sometimes blow it and forget about what matters most. You've written me and it encourages me.

And for that, I am truly thankful.

So keep up the good work, take a deep breath, and enjoy the wonderful day we call Thanksgiving with your family.

Be real.

NOVEMBER 26

Thankful for Encouragement

Hey Mom,

You know the great thing about God's timing is that He knows exactly when we as parents need to be encouraged. Usually it comes after we've been in the parent trenches for a while, battling it out on the front lines day in and day out.

Like most (read – ALL) moms and dads, we look at our children and their behavior and sometimes think, "We've failed…We've ruined them…Where did we go wrong?" Sometimes we get so discouraged that we can barely see straight.

And then it happens...like a cool spring of water to a thirsty soul, God encourages us in just the right way. Sometimes it happens when you see a large group of kids or teenagers at the mall, museum, or park, and they're acting cool, talking trash, and being as wild as jungle animals. Or maybe you overhear one of your kids saying something thoughtful or unselfish to a sibling that makes your heart smile.

It's as if God says, "Keep trying; your kids aren't as bad as you think."

He doesn't have to encourage us...but I guess He knows we need it, and He is good to give it.

For that I am thankful...and you should be too.

Be real.

NOVEMBER 27

Prudence Might Be Wrong

Hey Mom,

Sometimes I get conflicted, as do a lot of parents. Should we always do the wise thing or are there times when the wise thing is the wrong thing? See my dilemma? Then I read this article by Robin Hoffman in Ranch and Farm Living Magazine (no, I'm not a farmer). He helped bring things into perspective for me...and I hope it does the same for you.

Every time I see kids lost in the pure joy of snuggling with a puppy, splashing in a mud puddle or burrowing through a straw pile (like the photo he's describing), I find myself wishing I could be a kid again.

Then as long as I'm bending the laws of time and space, I usually go one step further and wish I could be a kid who knew THEN what I know NOW.

At least, that was the plan until I started thinking back to the day I shot the photo. While I envied the fun all those kids were having in the straw pile, I couldn't help thinking, "Boy, that's gonna be a long itchy drive home." And I realized that IF I'd known THEN what I know NOW, I'd have been the world's most boring kid.

Kids enjoy life more than we (dads) do because they don't think about the consequences. They see every new experience as an opportunity, as an adventure - and dive in headfirst.

As we grow older and WISER, we see more and more consequences, until sadly, we become so WISE that we can't see anything else.

Here's the kicker, Robin goes on to say, "Doing the wise thing isn't always the best thing."

You know he's right. Playing it wise sometimes keeps us from experiencing God's best as a parent. Prudence would say, "Don't play in the rain, don't have ice cream for breakfast, or don't waste your quarter on the gumball machine"... But maybe there are times when "prudence is wrong...and Robin is right."

So when the kids walk right through a puddle next time...sees if you can make a bigger splash.

Be real.

Unleash the Brain!!

Hey Mom,

It's starting to warm up as we continue digging out from a big winter storm. The kids love all the snow and bitter temperatures. And while it's mighty pretty, it sure does make life more difficult...that's the practical dad-side of my brain talking.

Actually, the practical dad-part takes up most of the room in my noggin, and the fun-dad part takes up an itty bitty part at the bottom of my brain.

Sadly, most of the time I lead with my practical dad part. It's more comfortable that way....especially when it's cold and snowy. For example: Sunday, the big snow hit. By the time we were home from church, the snow was deep and coming down good (that's snow talk). We had lunch and then I unsuccessfully tried to take a nap. When I got up, the house was quiet, and I found all my kids and my wife outside playing in the snow.

Did you hear what I just said? My WIFE was playing in the snow. My wife doesn't normally do snow. She likes warm and dry. But she knew what mattered. She was making me look bad and what's more is I knew she was having a great time outside with our kids. That's when I unleashed the tiny, fun-dad part of my brain, slipped on my snow suit and joined them in our winter wonderland of a yard. And it was wonderful, and a day none of us will ever forget.

We parents are experts at using the practical side of our brains...and when we do, we all suffer the consequences. So, my fellow practical parent, can I encourage you to dust off the fun-mom side of your brain and do something fun with your children?

It might be as simple as joining them in a game they're playing, initiating a round of charades, staying up late with popcorn and a movie, or freezing your nose off in the snow. Whatever it is...IT'S TIME TO UNLEASH THE BRAIN!!

Be real.

Just Imagine

Hey Mom,

Don't tell anyone, but we've been listening to Christmas music for a few weeks now. I love the sentimental songs. In fact, I was listening to a modern version of I'll be Home for Christmas with my oldest son and said, "That's one of the saddest songs."

I can picture 'our boys' stationed in Europe or on a tropical island listening to Bing Crosby's deep voice over the radio singing, "I'll be home for Christmas, if only in my dreams."

I get a lump in my throat just thinking about being away from family during the holidays, and yet for many homeschooling moms and dads, that is the way it will be this year.

We forget the huge sacrifices people in the military make so that we can enjoy everything they're missing. So can I challenge you to make it a point to not forget them? If you know a mom whose husband is stationed overseas, would you take her under your wing this Thanksgiving and Christmas?

Maybe you can invite their family for dinner, purchase gifts for them, do odd jobs, pray for them, or give them a money gift...something.

So how about this? You and I will let the song be our reminder. I'm going to ask God right now that every time we hear those words, "I'll be home for Christmas...if only in my dreams" it will serve as a reminder to take care of that part of the body that is often overlooked.

Be real.

NOVEMBER 30

'Tis the Season

Hey Mom,

There is a time for everything...and the time between Thanksgiving and the New Year is the time for family. Whether or not you like all the commercialism at Christmastime, you should certainly take advantage of all that the season offers families.

In fact, there's not a single month of the year that offers so many opportunities for dads and moms, husbands and wives, and children of all ages. When else can you snuggle down night after night to watch old Christmas video favorites*, go out in the cold and cut down a tree, gather on the doorsteps of neighbors to sing to them, drive along the road enjoying light displays, and overindulge the people you love more than life itself with tokens of affection? It certainly isn't in June...or October.

The month of December has it all. Not only can we spend the whole month emphasizing the birth of the Savior of mankind, but we also get to enjoy it with one of God's gift to us...our families.

So stop griping about the commercialism of Christmas and celebrate the Birth of the Savior AND the preciousness of your family.

You can do that by baking cookies to give to others, having a family night each week during the month, ordering and playing the wonderful Christmas game To Bethlehem**, volunteering to ring the bell for the Salvation Army, sleeping together around the Christmas tree, helping your children buy or make presents for family members, getting your wife a special gift and your husband the You 'da Dad Daily Calendar***, or attending a Christmas play, musical, or living nativity.

Oh Yes, Virginia, there is a time for everything...but the best time for celebrating family is upon us and it won't last forever. And whatever you do, don't let 'school' take its place.

Be real.

** You can find a great list of Christmas DVDs on our website. Just search 'Christmas DVDs.'*

*** To Bethlehem is just possibly the greatest family Christmas board game ever invented. You can find it on our website, Amazon, or CBD.*

**** If you want a gift for your husband that he'll like as well as you, then pick up a You 'da Dad Daily Calendar from our website. It's the greatest tool for dads since the cordless drill.*

DECEMBER 1

Ten Little Nail Holes

Hey Mom,

I'm not a game player; I just don't like recreational...thinking. So you can imagine the pain I was going through to finish up a rousing game of Battleship with my son Cal a few minutes ago. Actually, it would have been more fun if I could have just lounged around all morning in my PJs...but I needed to get moving...I had things to do...important things.

To make matters worse, I couldn't find his last ship. I filled up the board in white miss markers and was about to throw the game when I 'hit.' I was victorious...in more than one way. Not only did I win the game, but I spent my life on something that mattered.

I know I sound like a broken record most of the time always reminding you to enjoy your family...time is running out...over and over again. But it's true.

I was in the 'reading room' the other day thumbing through Reminisce Magazine and stumbled upon a little blurb about the nail marks left behind on a mantle of a house that someone had bought. The writer 'reminisced' out loud about how they were lovingly left by years of hanging stockings at Christmas time. The blurb couldn't have been four sentences long, but I've been pondering it ever since.

And then on Thanksgiving weekend we decked the halls at our house. As I went to hang the stockings by our fireplace I noticed that I had 10 nail holes ready to accept a nail. I projected time out 100 years and wondered if the 'new owners' would even stop to think about those holes and all the memories that they held.

Those ten holes may not matter to them, but they are a reminder to me of what matters and what I've poured my life into, BUT if I get too busy on 'important stuff' I just might miss.

Mom, can I encourage you to spend your weekend on what matters. Decorate the house for Christmas, hang some lights outside, cut down the family Christmas tree, hang the stockings…or play a round of Battleship.

Be real.

DECEMBER 2

My Inner Martha

Hey Mom,

Now don't spread this around...but I have a Martha Stewart side. In fact, as I thumb through her Christmas magazine and see a snowflake craft made out of wire and glitter, I think, "Ooo, we ought to try that."

It might be because I have so many fond memories of cutting red and green strips out of construction paper in a warm, little house in Broad Ripple near Indianapolis, IN. Back then, when I was just a sprig, holiday crafts ushered in the Christmas season. I made ornaments, sugar cookies, and a Christmas tree out of a Sears catalog.

There's just something about the days between Thanksgiving and Christmas that scream...holiday crafts and activities. My kids have begun the countdown. "Only 7 more days until we decorate," they announce as they walk by me. "Dad, when's our first Family Advent night?" they ask. Do we get our Christmas tree on the Friday or Saturday after Thanksgiving?"

It doesn't help that we had our first official snowfall today. They've been waiting for this day for weeks, and this morning they awoke to about a ½-inch of the white stuff. As is our custom, we gave each of the kids a small, first snowfall gift, and tonight we'll eat at Long John Silver's...it's just tradition!

So you can see that they're pumped up for the Christmas season...which brings me back to crafts and activities.

As I already mentioned, one highlight of our Christmas season is our Family Advent Nights. We set aside one night a week during the four weeks before Christmas to prepare for His coming. During the evening, we'll make a craft, read a Christmas book and some scripture, play our Christmas game (To Bethlehem), light a candle, and then eat a fun snack while sipping sparkling grape juice.

For several years, gathering up all the 'stuff' for crafts was a chore and kind of pricey which got us thinking. What if we do all the hard work so that parents don't have to, and all they'd have to do is have fun with their families?

That's when we started offering ready-to-assemble advent craft kits. Each kit comes with 4 complete crafts. All you have to do is bring one out each week and bada-bing, instant craft.

Be real...and don't tell your husband about the...Martha Stewart thing.

DECEMBER 3

Messing for the Holidays

Hey Mom,

Yesterday I told you I like crafts. What I didn't tell you are two important craft rules: Rule #1: crafts are messy. They involve things like glitter glue, scraps of construction paper, permanent markers, finger paint, and white paste. Rule #2: crafts are important ingredients for childhood.

Some of my best growing up memories involve making something with my mom. I don't have one single craft that I made left, but I can still remember making homemade Play-doh and its saltiness. I can still smell the fragrance of white paste as I pasted loop after loop of red and green construction paper into a humongous Christmas chain.

My mom made masks out of paper bags for Halloween, puppets from socks, and Christmas trees out of the Sears catalogue.

Did I mention rule #1? AND they sound like a big pain whenever my children ask to do them, BUT...rule #2.

So...we let our children make crafts...and messes. Sometimes we guide the crafts, but other times we just smile and let them make a craft on their own. Then, when they're all done and holler, "Look what I made!" we say, "That's beautiful," instead of griping, "You better clean everything up...and I better not find one sparkle of glitter on the floor..."

I still feel rule #1, but I KNOW and act on rule #2 (most of the time).

Be real and smile.

Board Games

Hey Mom,

I already told you that I don't like board games. I figure there is a reason they call them bored games. Fortunately, I know a bunch of dads who love board games and just last week posted a list of great family games on my website*.

Now, even though I don't like board games, I also know that games are like the laxative of the family world. Just about any game can take a family who needs some loosening up, and within minutes, people will be laughing and making memories. It's especially true for dads...because sometimes we have trouble having fun with our families. That's why we invented a Christmas game.

I know I said I don't like games, but I do like my family and Christmas and am always looking for something to give us meaningful family time during the Christmas season.

We searched but just couldn't find any good Christmas games (Christmas Monopoly and Bingo don't count). So...we invented our own, and since then thousands of families have played it, and we've been bowled over by the phenomenal response to To Bethlehem—A Christmas Game for the Entire Family.

Here's a little secret: I made it for your husband. I knew he needed some family laxative to loosen up and enjoy his family, and from all the responses we've received, it's working.

The game is a non-skilled, thought-provoking, goofy game for everyone in your family. The object of the game is to be the first to make it to Bethlehem. Along the way you might have to sing a Christmas carol, put your socks on your hands to keep warm, or wear a towel on your head to keep the sun away.

While traveling, you'll also stop for some meaningful questions around the campfire.

So from this non-game player who knows the value of family games (especially at Christmas), I ask what are you waiting for? Run over to the Familyman website and pick up your laxative...urrr, game To Bethlehem in time for the Christmas season. This is one game that will force you to...

Be real.

**Go to my website and search the words "Board Games."*

Christmas Cards

Hey Mom,

As of today I don't think we have received a single Christmas letter. I did my duty and wrote the annual letter from our home and as a critical Christmas card reader I thought I'd share my thoughts on Christmas letter writing.

First let me say I love getting Christmas letters. To tell you the truth, I get no warm, fuzzy feeling from a boxed card with a simple signature. I want to know stuff about families I don't ever visit but am curious to read about once a year.

At the same time, Christmas letters can be bragging platforms for insecure folks that cause some readers to feel worse about their own family or station in life. I was talking about the Christmas card phenomenon with a fellow, economically hard-hit dad when he mentioned how he hates seeing pictures of everyone else's exotic vacations.

So...here is the Familyman's Guide to writing Christmas letters.

1. Do not mention the words Hawaii/Disney World/RV and or balloon trips around the world.

2. People do not need to know your children were honor students/the top of their class/wrote a novel/started a successful business/or were nominated for the Nobel Peace Prize.

3. If you got a new car/boat/or expensive thing don't mention it.

4. If you wonder if it sounds like you're bragging...you are.

5. BE REAL - share at least one hardship/one failure/and one real moment from the past year.

6. If you include a photo, make sure the emphasis is your family and not the location it was taken or the clothing you are wearing.

7. As you review what you've written, think: will the receiver of this card feel better or worse because of getting this card.

Now go write your Christmas card.

Be real.

More Crafts

Hey Mom,

If I was a mom, I'd be a crafting kind of mom. I said, "If." In fact, some of my best growing up memories involved the smell of white paste and construction paper.

I cut orange pumpkins from crisp construction paper at Halloween, brown turkeys with brightly colored feathers at Thanksgiving, and wonderful paper chains to start the countdown at Christmas.

My wife, on the other hand, is a mom and is not a crafting kind of mom. She has gobs of talents and abilities…she just doesn't like crafts. That's basically how I see the division of mom-kind: those who like crafts and those who don't.

Problem is, those who don't…feel guilty for not, BUT they (read you) shouldn't. Just do what you were made to do and enjoy the ride.

So, if you're a craft-loving mom, go buy some white paste and construction paper; if you're not, go do what you do and don't feel guilty.

Be real.

7

Serving Others

Hey Mom,

Let me start this little treatise about the topic of serving others by saying, "You're a mom so you spend your whole day serving others!!!" Don't feel guilty for one moment about NOT serving every person or opportunity that comes your way.

Sure you can have the kids take some Christmas cookies over to the little old lady in your church or next door, have the boys shovel her walk, or do something else neighborly. But, I just know some of you spend most of your days feeling guilty about not doing more. So hear this, "At this season of your life, serving your family is enough…and is as servingish as serving gets."

So…go serve your children by snuggling up on the couch and reading a Christmas story with them, serve your husband by snuggling up on the couch tonight and watching a Christmas video with him, and serve them all by smiling, laughing, and enjoying these days leading up to Christmas.

For goodness sake, ease up on 'doing school' and enjoy your family.

Christmas is coming!!!!!

Be real.

Inexpensive Gift Ideas

Hey Mom,

I speak on behalf of husbands everywhere...like the Lorax of Husband-dom. What I'm going to share has all the makings for the best Christmas ever as far as your husband is concerned. And talk about inexpensive...it's all FREE.

The first thing on his Christmas wish list is a wife who smiles at him. This is not to be confused with a smiling wife but one who smiles AT him, FOR him, and BECAUSE of him. A smile says, "I like you...I think you're neat...I'm so glad you're mine." To be honest, most of us husbands don't get very many of those smiles. Instead we get critical comments, complaints, and looks of disgust and disapproval. So, especially on Christmas morning, smile even if he says the wrong thing, gives the wrong thing, or does the wrong thing. Look him right in the eye across the room and smile. Believe me, he'll melt.

Next, take all the unrealistic and lofty expectations you have for your husband and toss them in the trash. Quit hoping and hinting that he'll change and like him the way he is right now. Refuse to think, "If only he would lead us...if only he would be more...if only he would...THEN I could..." This year give him the gift of acceptance.

Lastly, give him the gift of yourself. Don't hold back. Don't worry about where it might lead or how he might read into it. Just give him YOU. Forget the thermal underwear and the amazing wrench, as seen on TV, all he really wants is YOU.

Thus saith the Husband-Lorax.

Be real.

Discovering Your Child's Gifts

Hey Mom,

The more I think about this topic, the more convinced I am that the real issue isn't discovering our children's gifts but ACCEPTING our children's gifts.

We live in a society that elevates certain gifts...marketable gifts...gifts that yield well-paying jobs like engineers, doctors, lawyers, politicians, world movers and shakers. Speakers and authors tell us how to "find and flame" those marketable gifts in our children causing us to ignore the just-as-important gifts that our children exhibit, leaving us frustrated and defeated.

The truth is that all of our children are gifted...all of YOUR children are gifted. I would just about guess you already know what those giftings are. But can you accept them?

You might have a child who is good with his hands, loves to pretend, or organize the garage, or a daughter who loves to mother her dolls or make lists. But no one writes books on how to fan the mothering flames, the car mechanic flames, or the janitorial flames in our children. Why is that? Because the world says that those aren't gifts.

Well, let me say, BALONEY!!!! Those gifts are every bit as important as doctoring gifts. There is no difference.

I'll tell you what; if you accept the gifts that God has given your children, you will have more direction in your homeschooling, greater joy in your homeschooling, and your children will like school more…and you more. And only then will you be able to help your children grow in the gifts that God has given each of them.

Besides that, I certainly hope you're enjoying the Christmas season with your children! That's way more important than, say...math.

Be real!

DECEMBER 10

Homeschooling with a Newborn

Hey Mom,

I'm no expert, but we seem to homeschool with a newborn all the time. The important thing to remember is to adjust. It is unrealistic, detrimental, and even ludicrous to think that you can add a newborn child to your family life and homeschool, and just keep on as you did before.

Yet, that's what many homeschoolers attempt, and then they're surprised when they feel overwhelmed and frustrated. You have to adjust. Your homeschool days might be shorter, less frequent, or you might have to take an extended break from the bookwork. It doesn't mean that your children will learn less, in fact, they might even learn more.

I know for a fact that my children learn invaluable lessons when we have a baby in our house. They learn to serve, pitch in, be selfless, and care for a baby.

But adjusting is required for many other reasons besides having a newborn. You might have to adjust for sickness, adoption, depression, hospitality, or celebrations. Adjustments are just part of life and demand that we flow with them and around them. Yet, we've been duped and misled into thinking that we just need to set the curriculum course and trudge through it no matter what life throws our way.

No more. Stop it. In fact, I'm going to ask you to do a little flexing this week...because it's Christmastime. Throw your schedule in the toilet and enjoy your children. Who cares if it doesn't fit with the school vacation schedule... it's Christmastime!!!

I know some of you barely take off Christmas day, let alone enjoy a Christmas vacation. May I say to you in my best Gomer Pyle voice, "Shame, Shame Shame"? Your children need the break and so do you.

So, close the books and make Christmas cookies with sprinkles instead. Believe me, that's way more important than geography lessons.

Be real.

DECEMBER 11

Listen to Your Bones

Hey Mom,

I love this time of year. Christmas is just a few weeks away, and I feel the giddiness in the air. I can remember how it felt as a kid in school. Everything seemed to be winding down around this time. We made Christmas gifts for our parents, the librarian read Christmas books out loud to us, and moms sent Christmas cupcakes to share with the class.

At home there were television specials during the evenings. We' d sit in the glow of Christmas tree lights and watch the Walton's Homecoming (which I watched last night), How the Grinch Stole Christmas, and A Christmas Carol.

On the weekends, we'd roll out sugar cookies and ice and sprinkle them until we had a heaping tray to dunk in milk. Oh, the house was filled with Christmas smells, sounds, and sights. It was wonderful.

Now that we're all grown up and have kids of our own it takes on a new perspective...but I still FEEL the wonder that calls us all home.

BUT sometimes homeschooling gets in the way of that. After all, we have stuff to accomplish, curriculum to finish, and projects to complete. The season still whispers to you, "Take it easy...stop and enjoy...you've done enough."

In fact, my wife said a few days ago, "It just FEELS like we should be done doing school and enjoy the season."

"You should," I encouraged her, but I knew she felt pressure not to stop yet.

You feel it too, don't you? You feel it in your bones that it's time to pack school away and enjoy your children and the time leading up to Christmas, but then there's that pressure that tells you otherwise.

Now hear me, Mom, and listen to your bones. They're right, you know. It is time to slow down and pack it all away. It's time to stop doing math and make cookies. It's time to put the school books away and get out your Christmas read-alouds or Christmas DVDs…stay in your PJs and snuggle up on the couch.

Oh, I know that you're thinking, but we've only scheduled two weeks for Christmas break…it's too early…

Who cares??! You don't have to justify it, count it, or feel guilty for it. Listen to your bones. Those bones of yours are linked to the Spirit of God. They speak for Him, not just at Christmastime, but all through the year.

When your bones say, I just don't like this curriculum, then listen to your bones and do something different. When your bones say, I think I'd rather go this direction…focus on this subject instead of that one…burn the harp…or take the kids to the park, listen to your bones.

Be real.

DECEMBER 12

Relax, It's Christmas

Hey Mom,

I'm feeling a little cynical and snappy. I'm sorry to dump on you, but even this topic of 'relaxing' fuels my Grinchy nature right now.

Relax? That's about all I tell homeschooling moms. "Relax and enjoy your children because they're going to be grown and gone before you know it," I say. I travel all over the country telling homeschoolers to relax. When moms email me and describe their homeschool situation, I say, "Relax."

BUT nobody's doing it!!!! Moms everywhere are tired, frustrated, and worn out, causing their children to hate homeschooling and everything they hold dear. They need to RELAX…but something tells them to push harder, plow through, and do more.

The TRUTH is: they don't need to do more, they need to RELAX.

BUT they don't listen. Oh they agree, nod in agreement, and say, "Yep, that's what I need to do…right after I do this, this, and this…and that and this…and then some of that…and I HAVE to finish this…"

And all that makes me think, "What's the use? I'm wasting my breath."

Because even if I tell them and you (like I do every Christmas at this time) to RELAX…you won't.

You've been duped into thinking that relaxing is 'bad' and doesn't fall into the real school schedule. So you say things to your children like, "If we work real hard this week maybe, just maybe, we can take off the time between

Christmas and New Years." Then you proceed to miss out on the important stuff while plowing through the unimportant stuff.

Whoa, did I say, 'unimportant?' Yeah, that's what I meant to say. UNIMPORTANT.

Again, I'm sorry for dumping on you. Just ignore me and go back to 'doing school.' Work hard, be diligent, mold young minds, make sure you get it all done, and don't rest until it's finished…I gotta go wipe a bottom.

I've got issues.

Being real.

DECEMBER 13

Taking the Stress out of Christmas!!

Hey Mom,

Stressed about Christmas? You should be!!! It's right around the corner…. and it's going to be over before you know it. If it will make you feel better, scream right now.

Feel better?!

Here's the deal: there are Martha's (not the Stewart variety) and there are Mary's. Some get stressed and some don't. My wife and I are one of each, and let me just say that we Mary's cause MORE stress for the Martha's. Mary's see all the fun and Martha's see all the things to be done. I'm not sure how you can change who you are…but maybe there are things you can do to be less stressed out.

That's why I'm asking my stressed out wife to give her thoughts (secretly I'm thinking it might help her as well). Here's my lovely, stressed-out wife's suggestion…marry someone who's understanding and loving!

Isn't she adorable…hmm…well, anyway I guess this turned out to be for those who DON'T get stressed out. We need to be understanding of our stressed-out spouses, AND we need to avoid adding to the stress by having such high expectations of fun and by being bothered when they are stressed out. That's just the way they were created. In fact, it's almost absurd to think that I, a non-stressed person, can instruct a completely, differently-wired, stressed out person to avoid the stress. Even Jesus, when he told Martha that she was missing out on the best, didn't offer any instructions…He just stated the fact.

So if you're stressed out, print this off and give it to your spouse, and if you're not stressed out, try to be understanding, let the comments roll off your back (easier to write than do), and ask your spouse how you might help lessen the stress.

Isn't marriage at Christmas fun?

Be real.

DECEMBER 14

Teaching Christmas

Hey Mom,

I don't mean to scare you, but the Christmas countdown paper chain my children made a month ago has shrunk drastically. Don't panic yet; there's still plenty of time to enjoy the remaining time with your family.

First thing to do is to put your homeschool into Holiday-mode, which means you elevate the fun part of family above the academic schedule you created. I know that may be tough for you, but you can do it if you make up your mind to.

So here's how you do it! You're doing school when an email comes across your computer (like this one) saying you should make some kind of Christmas craft. So you stop doing the 'normal' stuff and do a Christmas craft instead. Or maybe you wake up and everyone feels like going Christmas shopping. You ditch the homeschool schedule and go Christmas shopping.

One of the best educations you can give your kids is the ability to enjoy Christmas as a family and to know what matters most. They will only learn that by your example.

'Tis the season to be real.

DECEMBER 15

The Christmas Debate

Hey Mom,

Oh boy, I can hardly stand the excitement! My kids debate every morning whether it's 11 or 10, 9 or 8, and now 7 or 6 days 'til Christmas. Actually, one of the hardest concepts I think I've ever taught my children is…"Do you count today when you're counting days 'til Christmas?"

No matter how you do it, it's close. I still get goose bumps just thinking about it, and my heart is flooded by childhood memories of the last day of school before Christmas vacation. We'd have a class party, eat thick, frosted cupcakes, and take home our handmade gifts to put under the tree.

I can remember the excitement as the school bus made the trip home of how I had TWO whole weeks of Christmas vacation to look forward to. Ahhh…

Which leads me to my next comment: Don't jip your children out of an extended Christmas break from 'school!!!'

I'm telling you I get a little heated when I hear of the injustice of homeschooling moms, who like Ebenezer Scrooge look at Christmas as a day off, "but be in all the earlier the next day" kind of Christmas break.

Now hear me, you need to take a break. Your children need a break, and you NEED to enjoy each other without worrying about the schedule, the plan, or the curriculum. Fight the temptation to do even a little here or there. I don't want to hear about how your kids didn't finish their math, or that they'll forget all they've learned...because I don't care about the excuses. I just know that I needed a break back in the 70's, the teacher needed a break, and you and your kids need a break now. So if you're planning to do school today...DON'T!!! Tell your kids you're done for two whole weeks and that they can goof off today.

Don't accomplish...just enjoy.

Merry Christmas to all and to all...a good Christmas break!

DECEMBER 16

Todd's Tips for Gift Giving

Hey Mom,

Today I feel compelled by the spirit of fatherhood to talk about Christmas gift giving for husbands. In fact, with a little help from me, The Familyman, you can get an A+ in husband gift buying.

Just to get the ball rolling here are the Top 10 ways to know your husband doesn't like his Christmas gift:

10. He opens it and says, "Wow, I hope you got a really good deal on this...I mean a reallllllyyy good deal.

9. He opens it and says, "This will be perfect for the white elephant sale at Aunt Martha's tomorrow."

8. He opens it and says, "This will look good when I clean out the garage."

7. He opens it and says, "Boy, I like this one as much as the other one you bought me last year."

6. He opens it and says, "Honey you shouldn't have...and I mean it."

5. He opens it and says, "Where did you FIND this...a dumpster, the side of the road...?"

4. He opens it and says, "I like it...but what is the return policy at the store you bought it at?"

3. He opens it and says, "Of course I like it...what exactly would you call it?"

2. He accidentally backs over 'it' with the mini-van...twice.

1. You find him listing it on Ebay before lunch.

Does any of that sound familiar? OK here's what you need to do...think MAN.

Tip #1 - What does your husband talk about all the time? Sports, computer gadgets, tools, cars...then go to a store that sells those kinds of things, walk up to a man (that's important) and say, "What's the coolest 'thing' you have that is guaranteed to please my husband?" Then buy whatever it is that he says.

Tip #2 - Go to that pajama store in the mall and say to the clerk, "What's the coolest 'thing' you have that is guaranteed to please my husband?" Then buy whatever it is that she says and wrap it up as a special his-eyes-only Christmas gift.

Tip #3 - Buy my You 'da Dad daily Calendar (how clever of me). Go to my website and see all the testimonies from MEN whose marriages, families, and lives have been enhanced because of this light-hearted and practical little tool.* In fact, if your husband doesn't absolute love it after having used it for 6 months, he can...throw it away. BTW - It makes a perfect stocking stuffer for brother-in-laws as well.

Tip #4 - Throw away all the expectations you have for your husband. Love him just the way he is, even if he never becomes the communicator you want him to be, the spiritual leader you'd like, or spends too much time on unimportant stuff (another reason to get the calendar).

Follow those tips and you'll hit a homerun with your husband this Christmas. I guarantee it.

Be real.

* *"I got my husband your calendar two Christmases ago, and it has changed our family. My husband was already a wonderful husband and father but he became more sensitive and aware of our family and our needs. It has changed our family from a great homeschool family to an AWESOME homeschool family. It has been the tool to bring the homeschool family vision to my husband. Now 21 other ladies in our homeschool group are getting their husbands one for Christmas. Looking forward to 21 more, strong, homeschool families in Hampton Roads area of Virginia."*

DECEMBER 17

Christmas Mode

Hey Mom,

My wife told me I need to talk to our kids about not wanting to do school because they are in Christmas-mode!! So I said, Let's start Christmas break… NOW!!!

I'm telling you, there's just something in the air as soon as the Christmas tree goes up, and for us, that was a couple weeks ago. I know that most every mom reading this cringes at the thought of all the Christmas stress. It's kind of sad to me…but I know my wife feels it, too.

You have lists and responsibilities…gifts to buy, wrap, and make…goodies to bake…and costumes to sew…pageants to practice for…cards to write and address…and sheesh, I'm starting to get stressed just thinking about all the stuff that stresses YOU out.

But here's the deal: Christmastime is a gift To YOU. In the same way my entire family gets to enjoy the birthday of one of its members, you get to enjoy His birthday celebration along with your family.

Start by putting some Christmas music on, cancel school for today, make some Christmas sugar cookies or better yet, old fashioned Chex-Mix, and then play a family favorite game or read a Christmas book. The important thing is to remember the important thing…and it's not a thing or things. It's the people who call you Mom. It's not Christmas cards, Christmas lists, or getting people a stack of gifts. It's the relationships that matter.

Go on and enjoy the gift of Christmas.

Be real.

DECEMBER 18

Christmas Traditions

Hey Mom,

I know I say it every year, but this time I really mean it. "How did we get here so fast?!" I mean, we're only a week away from Christmas.

Now on to traditions. I can't imagine there being anyone who loves Christmas traditions more than me. I love them all: old classic TV shows, sleeping under the Christmas tree, advent nights, and a half a dozen other ones. Family traditions become cherished and convey what matters to the members of the family.

That said, sometimes I think I let the tail wag the dog in the tradition realm which is wrong. Sometimes the traditions become burdens to carry and endure. In fact, maybe a tradition each year should be to toss one of the traditions.

Maybe collectively you say, "This year let's NOT do Christmas cards, a gift for ALL the aunts and uncles, those three Christmas classics, or that one tradition that stresses Mom out."

They might kick and scream at first but I'm betting they'll never even miss the tradition. In fact, maybe it's just what you need to see what's most important.

Enjoy the last week before Christmas and…

Be real.

PS - If you haven't already done so, get off the computer (Facebook), bring school to an end, and just enjoy the days leading up to Christmas. That's an order!!

DECEMBER 19

The Biggest Lie of Them All

Hey Mom,

As I was reading the Christmas cards and letters that have been trickling in, I suddenly had this thought: the BIGGEST lie homeschooling moms TELL has to be, "I'm doing fine."

In reality, it doesn't take much digging to find out that most homeschooling moms (and moms in general) aren't doing fine. They feel defeated, worn down, burned out, and tired of dealing with kids, husbands, homeschooling, and LIFE.

Instead of admitting it like a sane person who should know better, they perpetuate the lie and say things like, "Oh, I'm doing fine."

Not only is it damaging to the person telling the fib, but it also has a truth-stifling effect on the one asking. Believe it or not, sometimes the people asking are hoping for a little crack so they can admit the truth of their own falling apart world to someone. As soon as they hear the lie though, they clam up tighter than an oyster.

I think it's time we stop telling the big lie and start telling the truth. We need some brave homeschooling moms who will say, "I'm not doing fine. I'm dying here. I can't stand my husband, my children, or homeschooling right now. If something doesn't change, I'm going to FREAK!!"

Can you imagine how freeing that would be, not only to the teller but to the asker? I'm sure many would respond with, I feel the same way.

Mom, would you be the ONE? Would you be the one who tells the truth the next time someone asks, "How are you doing?" Would you tell it like it is? Tell them how you feel? Tell them the ugly, freedom-producing truth. And, if someone answers you honestly, don't freak out when they tell you that things aren't going so well.

No more LIES. No More LIES!!!!!!

Be real.

Stay Married

Hey Mom,

Our snow was starting to melt around here when we were smacked in the face with another layer of wet, heavy snow. In fact, it whacked out our power for the entire day.

We stayed warm with our gas fireplace, but my concern was that we'd run out of water for the toilets so we filled the bathtub with snow and melted tubs of it on the stovetop.

Anyway, I had a great time last weekend in Kalamazoo speaking to a group of homeschoolers.* I love 'talking shop' with moms and dads. But it was the dinner conversation afterwards that left me thinking. We were all loaded up and met some friends for dinner at Finley's.

At one point, we talked about a dad we both knew who had ended his own life, since the trauma of the event was still fresh. We were lamenting the pain the kids must still be dealing with when my friend said, "I still feel the trauma of my parent's divorce."

What blew me out of the water was that this 60-year-old man used the word 'trauma' to describe what he STILL feels about his parent's divorce that took place many years ago.

I guess it shouldn't have surprised me, because anyone who says kids are okay after a divorce is not being honest. They may stuff it, smile, and move on, but God designed moms and dads to stay together.

Here's the deal. I'm not sharing this to lay guilt on you if you've gone through a divorce...but what I am trying to do is encourage you to STAY MARRIED. You may be at the end of your marriage rope, wondering how much more you can take...but STAY MARRIED.

It's not just about you and your husband...it's also about those children of yours who will never get over the trauma and will talk about it 50 years later. Your children need you to work it out, hang in there, and STAY MARRIED. Is it easy? NEVER.

Be real.

**You can have me speak at your group too. Go to our website and click on the "Have Todd Speak" button on the tool bar. www.familymanweb.com*

Slowing Down for Christmas

Hey Mom,

One of the greatest sounds in the world is the passing of a train. I used to lie in bed and listen as the train 'clickety-clacked' its way past my grandparent's house. Now I live not more than 75 yards from a busy train track. We've laid pennies on the track and walked its rails, and at night I can tell which direction it's going just from the number of whistles blown.

I love those sounds. I love the whistles, rattles, and squeals. I love the sound of the engine gearing down, the slow wum, wum, wum of the giant steel wheels on the track, and the overall feeling of quiet as the train slows to a stop. Ahhh.

As the old adage goes, my fellow homeschooler, make like a train…and slow down for Christmas. You don't want to go screaming into Christmas; you want to gear down, apply the brakes, and wum, wum, wum your way into the most wonderful time of the year.

So, start right now as you read this email. Take a deep breath, hold it, and then slowly exhale (I mean for real). Then, make a mental decision to put school away. You know you want to. Your kids have been asking.

Listen to the softness of my voice and put it away. And don't feel guilty for one second. I mean it!!!!

Ahhhhhhh.

Be real.

Thanks Mater

Hey Mom,

D you ever feel like your kids are destroying your house, cars, and…everything? I've begun to notice that all the stuff that I reupholstered, repainted, repapered, and reworked is looking pretty dinged and banged up…thanks to my children. Normally I would feel a bit bothered by all their destructive qualities, but not after the powerful lesson Mater taught me. In fact, instead of fixing all the dings and dents, I'm thinking of having the kids sign each work of art.

Yes, I'm referring to THE Mater…Tow Mater from Radiator Springs. He made his powerful point in the second Cars movie that we saw at the dollar theater a few days before we hit the road.

At the beginning of the movie, Mater and Lightning McQueen finished up one of their adventures. They were headed back to park for the night when Mater noticed a NEW dent on his dented and rusted body. Instead of being bothered by the new dent, he recognized it as a trophy of the time spent with 'his best friend.'

Later, when some slick, little female sports car wanted to remove it, he said, "No way…that's a reminder of my time with my buddy." As the movie moved on to the new scene I thought how that old truck would make a good dad. After all, 'dents' are inevitable and really serve as reminders…not of the dents…but of the special people who made them.

In my case, it's of my children. So I need to quit lamenting the scratches, gouges, rips, and dents and let them remind me of my children who left their mark behind for me to remember…forever.

So do you. I know they ruined your best_______ , make messes faster than you can keep up, and will break their new Christmas gift within 24 hours of unwrapping it. Those things just serve as reminders of what matters.

So, thanks Mater…you're OK, buddy.

Be real.

DECEMBER 23

Tradition!!!

Hey Mom,

It's beginning to look a lot like Christmas!!! Last night, we got dumped with more heavy, wet snow, knocking out the power for 12 hours. The kids think it's wonderful and have been outside making snowballs, snowmen, and sliding off the shed roof (until I saw them). Tonight, we're thinking about going to Long John Silver's since we weren't able to do that on the first snow night. It's tradition.

It's funny how some of the best traditions start. You don't go looking for them…they kind of find you. Take for example our LJS tradition. Several years ago we were on our way somewhere when it started snowing and it was not the powdery, dusty kind of snow but the big, goose-down kind of snow.

It was dinner time and we pulled into a LJS. I can still remember walking from the van to the front door as the snow filled the sky in softness. It was magical. Ever since then, when we get those big kind of snowflakes that stick, the kids, who normally hate LJS, beg us to eat at Long John Silver's. So tonight we're going…probably.

Those traditions are powerful tools in the parenting toolbox. They somehow tie the tradition or memory to a person and what's important. I know that when

I'm long gone and my sixty-year-old children find themselves surrounded by millions of feathery snowflakes they'll not only get this insatiable desire to eat at LJS, but they'll remember their dad who made a big deal about everything, risked life and limb to drive to LJS in blizzard-like conditions, loved to snuggle around the fire and watch old movies, and got tears in his eyes when he thought about his kids growing up.

All that from a silly tradition that I didn't even try to create…it just happened. The important thing, Mom, is to be there when it happens. It saddens me to think that so many moms are too busy doing school that they miss out on traditions, and when their kids are sixty and surrounded by a million feathery snowflakes, they won't have those traditions to remember.

So slow down, Mom. Put your to-do list aside and let the traditions find you.

Be real.

DECEMBER 24

The Richest Mom in Town

Hey Mom,

Well, I'm ready for Christmas. I've wrapped my wife's gifts, and I think we've officially watched all the 'must see' Christmas videos, including at least a half dozen versions of A Christmas Carol (our favorite is Scrooge – the musical).

Maybe it's my season of life right now…but I found myself moved by Jimmy Stewart's "It's a Wonderful Life". The story is about the ambitious and talented George Bailey who has planned to leave tiny Bedford Falls and do something big with his life.

Through a serious of events, George finds himself 'stuck' in Bedford Falls, doing a job he doesn't like, driving a beat up car, and living in an old, drafty house. The low point comes when his forgetful Uncle Billy loses a large bank deposit…and George tailspins into the depths of despair.

Well, you know the rest of the story…he meets Clarence the angel who shows him what life would be like if had never been born.

Now comes the emotional part. At the very end of the movie George is surrounded by his family and friends when his war hero brother enters the room and everyone cheers. His brother Harry lifts a glass and makes a toast, "To my big brother George, the richest man in town."

As he said those words, a wave of emotion washed over me, and I knew Harry was right. By the standard of what really, really, REALLY mattered—George Bailey was rich.

So are you, Mom. You may have an old car, a cramped house, and not enough to go around…but in what really matters, "You are the richest mom in town."

That's not just a quaint way to look at things…It's THE TRUTH!

So with that thought, let me wish you and your family a very merry Christmas.

Be real.

DECEMBER 25

Try, Try Again

Hey Mom,

I mean well…honestly, I do. I have this vision in my head of making Christ the center of our Christmas celebration. I picture me sitting in our family room surrounded by my children in rapt attention, drinking in every word as I read a portion from Scripture and then point out the nuances to their little, attentive brains.

They bow their heads and prayerfully dedicate themselves to godly living, sharing the Gospel, and honoring their parents.

Yeah, right. I know…I'm living in a dream world. But you know what? I keep trying.

For example, I really like the idea of a Christmas countdown. It started when I was a kid. I made countdown chains from green and red construction paper. For at least two days, I'd carefully rip a link from the chain. Then I moved onto other things and later threw away a paper chain with at least 22 links.

As I've gotten older, I've tried other things…like the Christmas tree banner that my sister made us with countdown ornaments and the 25 votive candle set that we got at Goodwill on our travels (very cool).

Two years ago, I got a wooden Christmas tree box with 25 little doors. We made it through about six doors before we gave up. But one thing about me is…I keep trying.

So this year, I'm back at it. I decided to stick a verse in each of those little doors and read them during our morning devotions. So far, so good. Don't think too highly of me…it's not very spiritual. We just read and pray and some of them look bored out of their skulls.

You may have tried something in the past to make Christmas the center of your celebration…and maybe you failed. It doesn't really matter…but go ahead and try again. That's what moms do. We never stop trying…especially at Christmas. Christmas isn't about the destination; it's about the journey… and a child born to save the world.

Merry Christmas.

The Aisle of Change

Hey Mom,

Hope you had a great Christmas with your family and are still enjoying that wonderful time between Christmas and New Year's. We had a great Christmas… although it never goes like we expect.

Last Saturday we attended our first "friend's kid's wedding." We've known the father and mother of the bride for a long time. In fact, my wife went to Kindergarten with the dad, and the mom was one of the bridesmaids in our wedding.

We were young couples back then. No kids, first-time home owners, and just getting started in life. Actually, in our wedding day video, the father of the bride can be seen anxiously waiting for his cue to leave the auditorium because it was his job to go get their three-month-old daughter and bring her back to the bridesmaid mother to feed her. That moment was captured on video.

Last Saturday, that little three-month-old daughter walked down the aisle… the aisle of change. As the ceremony took place, I found it hard to breathe at times and wondered how we got there so quickly. She was just a baby…and now…she's getting married.

Then, I thought of my little daughter, Maggie Rose. She's all giggles and emotion and growing up just as fast as that new bride did. This time, the emotion I felt…was guilt. My little Tinkerbell wears me out, and too often I find myself brushing her aside or giving her my half-listening ears as I do my 'important stuff.'

"She's going to be gone soon," I heard that voice say in the middle of the ceremony.

"I know," I responded.

"You better do a better job of loving your girl," it said and then faded away.

You know, Mom, I'd better do a better job of loving her because it won't be long before she walks down the aisle of change, and I will wish I had my little girl back home to love on some more.

You're going to feel the same, Mom. So let me be the voice that says, "They're going to be gone soon…you better do a better job of loving your little ones." What a great time of year to do some of that right now.

Be real.

National Pray for Homeschooling Moms Day

Hey Mom,

Buckle your seatbelts—the Familyman Mobile is pulling out of the driveway in a few weeks. I feel a little like Gilligan heading out for a routine three-hour cruise. You know how that one ended up.

I'm not sure we're ready. We just de-winterized it yesterday and packed our clothes this morning. I usually like all that done at least a week before lift-off. Not this time. Just to make sure nothing was majorly wrong, I ran it down the road three miles and it purred like a panther.

Anyway, first stop...Montgomery, AL. I'm hoping for some nice warm weather. We were in Cincinnati a couple of weeks ago, and it was cold. Aside from the not-so-stellar weather, it was great to meet lots of homeschooling parents. I feel so grateful to be on the same team as you.

One thing I noticed was how many moms and dads are struggling (read—all of us). There are moms whose marriages are on the rocks, whose kids are in trouble, who are jobless, hopeless, and about to toss in the towel.

As I felt its heaviness today, I thought we need to really pray for homeschooling moms. So by the power vested in me as the Familyman, I declare this National Pray for Homeschooling Mom's Day.

Would you stop right now and pray for those unnamed (and those you know) moms who need God to work in their lives.

Pray for:

-moms whose husbands are without work,

-moms who are fighting for their marriages,

-moms whose hearts are broken for their children,

-moms who NEED to be fighting for their marriages and families,

-moms who are about to do something...bad,

-moms who are just tired and ready to give up,

-And while you're at it, pray for this dad who wants to love his wife and children more than anything.

Be real.

Ease Back Into It

Hey Mom,

Don't you dare ease back into the school schedule before the New Year! Don't even think about lesson planning, school subjects, record keeping, or any word with 'homeschooling' in it.

Instead, think happy thoughts of playing with new Christmas games, 'hanging' in your PJ's, watching videos during the day, taking naps, cleaning up Christmas messes, and enjoying each day without 'school.'

In fact, you shouldn't even be reading this…you need to turn off your computer, forget your blog or Facebook account, and go do some family stuff.

I'll do the same.

Happy New Year!

DECEMBER 29

Teaching Common Courtesy

Hey Mom,

Before I spout off all my vast wisdom concerning common courtesy, let me just remind you that I AM A MAN, and everyone knows that men have a different approach regarding acceptable behavior among people.

Let me begin by just asking the question, whose idea was the 'thank you' note anyway? Obviously, it wasn't a man's. It just doesn't make sense to me. On Christmas morning, if someone gives you a tie shaped like a fish, you open it, and then turn to the person who gave it to you and say, "Thank you."

That's it. Then along came some sadistic woman who decided that it wasn't enough to offer a verbal "thank you", but that you also needed to send a written "thank you."

Ever since then, women have been living under the burden of having to write thank you notes (men just don't). Why, I even know people who hate having babies or getting Christmas and birthday gifts, just because it means they have to add writing thank you notes to an already impossible schedule.

So, here's my advice for the New Year…quit writing and expecting thank-you notes. The next gift you give, kindly inform the recipient that you don't want them to write you a thank you note…and mean it. That's almost a better gift than the actual gift.

Looking Back

Hey Mom,

As we say good-bye to the old year, it's time to do what all self-respecting writers do to fill space and that is…to devote the page to reviewing the past year, looking at the most important, world-changing, significant events and people of the last year.

However, unlike most self-respecting writers, I'm not going to mention republicans, democrats, or even 'grass roots' Christian underdogs. I won't fill this column with INTERNET buy-outs, technological breakthroughs, or teenage-billionaires.

I'm dedicating this space to the REALLY important stuff like…wiping noses, bottoms, and perpetually syrup-covered counter tops…and moms and dads who give everything they have only to be told by a six-year-old who doesn't even vote yet that, "You don't love me."

You want courage and bravery? Let me tell you about the multitudes of homeschooling mothers who drag themselves out of bed every day (or almost every day) trying to make a difference but most often feeling like big failures.

In fact, if I had to name the person of the year, I'd name YOU. Don't believe for one moment that all that tripe that fills the papers and news channels is what's important; it's not. What you do every day is not just important…it is the MOST important. The world may not applaud you, but God does…and so do I.

So congratulations on being selected as the Familyman's Mom of the Year. But I'm afraid you can't bask in the glory long…because your youngest just stuck your favorite shoes in the toilet…and so begins another year.

Be real.

And the next gift you receive, tell the giver, "Thank you so much for the gift. I really love it…but I won't be sending you a thank you note… told me not to."

My wife began doing this a while ago and people love the freedom it gives. In fact, if we all do this, we can right this terrible wrong and once again begin to enjoy the giving…and the receiving.

Besides that, about the only other common courtesies I can offer are:

- Don't spit at the table, into the wind, or in public buildings.

- If you must belch at the table, the acceptable comment afterwards would be, "Let me see you top that!"

- Don't eat soup and whistle at the same time.

My only other advice for the coming year is to…

Be real.

DECEMBER 30

Setting the Stage

Hey Mom,

I feel a little like Bob Cratchit when he showed up late at work the day after Christmas. I'm having a little trouble getting back into the swing of things. So, I thought I would set the stage for a great new year by taking the kids sledding in a few minutes.

That's why I've got to make this quick. Let me just say that if you want this to be a great new year, you need to do what you KNOW to be important and not what you FEEL to be important.

Instead of reacting to what all the experts tell you to do, DO what you KNOW God would have you do. That said; if you're going to err this coming year, err on the side of spending too much time enjoying your children.

This year err on spending more time playing games, reading books, building forts and sledding than on less important stuff like…physics.

Now to REALLY set the stage for the year, start the day out by doing something fun. Prove to your children that you DO what you believe.

Gotta go…my kids are 'swishing' around in snow gear.

Be real.

PS – Still don't know what's really important? Then stop over at our website and pick up a copy of Lies Homeschooling Moms Believe.

Dads need encouragement too.

Check out all our great products at
familymanweb.com

About Familyman Ministries

Familyman Ministries' mission is to remind moms and dads about what's most important. They produce books, seminars, audios, and products to encourage homeschool moms and help dads be the men, husbands, and fathers they were created to be.

If you would like to learn more about Familyman Ministries or have Todd speak to your group, go to **www.familymanweb.com**.